The Web of the Universe

John Hitchcock

The Web of the Universe

JUNG, THE "NEW PHYSICS" AND HUMAN SPIRITUALITY

Paulist Press
New York ◇ Mahwah, N.J.

The Photographs in the Text

Sixty years have now passed since the initial publication of the photographs (Figure 1) which first provided an accurate visual representation of the various patterns which can be assumed by hydrogen atoms. The pictures which are reproduced here have been taken directly from the June 1, 1931 issue of Physical Review. (Harvey E. White, "Pictorial Representations of the Electron Cloud for Hydrogen-like Atoms." *Physical Review*, vol. 37, p. 1416. The photo is from p. 1423.) Permission to do so is granted in the pages of that journal, provided that the source is acknowledged. The author holds in grateful remembrance the openness which was characteristic of those times.

Of similar openness is the permission granted by Dover Publications to use up to ten images of snowflakes without written authorization from them (see Figure 2). Their wonderful book, *Snow Crystals*, by W.A. Bentley and W.J. Humphreys (with 2,453 illustrations), is highly recommended for meditative perusal. Interestingly enough, these photographs were originally made available to the public in 1931, the same year that the hydrogen atoms appeared.

The author is grateful to Dr. Thomas Goreau, the grandson of the photographer, for permission to use the "rotating chemical reaction" images in Figure 5.

Library of Congress Cataloging-in-Publication Data

Hitchcock, John L., 1936–
    The web of the universe: Jung, the "new physics" and human spirituality/by John Hitchcock.
        p.   cm.—(Jung and spirituality series)
    Includes bibliographical references and index.
    ISBN 0-8091-3267-2 (pbk.)
    1. Psychology, Religious. 2. Jung, C. G. (Carl Gustav), 1875–1961. 3. Physics—Religious aspects. 4. Spirituality. I. Title. II. Series: Jung and spirituality.
BL53.H557   1991
150.19'54—dc20   91-24868
                                                                       CIP

Published by Paulist Press
997 Macarthur Blvd.
Mahwah, N.J. 07430

Printed and bound in the United States of America

Contents

CONTENTS

PART IV: PROSPECT

DEDICATION

To That which Desires
to grasp us and
Thrust us into Life—

And to our Response!

and to the memory of
Sheila Moon (1910–1991)

ACKNOWLEDGMENTS

The Publisher gratefully acknowledges use of the following materials: Carl G. Jung, *Memories Dreams and Reflections,* translated by Richard and Clara Winston. Translation copyright © 1961, 1962, 1963, by Random House Inc. Reprinted by permission. Ilya Prigogine and Isabelle Stengers, *Order out of Chaos.* Copyright © 1984, by Alvin Toffler. Reprinted by permission of Bantam, a division of Bantam, Doubleday, Dell Publishing Group, Inc. C.G. Jung, *Psychological Types, Collected Works,* vol. 6. Copyright © 1971, by Princeton University Press. Reprinted by permission of Princeton University Press. C.G. Jung, *The Structure and Dynamic of the Psyche, Collected Works,* vol. 8. Copyright © 1969, by Princeton University Press. Reprinted by permission of Princeton University Press. C.G. Jung, *Psychology and Religion: West and East, Collected Works,* vol. 11. Copyright © 1969, by Princeton University Press. Reprinted by permission of Princeton University Press. C.G. Jung (ed.) *Man and His Symbols,* Aldus Books, 1964; permission granted by the J.G. Ferguson Publishing Company.

SERIES FOREWORD

The *Jung and Spirituality* series provides a forum for the critical interaction between Jungian psychology and living spiritual traditions. The series serves two important goals.

The first goal is: *To enhance a creative exploration of the contributions and criticisms which Jung's psychology can offer to religion.* Jungian thought has far-reaching implications for the understanding and practice of spirituality. Interest in these implications continues to expand in both Christian and non-Christian religious communities. People are increasingly aware of the depth and insight which a Jungian perspective adds to the human experiences of the sacred. And yet the use of Jungian psychoanalysis clearly does not eliminate the need for careful philosophical, theological and ethical reflection or for maintaining one's centeredness in a spiritual tradition.

Thus the second goal is: *To bring creative insights and critical tools of religious studies and practice to bear on Jungian thought.* Many volumes in the *Jung and Spirituality* series work to define the borders of the Jungian and spiritual traditions, to bring the spiritual dimensions of Jung's work into relief, and to deepen those dimensions. We believe that an important outcome of the Jung-Spirituality dialogue is greater cooperation of psychology and spirituality. Such cooperation will move us ahead in the formation of a postmodern spirituality, equal to the challenges of the twenty-first century.

Robert L. Moore
Series Editor

Daniel J. Meckel
Managing Editor

Preface

In 1952 a very remarkable book appeared. Perhaps the most remarkable fact about *The Interpretation of Nature and the Psyche*[1] is that it was a collaborative effort by C.G. Jung and the eminent physicist Wolfgang Pauli. In it Jung drew upon recent developments in physics which indicated that "causality" did not necessarily hold in the microphysical realm, and on that basis he formulated his principle of "synchronicity." Jung's part of the book appears in Volume 8 of his *Collected Works.*[2] To complement the sharing, Pauli wrote an essay drawing upon Jung's concept of "archetypes" and used this work to document some occurrences of the influence of archetypes in the history of physics.

The mutual support of physics and psychology, recognized early by these two great men,[3] sets the tone for the present effort in more than one way, as will be seen. The fact of the collaboration has been noted here at the very beginning, for the benefit of any scientist who might pick this book up. It is a serious undertaking, with a history of excellence.

It seems to be more and more clearly the case that there is a unified reality behind the diversity of the living cosmos. As a result, the clarity to which physics comes concerning physical reality should illuminate our view of other parts of the human enterprise. Moreover, in setting physics to this task of illumination, the high standard of experimentation and thought to which physics holds itself can make its own contribution. In the light of the goal that this be so, my work is to make as certain as I can that what I accept from psychology, philosophy, or theology is "good physics." Good physics, for me, does not focus primarily upon mathematical development or quantification, but rather upon an adequate *conceptual* understanding of physical reality. Though mathematical *foundations* change, *facts* remain to be explained. And though mathematical formalisms can be

1

suggestive of applicable concepts, it remains for the concepts themselves to satisfy us as to our understanding. If it were not so, we
would need no text to accompany mathematical argument. The manner in which this conceptuality will be employed will become clear as
we go along. That concern will make its presence felt throughout
this book, beginning with the Introduction. I urge the reader not to
skip it.

My own efforts are an attempt to continue building the edifice,
the strong foundation for which has been begun by Jung and many
great physicists. The names of the latter which one will most often
find in my work are: Einstein, Bohr, Heisenberg, Wheeler, and Prigogine. Though he was not a physicist, Teilhard de Chardin has been
tremendously influential, contributing much to the language of the
discussion, but more importantly to the vision of science and the
scientific attitude.

DESCRIPTION OF THE BOOK

Part I, "SCIENCE AND SPIRITUALITY," contains the Introduction and a chapter which defines "spirituality" as used in this book.

The Introduction explores the relationship of Jung to science.
"Post-Jungianism," now popular, *aborts* Jung's essential vision of the
spiritual integration of humanity, which he called "individuation." It
does this by reasserting the nineteenth century assumption that intellect alone can cut through to the heart of the cosmos. For Jung, only
when our intellectual knowledge is also integrated at the feeling level
and expressed through our *living* can we say that we *understand*.
While acknowledging the power of differentiation, we must not lose
the new paradigm offered by the "new physics," which forbids the
separation of the human from the nature of reality, and which acknowledges the non-rational nature of physical facts. The so-called
scientific outlook is not truly scientific at all, since it overlooks the
fact that our rational consciousness can only comprehend parts and
pieces of the total worldfield. We know with certainty that our rational concepts do not afford an adequate description of microphysical
entities, and that this limitation extends to our everyday world as
well. Contradictory attributes must always be ascribed to the simplest of elementary phenomena for a full description, if the phenom-

ena are described by means of such concepts. But, as Niels Bohr pointed out, these are the very and only concepts by means of which we communicate.

Chapter 1 is titled "What Is Spirituality?" From the point of view of Jung and physics, spirituality means the refinement of spirit-matter, but as we see with regard to the solution of problems of the earth, the process is not sequential. We must maintain our present refinements, while yet using crude methods to attack crudity. The essence of humanity is seeing beyond the surface of things to inner necessities, and *loving* this great experiment for what it *is*, as well as for its potentials. From the point of view of physics, the physicist cannot avoid dealing with spirit, but must take account of the spirit aspect of spirit-matter, its patterning and dynamism. We don't have the intellectual luxury of cutting spirit off since we are a part of the natural realm. A physicist will avoid doing anything intentionally mysterious with "spirit," but we also recognize that our "models" evolve toward greater and greater depth and subtlety. The case, as now understandable, amounts to a *spiritual imperative*.

Part II is called "CONSCIOUSNESS: THE CONDITION FOR SPIRITUALITY." Its two chapters present consciousness as a waking up in a moral context.

Chapter 2, "The Analogy of Waking as a Gauge of Spirituality," sees waking up, becoming conscious, as an infinite process. We are indeed partly awake, but there is no potential stopping point for this process, no sort of "complete" awakeness. We can, however, evolve good criteria for awakeness, and outline some steps to be taken by humanity in general, in the next few centuries, perhaps. The waking up process is closely related to the involutions to be presented in Chapter 8.

Chapter 3, "Consciousness and the Moral Dimension," draws upon Jung's *Answer to Job*. In this book, the one with which Jung was most satisfied, he demonstrates the essential connection of consciousness and morality. We usually associate consciousness with either of two extremes: with our everyday thoughts and awarenesses (and sometimes those of other living forms), or with the divine. But, on the one hand, our everyday life is usually quite unconscious of the essentials of its own life, and, on the other, Jung powerfully presents the unconsciousness of the divine. The essence of our growing is the awareness of inner conflict, the obstacles in our vision of perfection, which we so conveniently pass off, and leave in an unconscious state. Carrying opposites consciously is a burden, and can only be undertaken with an appropriate attitude.

Part III is titled "THE PATH: THE DYNAMICS OF SPIRITUALITY," and describes our search for what can only be termed the "hidden Center," also showing forth the phenomena from modern physics which provide models for this search. After an Introduction on the Center in Chapter 4, it is shown that the dynamics of consciousness in Jung's sense entails the qualities of circumambulation, oscillation, opening and deepening, transformation, and integration/consciousness/seeing. Together, these qualities of the process constitute a "mystic spiral" of spiritual development. Each of these points to a Center, or Attractor, which guides the development of the individual. The five chapters present alternately the material from Jung and from the New Physics.

Chapter 5, "Oscillation," shows that the dynamic of our lives is not merely movement and change, but specifically an oscillation between opposites, which Jung called the "transcendent function." This is a dynamic in concrete life, actually being there, as distinct from merely meditating upon such changes. Of course, meditation is an important tool in approaching the concrete weaving which oscillation is.

Chapter 6, "The Opposites in Physics as the Web of the Physical Cosmos," shows how the opposites arise in the evolution of the cosmos. Because of these opposites, it is necessary to deal with phenomena in aspects which are mutually exclusive, so that what happens in a given experiment is necessarily partial, however definitive it may seem.

Chapter 7, "Circumambulation," includes material from Jung and physics in one place. In contrast to the real "mystical spiral," we have been *fascinated* by the images of spiral, wandering, the labyrinth. What might it mean actually to *live* it in the course of a modern life? This is the issue of actualization in spite of an *essential* uncertainty. Parallel to this is the statement of a prominent physicist that the relation of the opposites in specific circumstances is "by no means obvious." What has the potential of obviousness is the rational, whereby figure and ground are clearly distinct. The hard-won discovery of non-rationality in modern physics at once corroborates and clarifies the psychological condition of humanity and consciousness. The fact that physics continually shifts its foundations, as from those of Newton to those of Einstein, constitutes a true circumambulation. The world of the physicist is one of continual, continuing discovery: a revelation through the efforts of our search, our attempts to penetrate the surface of things while living in the world of concrete fact. This orientation is a commitment which excludes the possibility that the ultimate nature of things was revealed in the past, and excludes it because of the errors of fact contained in all such worldviews.

In Chapter 8, "Jung and Transformation," it is shown that the real path of transformation must touch and restructure that which concerns us most deeply. Jung likened this process to crucifixion. It is at once an involution and an opening, a psychological death which leads to a new birth of consciousness, that seeing-in-depth which is the hallmark of evolved humanity.

Chapter 9, "The Physics of Awakening and Transformation," demonstrates that we finally have a physics of awakening and transformation through Prigogine's work on "irreversible" and "far-from-equilibrium" processes. With these he is able to explain involutions as awakening to a new coherence and awareness of wider, more subtle, fields. The latter is a good criterion of spirituality, though not the only one. We can show the evolution of spiritual beings as a series of evolutionary involutions.

Part IV, called "PROSPECT," has just one chapter, "Theonomy: The Self-Integration of Freedom and Consciousness in the Cosmos." "Theonomy" is a concept adapted from Paul Tillich, for whom it pointed to "the Ultimate *in* every creative human function." It also draws upon Ernst Mayr's "teleonomy," which recognizes the *internal* goals of organisms, both as individuals and evolutionarily, as distinct from the *external* goals of teleology. The implication of an internal, self-revealing Other is consistent with the concept of spirit-matter as Godstuff, and of the evolutionary process as Godding.

ACKNOWLEDGMENTS

Chapters 8 and 9 are adapted from an address given in 1988 at a Symposium on Science and Spirituality which was sponsored by the

Swedenborg Foundation, and later printed in the Spring 1989 issue of the Foundation's journal, *Chrysalis*. I am grateful to the Swedenborg Foundation for the support of this work, and to *Chrysalis* for permission to use this material.

I have had the help of many readers. By far the greatest influence on the book, in terms not only of style and clarity, but also in the contribution of ideas and images, has been that of my former wife, Dorinda Hawk. Her conviction that the symbols from science can carry religious meaning for many people, and her daily demonstration that this is indeed so for her, have been a wonderful inspiration, and a source to me of courage to persevere in writing about this possibility. As central as this inspiration has been, a simpler statement is most to the point here: she took a book which was manifestly unreadable and made it readable.

Hal Childs read and commented on not only the material which is to be found in the book, but a great deal besides, which did not, in the end, find its way into the present pages. The support of his interest and energy has been a great help, far beyond the changes which were inspired by his insights.

Judith Anders-Richards also contributed most helpful comments from a full reading of the text, and has been a great and continuing support.

My colleagues in the UW-L Physics Department have given much moral and physical support. In particular, Dr. Frank Barmore provided a detailed critique of Chapter 7, which led to many improvements. I am also grateful to him for ongoing discussions concerning the implications of quantum physics. Dr. T.A.K. Pillai contributed to Chapter 6 from his knowledge of Sanskrit. Dr. Dell Fystrom's concern that my work shows not only the symbolic contribution of physics to spirituality, but the flow in the opposite direction as well, led to the inclusion of Appendix 4: "The Spiritual Imperative in Physics."

Daniel J. Meckel, Managing Editor of the Paulist Press series "Jung and Spirituality," made important stylistic suggestions throughout the text. Because of his interest and thorough work, the book is significantly better than it would otherwise have been. I deeply appreciate his encouragement, and his efforts in facilitating publication, including the odious task of obtaining permissions to use the quotations.

Robert L. Moore, the Series Editor, invited me to submit my work to the Series after hearing the symposium presentation mentioned above. Otherwise the book would not have come to being. His continuing support has been deeply felt.

Beyond these few specific acknowledgments, I feel the presence of a "support system" of friends and teachers, near and distant, and of the circumstances which have permitted me to study and to write. I hope that those who feel part of this will forgive me for omitting so long a list of individual contributions, and will know that they are in my thoughts.

Notes

1. The German version, *Naturerklärung und Psyche* (Zurich, Rascher Verlag), came out in 1952. The English translation was published in 1955 by the Bollingen Foundation (New York, Pantheon).
2. *The Collected Works of C.G. Jung,* Bollingen Series XX, translated from the German by R.F.C. Hull (Princeton, Princeton University Press). In view of the prominence of Jung quotations in this book, all references to the *Collected Works,* after the first reference to a title, will be given as *CW,* followed by volume and *paragraph* number. The article in question is "Synchronicity: An Acausal Connecting Principle." Synchronicity is the *meaningful* connection of a material happening with a psychic state, perceived as such by a subject.
3. When the creator of the Soviet theoretical physics establishment, Lev Landau, was praised for his critical intellect, he once responded, "You haven't met Pauli."

PART I
SCIENCE AND SPIRITUALITY

Introduction: Jung and Science

The great wisdom to be found in the writings of C.G. Jung extends to his treatment of the realm of science as well as to spirituality. Since the word "science" means many different things to many people, it may be helpful to point out some of these meanings, and to say how "science" is to be used in this book. The overall purpose of this introduction is to justify the association of Jung with science in the face of criticisms which have unfortunately arisen, that Jung is "unscientific."

1. Science is often *identified* with technology. Technology, however, is the *mechanical application* of principles and phenomena which are discovered in the course of scientific research. The illusion of the identity of technology with science is enhanced by the fact that technology is fully exploited in scientific research. We see a photograph of an advanced laboratory, have the thought that *this* is science-being-done, and fail to notice that the technology is here serving as a *means* to do science. Science, as such, is the discovery and understanding of principles on which the physical universe "works."

2. Because of the efficacy of *mathematics* as a descriptive language in which to express the fundamental principles of the cosmos, doing science is often identified, even by scientists, with doing mathematics. But mathematics, as with *any* language, only affords us a "way of putting it."[1] The "it" which we attempt to describe remains elusive, which is why any current theory must be held as provisional. There are always going to be *new phenomena* to incorporate into theory, which are not currently predicted by theory. The *potency* of the logic of mathematics to show implications of currently known phenomena lends a powerful *predictive* quality to theoretical physics, and indeed one can sometimes anticipate the discovery of new phenomena by such means. Even the greatest theoretical minds tend to

11

get carried away by this power. In fact, mathematics stands in a similar relationship to doing science as does technology: it is a powerful and sophisticated *tool,* but does not in itself constitute either our *discovery* or our *understanding* of the cosmos. Our understanding is *conceptual,* i.e. it is concerned with the *content* of the symbols which are manipulated by the mathematician, and which represent physical quantities. Mathematics is concerned only with the *rules* for manipulating the symbols.

A final comment here, concerning mathematics, is that mathematics itself evolves in the power of its methods. The mathematics which will exist a century from now will be much more able to describe what we know, and whole new branches will be invented just for the purpose of such descriptions. The workings of the cosmos, however, are not susceptible of description in an ultimate sense. They are a "patterning"[2] of physical reality, toward the understanding of which we must eternally reach.

3. Jung's view of science is grounded in *factuality,* but his interpretation of factuality is also important. He often stated that religious beliefs are *psychic facts:* it is a fact that enormous numbers of people hold specific beliefs, however diverse from those of other religions, and that these beliefs are the rocks, the massive foundational points, of their psyches. The truth or falsity *in physical terms* of these beliefs, e.g. those concerning the reality or the nature of life after death, is not at issue, but the *psychic* fact is the shaper of psychic effects, which have such physical issue as wars in which physical people physically die. Jung's view of science is amplified in a passage from *Memories, Dreams, Reflections,*[3] which is somewhat lengthy but needs to be seen in its entirety.

> Today I can say that I have never lost touch with my initial experiences. All my works, all my creative activity, has come from those initial fantasies and dreams which began in 1912, almost fifty years ago. Everything that I accomplished in later life was already contained in them, although at first only in the form of emotions and images.
>
> My science was the only way I had of extricating myself from that chaos. Otherwise the material would have trapped me in its thicket, strangled me like jungle creepers. I took great care to try to understand every single image, every item of my psychic

inventory, and to classify them scientifically—so far as this was possible—and, above all, to realize them in actual life. That is what we usually neglect to do. We allow the images to rise up, and maybe we wonder about them, but that is all. We do not take the trouble to understand them, let alone draw ethical conclusions from them. This stopping-short conjures up the negative effects of the unconscious.

It is equally a grave mistake to think that it is enough to gain some understanding of the images and that knowledge can here make a halt. Insight into them must be converted into an ethical obligation. Not to do so is to fall prey to the power principle, and this produces dangerous effects which are destructive not only to others but even to the knower. The images of the unconscious place a great responsibility upon us. Failure to understand them, or a shirking of ethical responsibility deprives us of our wholeness and imposes a painful fragmentariness on our lives.

One might at first say that the ethical dimension asserted here applies only to psychic facts, but a little reflection reveals that the same stopping short with mere "scientific" understanding of physical reality, the lack of ethical realization, yields the very same destructive results. Of course some of our greatest scientists have been sufficiently complete scientists to see this need; to omit it yields phenomena which are destructive to the physical and psychic environment. In this sense, science as such strives for a comprehensive understanding of the *whole,* and all of the inter-relationships which comprise it.

The need for completeness, in seeing not only the whole but *all* of its parts, is reflected in another of Jung's statements:[4]

Consciousness is phylogenetically and ontogenetically a secondary phenomenon. It is time this obvious fact were grasped at last. Just as the body has an anatomical prehistory of millions of years, so also does the psychic system.

This "obvious fact," that consciousness, far from being antecedent to evolution as most people assume, is a latecomer to the planet, has been missed by philosophy, psychology, theology, and even physics. As a result, all these fields of thought have been led into hopeless erroneous bypaths. For instance, Freud's assumption that the only contents of the unconscious are items which have been repressed from human living is founded upon the error of not grasping the above fact. It assumes human consciousness as a given. Since evolution is a fact, science, the understanding of the whole, requires us to perceive that Freud was wrong in this most fundamental of his tenets. The *whole* begins as unconscious, and consciousness arises later. This may not be clear immediately to the reader, for it is not easy to rearrange our assumptions, our massive psychic rocks. The fact that consciousness is a secondary phenomenon in the physical universe is the single "guiding fact" for the whole of my *Atoms, Snowflakes & God*, to which the reader is referred for a fuller presentation.

4. Science has been assumed to be fundamentally a rational endeavor. Rational clarity and logical consistency have been taken as primary prerequisites of the resulting understanding. We now know, however, as I stated in the Preface, that physically simple entities, such as electrons and photons, manifest logically contradictory properties. We are certain now that physical reality is not founded upon rational entities! Science must still, in a sense, hold tenaciously to its assumption of rationality. If it were let go, all sorts of gobbledegook would become science. However, the scientific *attitude* must not shrink from the knowledge of the ultimate non-rationality of physical reality when we have held onto the rational until it has been confuted by reality as such. The recognition of Jung's "obvious fact," which was presented just above, illuminates this apparent impasse as well, in that it is *clear* as a *fact*, but so many of our cultural assumptions are based on the picture of a humanity set down upon a finished earth, rather than having evolved with the rest. It follows that our consciousness can perceive only a part of that which is manifest out of the worldfield: there are aspects of the greater reality which it simply is not developed or suited to see. Science is indeed the *rational* pursuit of understanding of the cosmos, but science must not lose touch with the seeing of the non-rational unity of the whole, or the non-rational character of any part which is visible.

5. An aspect of the "hard sciences" which can be mistaken for the entire enterprise is that it is the realm of number and measure. Since "quantifiability" is popular at present, e.g. in educational and psychological testing, it may be difficult at first to see that those aspects of reality which are subject to such measurements do not

comprise the whole of reality. One way to grasp that they do not is to reflect again upon point 3 above (seeing the ethical dimension of knowledge as such) in relation to the educational testing just mentioned, or other forms of testing, in which *knowledge* of the facts or results brings up ethical problems in the very possession of the knowledge, because the knowledge can be used for *power* over people. Or else we might reflect upon the fact that "scientific" statistical sampling, while helpful to the power-oriented purposes of politicians, leaves out the individual's conscience. Or think, too, about the structure of human service systems, in which quantified criteria for receiving assistance often blocks help to many who need it under a non-quantified human judgment, e.g. those who just miss the cut-off in the financial category but who may actually be *more* needy if other facts were considered. Any application of measure-rules, from taxes to grades in class, leaves out not only that quality of compassionate judgment, but one of the most fundamental facts of human existence, namely love. Any clear look at the whole of humanity would have to register love as a most salient and ubiquitous phenomenon to be seen. Number and measure are deeply profound as tools in the quest for understanding, but by no means do they comprise the essence of a true science. When they are seen as such, they bespeak a deep woundedness with respect to love. Jung's final statements in his memoirs, which reflect the attitude of healing with which he lived his career, give his sense of wonder at the phenomenon of love.

Misunderstandings of the aspects of science presented above, especially with regard to rationality and quantifiability, have caused many to see Jung as "unscientific," while appreciating him as a precursor to a more "modern" way of thinking. In fact I regard Jung's writings, and especially his memoirs, as among the greatest scientific documents of the century, and that from the perspective of a scientist.

A physicist has a vantage point, normally inaccessible to professional psychologists, from which to evaluate Jung in relation to Jungians and post-Jungians. Here the stringent condition for thinking about the issue is that descriptive psychology, or, if you will, theoretical psychology, should be what I call (and will shortly define as) "good physics." At least Jung himself would be so concerned, perceiving as he did an ultimate unity, the *unus mundus*, behind the manifestation of both spirit and matter. That is, the form of the spirit-side of reality, which in part is represented by psychology, should be consistent with the structure of physical reality. In fact it is precisely this perception which attracts the present physicist to the endeavor of writing this book. Jung's psychology, as distinct from much of Jungian and post-Jungian thought, is *good physics*.

Being "good physics" entails primarily the satisfaction of two of the criteria of science given above: first, the honoring of the non-rational unity of opposites in the description of reality, and, second, the fact that *all* of physics is done by analogy, since we do not know the "thing-in-itself."

The best known example of the non-rational unity of opposites in physics is the so-called "wave/particle duality." The oppositeness of wave and particle lies in the notion of continuity: a wave is something continuous, while a particle is something discrete or discontinuous. To say that something is both continuous and discontinuous is a logical contradiction. Yet the simplest physical entities, electrons and photons, exhibit both characteristics, though not at the same instant. But even the possibility to manifest contradictory properties in different circumstances means that the nature of the simplest things is non-rational. At the same time, the self-identity of the electron gives the unity to the opposites. Much will be said in the book as a whole concerning the unity behind the fundamental human opposites.

The clearest approach to the second criterion is through an anecdote, which I have often told, of an immensely formative experience I had in an astrophysics class. The professor had developed the four equations which describe the basic structure of stars. Since the equations are very difficult to solve all together, usually only by means of crude approximations or by laborious calculation, the professor sàid, by way of encouragement, "After all, the star has to solve these equations." Eventually I realized, of course, that a star doesn't solve any equations at all! What can it mean, then, that these mathematical formulae can describe what happens in the star, when the star doesn't do any mathematics? It can only mean that the mathematics is merely an attempt to describe what the star actually does by means of some kind of patterning, or non-chaos, in the nature of physical reality. There are what we call temperatures, pressures, energy flow, gravity, etc. What are they, really? We understand that when we define and measure these "quantities," we get something reproducible which reflects an understanding of the reality, without really knowing the reality itself. Our "quantities" are *names* which we apply to experience.

But this leads us to a deeper point. What is *experience?* When we "see" something, an examination of the physiology of the nervous system shows that millions of single nerve impulses are arriving at the brain. What makes it possible to "see" *an object* as a result of all these impulses? What enables us to form what appears to be an image or *gestalt?* Jung makes much, and rightly so, of the fact that every image, in fact everything we know or can conceive, is *psychic* in nature, rather than the physical impulses. This is a tremendous mystery, this factuality of something which holds together the disparate and gives it form. Philosophers also, especially Immanuel Kant, have shown convincingly that the intervention of *perception*, by means of our psychic capacity for perception, means that what the object is will not be that which we perceive, for we perceive by means of our own definite and limited capacities, not by means only of the properties of the "object."

A corollary of the second criterion for "good physics" is that physics does not indulge in the notion that it "proves" its theories. It will be seen that misconceptions concerning these criteria of "good physics" underlie the departures of the "post-Jungians" from Jung.

In particular, Jung's care for the balance of opposites has been lost in overstressing the *intellectual* understanding of the reality which the psyche is, and not including the fact of non-rational understanding as well. That which balances the refined intellect is a refined feeling for form. This inner understanding is the same sort of sense of rightness which we have indeed developed for the comprehension of art. We must, therefore, as has been intimated in the discussion of science above, use our intellectual understanding (our knowledge of the *fact* of non-rationality) to hold the intellect in leash. But it also requires emotional wholeness to accomplish.

In *Jung and the Post-Jungians,*[5] Andrew Samuels has done us a great service in summarizing the history of the various offshoots of Jung's work. The problems to which I refer in the opening paragraph are expressed particularly well by Samuels, as he presents his summary and defense of "post-Jungian" thought. In view of this, the rest of this Introduction will respond to several of his statements in order to clarify the attitude taken in this book.

Samuels speaks of Jung's need of the post-Jungians in order that his work may be extended into the future, but we must be careful to differentiate an extension which merely has its *impetus* in Jung's work and one which is an actual extension of that work. It is clear that both kinds of extensions exist.

One primary criterion to use in making this distinction is the balance of the rational and the non-rational just described. Any undue stress on intellectual criteria and "scientific validity" (in the sense of causality or of deductive logic) is a clear indication of a departure from Jung's point of balance.

In fairness, it needs to be said that the misconception of science that characterizes the post-Jungian attitude is much more widespread than that group of individuals. We need, quite universally, a restructuring of what is called "science." It has been seen as a process of developing a *rational* explanatory theory founded upon "first principles" by a deductive process. Now it needs to be recognized as a process of developing an *understanding* founded on descriptive conceptual aptness. We have all had some experience with understandings which are not fully rational, especially mysterious connections or meetings, or our experiences of love. On the basis of the restructuring of the concept of science suggested in the above, it can be stated that this book is by no means a regression to an unscientific mysticism. Rather, it points out the fundamental error of the usual conception, which Jung, in the quotation below, calls a haven for intellectual mediocrity.

It may be that the sheer power of Jung's intellect has so dazzled his later "followers" that they have missed the living power of the non-rational in his work. In a later chapter I will document his comment that a one-sided intellectualism is a western form of "barbarism."

It is my impression that many of the "serious objections . . . to Jung's work"[6] have impelled Jung's "defenders" to take refuge in intellectual one-sidedness. Samuels himself declares that he is pushing for greater "scientific validity." In stressing this very point he seems to have fallen prey to the devouring monster of rationalism in spite of the fact that he quotes one of Jung's warnings against it:

for a certain type of intellectual mediocrity characterized by en-
lightened rationalism, a scientific theory that simplifies matters is
a very good means of defence. . . .[7]

In the quotation Jung goes on to say that religious dogma does a
better job than theory of "rendering an irrational fact like the
psyche," because it uses imagery, and thus avoids an exclusive dependence upon the rational.

In his memoirs as quoted above, Jung does stress that his
"science" saved him from a hopeless entanglement with the irration-
alities of the unconscious, but in making this point he is finding the
balance from the other side of the fence. His use of "science" here
was to find the *image* which went with the emotion, which hardly
points to an excessively rationalistic attitude. Jung's science was an
empirical science in which he always remained aware of the necessity
of contradictory descriptions to do justice to the reality. This is
precisely the lesson of modern physics.

Samuels devotes a section of his first chapter to "the place of
theory." To show that Jung did indeed attempt to formulate theory,
in contrast to Jung's commonly recognized claim that he used ideas
only as flexible guideposts, which in any case had to be suspended
when working with a patient, Samuels finds it necessary to quote an
exceedingly early passage in Volume 4 of the *Collected Works*.[8] There
Jung says that he applies a theoretical formula in his clinical work
until it is "confirmed, modified, or else abandoned." It is not at all
surprising that Jung would have written something like this in his
early works, before he was well established in his own right. And, of
course, it makes all the difference whether one considers theory as
descriptive of that which does occur regularly, or as the logical consequence of "first principles." It is clear, from Jung's entire *opus*, that
he considered theory exclusively in the first sense. In fact, in the
same early volume he gives clear evidence of the empirical approach
to which he remained true all his life:[9]

Why does the psychoanalytic school apparently demand far less
exacting proofs of its formulations than its opponents? The reason is simple. An engineer who has built a bridge and calculated
its load needs no further proof of its holding capacity. But a
sceptical layman, who has no notion how a bridge is built . . . will

demand quite different proofs of its holding capacity. . . . Freud
is anything rather than a theorist. He is an empiricist . . . for
psychoanalysis is essentially empirical. . . . In the field of theory
there are many uncertainties and not a few contradictions.

This passage in defense of Freud is especially interesting, for it holds
clues to the role that insistence upon an empirical rather than a theoretical approach may have played in Jung's break with Freud. Jung
was clearly attracted to that element of Freud's work. Later he became dismayed that Freud could not see the phenomena of the spirit,
but rather held to the sexual theory on theoretical grounds.

When Samuels says that "theory is not *inferred* or *deduced* [em-
phasis mine] from the facts," but that "it may be tested against them,"
he gives no accounting for how a theory comes to be. Its coming to
be most certainly is *related* to the facts which it arises to explain!
While it is true that the relationship is not inference or deduction,
theory would not exist without the facts *along with* the inner impetus
to seek to understand. Indeed, "intuition" plays a role in the analogy
formation which theory is, whether the analogy is mathematical or
verbal. In other words, the unconscious is active in inspiring the
conscious mind with theory by means of "associative thinking."[10]

It would be easier to pass over such silly statements as, "The
theoretical entities mentioned in this book [e.g. 'the physicist's positron, photon, electron, the biologist's gene'] do not exist,"[11] but they
must be dealt with. By every conceivable definition, the *effects* of that
which physicists call "electron" or "gravity," or of that which Jung
calls "archetype," *exist*. By common consensus, physicists use a
shorthand expression in saying that electrons exist, or that gravity
exerts real effects, even though they know that the entities so named
may be understood quite differently in the future. The visible effects
which are observed at present will still be the same. These effects are
regular and identifiable, and one has much information when the
term "electron" or the term "gravity" is employed. It is not possible,
upon investigation, to mistake the effects of the one for those of the
other. The statement that "gravity is a totally contrived invention"[12]
to a physicist is utter nonsense. The theoretical contrivance cannot
force anything to fall with the particular measured rate of acceleration
that is observed. What must be "contrived" is an adequate description of that which does occur, not an invention of an occurrence!

Samuels goes on to such statements as the following:

There are two scientific challenges to Jungian psychology. The first is levelled against all depth psychologies which are held to be unscientific because they deal with unprovable areas.[13]

Such charges could only come from a point of view which is unaware that physics, too, while obviously among the hardest of the "hard sciences," also deals with "unprovable areas." As noted earlier, no physical theory is *ever* "proved." The only result of a physical experiment is affirmation that the theory is *consistent or inconsistent* with the facts. From the history of physics, we assume that other theories which are consistent with the same facts, and which will explain even more facts, will be discovered. In addition, as Einstein's understanding of "gravity" is different from Newton's, so also other understandings will be totally transformed.

In this sense, Jung's approach to descriptive psychology is completely consistent with the approach of physics in its attitude. At the same time, no one would deny the advantage which physics enjoys with regard to precision of measurement and to reproducibility of experiments. This is a consequence of the relative simplicity of physics as an endeavor. And with regard to language, mathematics, the "language" of the hard sciences, still provides a merely descriptive analogue, as is the case with any other conceptual language. The differences cited are all quantitative, and not differences in *kind*.

The usual concern for "scientific validity" pushes in a direction which might even be called *alien* to Jung's concern for life and healing. It pushes in a direction of *conventionality* with regard to the acceptance of Jung's work and in so doing endangers its very spirit. In fact, it deletes spirituality as such as a goal of that work.[14] *From first to last, Jung's is the development of a work of healing, not of a concern for theoretical validity.* Psychologically, healing embraces the opposites, and therefore must remain as much non-rational as rational.

Post-Jungianism *aborts* Jung's essential vision of the spiritual integration of humanity, which he called "individuation." In Jung's view, humanity will be integrated as individual humans are integrated.[15] As we have seen, the post-Jungians do this by reasserting, perhaps somewhat unconsciously, the rationalistic nineteenth century assumption that intellect alone can cut through to the heart of the cosmos. This view entails a puerile conception of consciousness, as well as an erroneous assumption of the human as "given" rather than as evolved from the primal hydrogen of the cosmos. The most telling, and the most relevant, example of the assumption of givenness, as noted earlier, is found in Freud's assertion that there was nothing in the unconscious except what had gotten there through the senses, or by some form of repression. On the other hand, if one acknowledges the reality of evolution, it is easily and clearly seen that the unconscious must contain all future human and post-human potentials, just as the human is a potential of the unconscious hydrogen of the early cosmos.

Since such consciousness as we have has evolved from that primordial unconscious stuff, the "hypothesis" of the unconscious, far from being unscientific, acquires the greatest explanatory power in relation to human nature. This is the epitome of good theory. The unconscious thus becomes a necessary field of exploration. Because of the persistence of rationalism, our *intellectual* endeavor remains unconscious and fails to fulfill its promise.

In contrast, Jung's models of "circumambulation" and "the transcendent function" (oscillation between opposites), which we will explore in Part III, recognized a *perpetual* nearing of that goal, a perpetual deepening of our understanding of the cosmos, but a cosmos infinitely deep, so that humanity and its offspring will never *fully* understand it.

For Jung, only when our intellectual knowledge is also integrated at the feeling level and expressed through our *living* can we say that we *understand*. While acknowledging the power of intellectual differentiation, we must not lose the new paradigm offered by the "new physics," which forbids the separation of the human from the non-rational nature of reality.

Notes

1. Eliot, T.S. 1943. *Four Quartets*. New York: Harcourt Brace and World, Harvest Books. "East Coker," II & V.
2. Hitchcock, John L. 1986. *Atoms, Snowflakes & God*. Wheaton, IL: Theosophical Publishing House, Quest Books. *Passim*.

3. Jung, C.G. 1963. *Memories, Dreams, Reflections*. Compiled and edited by Aniela Jaffé. New York: Random House, pp. 192–193.
4. *Memories*, p. 348.
5. Samuels, Andrew. 1985. *Jung and the Post-Jungians*. London: Routledge and Kegan Paul.
6. *Jung*, p. 1.
7. Jung, C.G. 1969b. *Psychology and Religion: West and East. CW* vol. 11, par. 81.
8. Jung, C.G. 1961a. *Freud and Psychoanalysis. CW* vol. 4, par. 685.
9. *CW* 4, pars. 320–322.
10. This is one of two kinds of thinking; the other being "directed thinking." See Jung, "Two Kinds of Thinking," *CW* 5, paragraphs 4–46.
11. *Jung*, p. 5.
12. Ibid.
13. Ibid. The second challenge, as presented by Samuels, is no different from the first except that it involves Freudians calling Jungians unscientific. Samuels rightly points out that neither side is less vulnerable than the other.
14. The fact that Jungians object to Jung's spirituality was shown when Laurence vander Post's films on Jung came out. At that time, some objections were heard from within the San Francisco Jung Institute that they were too religious. It is noteworthy that the titles of the last two of the three films, "67,000 Dreams," and "The Mystery That Heals," combine the analytic and the synthesizing sides of the psyche. The analysis of that many dreams laid the scientific foundation of the work, whose sole aim was healing.

    Another example comes from the place of my own training in Jung's work, which has spanned more than twenty years. This is the Guild for Psychological Studies in San Francisco. When the San Francisco Jung Institute was formed, the founding leaders of the Guild were excluded from it in part explicitly for the reason that it was "too religious." The other reason was based on the mistaken impression that the Guild was doing group therapy.
15. Jung regretted that the word "wholeness" came to be employed as nearly synonymous with "individuation." He said (to one of the founders of the Guild for Psychological Studies) that he really meant "specificity of consciousness." Integration occurs as the inner centrality, the Self, regulates the life so that all which *belongs* to the life will be available to it. (*Answer to Job, CW* vol. 11, par. 745.) Since some of what *belongs* to a life always remains alien to the conscious attitude, the assimilation of these contents does yield a form of wholeness, but still *specific to the life.*

Chapter 1

What Is Spirituality?

To thine own self be true.

—Shakespeare (Hamlet, I,3)

Clearly there are many ideas of what spirituality is. The meaning it will have in this book is strongly influenced by the fact that I am a physicist and that I find Jung's view of human nature the most relevant among psychologies. As we will see, Jung's psychology is also the most compatible with physics, which now is founded upon a non-rational unity of opposites. Jung's care in this area amounts to an exemplary integrity, which he achieves in his writings in the balance of such opposites as intellect/emotion and spirit/matter.

To approach the meaning of spirituality, I will begin by making four independent points, which already reflect the two major influences just mentioned, Jung and physics. The presentation of these points will be followed by a description of "spirit-matter." This term was coined by Teilhard de Chardin as a more *accurate* designation of the stuff out of which everything in the cosmos is formed. Teilhard recognized the fact that in order to see the sweep of evolution as a whole, and as the unfolding of a divine potential, we must perceive the presence of spirit in the simplest atomic forms. As an example, one of the spiritual potentials of humanity is freedom. We can see elements of freedom in the nature of atoms, and for this reason Teilhard called atoms "elementary freedoms" in *Human Energy*. Actually, he argued the other way around. Evolution of spirit-matter has produced us, with our distinct though rudimentary freedom. Therefore, on the basis of the continuity of evolution, there must be elements of freedom in the atom. I have shown these elements explicitly in *Atoms, Snowflakes & God*. What we have called "spirit" and "matter" are in reality inseparably united, even at the most elementary physical level.

The influence of physics leads us toward an ideal of pure form, unladen with dogmatic interpretations. The pure forms of reality which physics strives to perceive may now carry the numinosity of the meaning of the individual in the cosmos. These pure forms of physical reality will be presented later in the chapter.

Following the fuller description of spirit-matter, the chapter will be summarized in a table of qualities of spirituality.

FOUR INTRODUCTORY POINTS

First, spirituality is both a *goal* and a *process* of movement toward that goal, undertaken consciously. As a goal, spirituality consists of images which are present to us as a vision of the divine. But as we know, the divine is always elusive in some way, so that it is not possible to formulate a clear and permanent definition. Spirituality as a goal always remains infinitely distant. We might be tempted to name a particular *person* as "spiritual," with the implication that such a one embodies the *fullness* of spirituality, that the person has completed a process of becoming spiritual. To identify an individual with a complete spirituality, no matter how spiritual the person is, is always deceptive. In principle, *no one* has achieved the ultimate potential of human spirituality, nor ever will. Only this *reserve* allows for unending evolution of consciousness and of spirituality.

As a process, spirituality consists of movement in a comparative sense, e.g. "greater complexity," "clearer seeing," "deeper feeling." Again as a process, spirituality is a transformative change, so that things which are unpredictable from the previous state come to view, and we see as if with new eyes. Another example of transformation is the availability of a new source of nourishment for the soul. In this book, then, we will focus largely upon spirituality as *process* (Part III) while still encountering the vital and numinous images of spirituality as a *goal*.

Second, we need a clear distinction between *a* discipline or skill as a recognizable performance level, and discipline as an attitude and a dedication of energy. Especially in organized religions, disciplines of the former kind are sometimes accepted as plateaus of *spiritual* development. A "neutral" area may be used to illustrate the difference between the kinds of discipline. For example, a professional musician must master the technical aspects of an *instrument* and also master *music*. I am referring to the mastery of the instrument at a recognizable level of performance skill as the mastery of the specific discipline. The mastery of music, becoming an individual interpreter of music, is much more akin to the concept of spirituality which I am presenting. In this case, the attitude and dedication of energy are primary, and not merely the means to a specific skill. The musician will meditate deeply upon the *meaning* of the piece, as that which she or he wants to get across. Then, in working with the music and in the performance, there is always an element which comes as if from outside, which combines with the inner depth of the artist, to weave together all of the preparations into the beauty and meaning which may be transmitted to the listener. The two masteries, of the instrument and of music, are masteries of different kinds.

The mastery of disciplines is good, even essential to human living at our present level, but my approach to spirituality proceeds along different lines. The specific disciplines are something for which a certificate of achievement, a diploma, or a degree might be issued for a particular recognizable level of performance. Spirituality is not such a thing. Given this distinction, it perhaps needs to be remembered that the application of discipline to the mastery of the specific discipline generally does yield a direct benefit of spirituality.

Third, as will be evident from the consideration of music in the last point, spirituality is not *specifically* religious in any conventional sense. It does not have to do with specific religious practices. Such practices may be employed as *aids* to the process of increasing spirituality, but other practices will also work for the purpose. The examples given above, "greater complexity," "clearer seeing," and "deeper feeling," show this to be the case.

Fourth, spirituality means, at least in part, the refinement of spirit-matter. Since spirit is now seen as intimately involved with matter at the micro-physical level, *spirituality* necessarily affects what we have seen as the material or physical aspect of our living.

The refinement of spirit-matter is something which proceeds on many levels at once. We can see this when we consider our attempts to find solutions to the problems of the earth. For example, it seems that we must maintain our present refinements, such as the fine arts, while yet using crude, warlike methods to attack crudity. It was, for instance, absolutely necessary to employ the very unspiritual methods of war against Hitler, even while hating the fact of that necessity. On the complementary side, while we work for social justice and the liberation of oppressed peoples, we still must push forward with the *whole* philosophical enterprise, and not, for example, only political intellection. Such seeming contradictions as honoring the spiritual side of life when the more material aspects of life are in such disarray need not deter us from doing what we can, where we can, with the means available under the circumstances. Some psychologists will concentrate on the obvious problems of substance abuse, incest, spouse battering, and the like, while others will work with healthier souls for spiritual growth. Both sides are needed.

To summarize the four points just made:

1. Spirituality is both a goal and a process; the *vision* is the goal, but we *work* at the process.

2. Although there is no spirituality without discipline, spirituality is not the mastery of a *particular* discipline.

3. Spirituality is not specifically religious, though it may be facilitated in a religious context.

4. Spirituality "proceeds" on many levels at once.

The essence of humanity is seeing beyond the surface of things to inner necessities, and *loving* this great experiment for what it *is*, as well as for its potentials. Some of us may push at the potentials of subtlety of thought, while others may, e.g., simply act from love of those with handicaps.

Clearer seeing and deeper feeling are forms of *perception*, forms of subtle energy exchange. By this I refer simply to the fact that such things *move* us, and moving things takes energy. Another way to put the same thing is that spirituality involves sensitivity to, being moved by, subtle "fields." A familiar example of a field is the "gravitational field" or sphere of influence of a massive body such as a planet. If an object falls into a gravitational field, it is physically drawn to the source of the field. A satellite orbiting the earth is also being drawn to the earth, is in the earth's field. We picture a field as an influence extending beyond the body or center doing the influencing. It will be important to picture the field as an extended influence when we describe atoms later in the chapter. Picturing the fields of atoms will help us to develop a useful analogy to spirituality *as being moved by a patterned field of energy forms*. When a bell is rung, is given energy by striking it, the atoms in the metal of the bell, held together by molecular forces, *move each other* in vibratory patterns, exchanging energy as they do so. The bell is shaped and reshaped by the energy patterns which it contains because of being struck. These same patterns move the air around the bell, and these vibrations carry the energy of the sound to our ears. We will also use the wave shapings of plucked strings. The visualization of such processes gives us a most helpful analogy, which is indeed often used to picture spirituality, as sensitivity to subtle tones or vibrations, or the reception of subtle forms of energy, deep feelings, or inspirations. The term "morphogenetic field," as developed by physicist Michael Polanyi in the 1950s in *Personal Knowledge*,[1] includes an element of *reaching* for something not yet known:

> All mental unease that seeks appeasement of itself will be regarded as a line of force in such a field. Just as mechanical forces are the gradients of a potential energy, so this field of forces would also be the gradient of a potentiality; a gradient arising from the proximity of a possible achievement. Our sense of approaching the unknown solution of a problem, and the urge to pursue it, are manifestly responses to a gradient of potential achievement, and when we identify a morphogenetic field, we see in it in fact a set of events coordinated by a common gradient of achievement.

We can get some initial idea of the nature of these fields by looking at the "pictures" of atoms and photographs of snowflakes which occur a few pages hence. What is pictured there is the "quantum state," within which fields interact with fields most delicately, to move us in major ways. Only a brief introduction will be given here. The visualization is amplified throughout the book, but especially in the chapter "The Physics of Awakening and Transformation." The material which now follows will also lay the groundwork for numerous other visualizations which will be encountered in the book, e.g. models of complexity, dynamism, and entelechy.

SPIRIT-MATTER

Spirituality is the development of the potentials of spirit-matter, the stuff of which we are formed, focusing upon the spirit aspect, or spirit as distinct from its matter aspect. But what is spirit, and what can a physicist say about it? Some hints have been given. We use the term spirit for energy or dynamism, and we use it for form or shaping. It is that which can move us at any level of our being, from the lowest to the highest urges. By means of the field-concept given above, for which physics provides numerous examples, we can deepen our feeling for the presence of spirit at all levels of being and existence in the cosmos, from the most material to the most sublime. Again, the feeling for the *oneness* of all things in the cosmos stems from the fundamental unity of spirit and matter in spirit-matter. Thus, the physicist's descriptions are not merely analogies, but statements of the realities of the spirit as such.

If we agree with Teilhard de Chardin that "the stuff of the universe is *spirit-matter*," we have a whole realm opened by physics for the elucidation of spiritual potentials, or, to use Teilhard's formulation again, for the articulation of "the spiritual power of matter."

The palpable "stuff of the universe" consists of atoms, each of which has a massive "nucleus" surrounded by "electron clouds" such as are pictured in Figure 1. The term "cloud," which is applied to the fuzzy images in each frame of the picture, is a way of referring to the fact that the electron, which can manifest itself as either "wave" or "particle," is in its wave-like state, or "quantum state," as physicist and Nobel laureate Victor Weisskopf puts it.[2]

The delicate quantum state lies behind virtually all of our experience and our *capacity* for experience. It is responsible, as we now realize, for the very stability and structural strength of matter, as well as for the chemical bonds which yield an infinite variety of substances from the ninety-odd chemical elements. From stone and metal and the properties of water and carbon, so essential for physical life, to life processes themselves, including digestion and the miraculous network of nerves by means of which we think and feel, it dominates our existence. Let us then devote some space to developing the visualization of it.

In identifying the wave-like state with the quantum state,

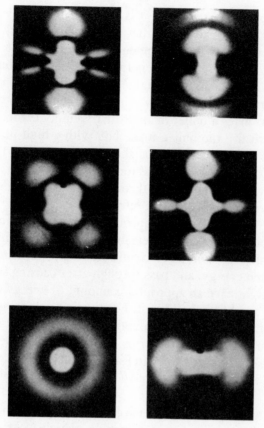

Figure 1. Photographs of the electron cloud for various states of the hydrogen atom as made from a spinning mechanical model.

Weisskopf is pointing out that it is only when the wave aspects of matter are important that quantum phenomena appear. Practically, this is the same as saying that the quantum state is something which occurs at low energies. At high energies not only electrons and other "normal particles," but even "light" waves[3] behave as particles.

In order to form an analogy of the electron in an atom, let's say we wanted to place a bullet in an ordinary empty cardboard box, so we decided to fire the bullet at the box with a high-powered rifle. One way of describing the mistake which we would be making would be to say that the bullet has too much *energy* to be contained in the box. It would simply pass through it as if it didn't exist. The *energy of motion* to which we are referring is called "kinetic energy." We could even calculate the appropriate amount of kinetic energy the bullet could have and still remain, or be "bound," in the box.

In a similar manner, an electron speeding toward an atom might have too much energy, and pass through after causing some disruption, or it might have an appropriate amount of energy to be caught by the atom and be "bound" to it. For that it needs an appropriately *small* energy. Upon becoming bound, it enters the quantum state, and the characteristic patterns or forms of that state become prominent. Some of these forms are shown in Figure 1, on page 31. According to Weisskopf, these forms produce *all* of the symmetries which we see in nature.

If an atom is hit with too much energy, the quantum state itself is destroyed: the wave becomes a particle, which is its opposite, or high-energy, manifestation. The wave-like quantum state occurs only at low energies, but in a relative rather than absolute sense.

As indicated above, the quantum state is predicated upon *confinement*, on being bound. In order to see this we can employ an analogy from the strings of a musical instrument. This will show us further why the quantum state consists of discrete or distinct states. The states of vibration shown in the picture can be produced on a guitar or violin. The fact that organ pipes or wind instruments produce definite musical pitches has a similar explanation. On page 33 the diagram shows four different "standing wave" modes of vibration for a string of a given length. The idea of confinement is twofold: first, the given length, and, second, the fact that the *ends* of the string cannot vibrate, being tied down to the instrument. The pictures show one, two, three, and four "loops" in the pattern. Each

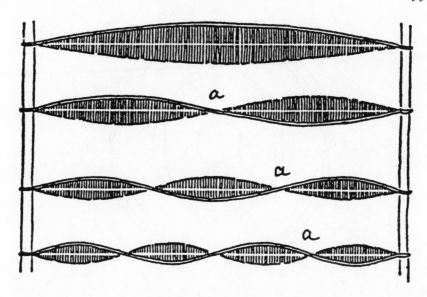

loop is one-half a wavelength, or two loops make up one full wavelength. E.g., the third picture shows three loops, or one-and-a-half wavelengths. It is common for a violinist to produce very high notes by inducing the string to vibrate in one of the "higher harmonic" modes, with two, three or four "loops" in the standing wave pattern. This is done by placing a finger lightly at point "a" in the appropriate diagram to suppress the vibration there. If the finger is placed at the midpoint of the string, for example, the two-loop pattern would ensue. If the finger is placed one-third of the way along the string, the three-loop pattern appears, etc. The energy in the string will then be induced to flow into the mode indicated. Such patterns are the *only* modes in which the string can vibrate to produce a *tone*.

To carry the analogy of the vibrating string to the picture of the atom, the electron in its wave-like state must "tie in" to itself in being wrapped around the nucleus of the atom. This is shown in the following diagram, but with this difference: since the string in the above diagram had *two* ends, it could have whole-numbers of *loops* in its patterns. Now those two ends become *one,* and this means that we need whole numbers of whole *wavelengths,* or pairs of loops, as shown:

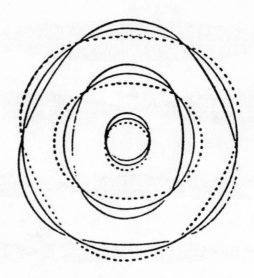

This diagram represents an intermediate concept between the standing waves in strings, and the complexity of electron waves in real
atoms. Here, waves are wrapped around a center: the innermost circle shows two loops or one wavelength, the second shows four loops
or two wavelengths, and the third shows three wavelengths. With
atoms, the waves are wrapped around the nucleus of the atom.

A few of the less complex patterns of hydrogen atoms are shown
in Figure 1 on p. 31.[4] Here we will focus upon visualizing *spirit*, and
will present only what moves in that direction.

The atom pictures show the fundamental *tones* of the cosmos.
This is the intended analogy with the tones and harmonics produced
in the strings of musical instruments pictured above.

These are the quantum waveforms. They represent three-
dimensional shapings. As *shapings*, they show an aspect of spirit-
as-such. Our main goal is to develop the ability to visualize the
shaping quality of spirit, or of the Patterning. "Spirit" has meant
numerous things to us, but it usually speaks of a form or character, as
in the "spirit" of physics, and it speaks of a dynamism. *Visible* spirit is
a sort of *shaping energy*—that which comes through beings or art as
conveying energy or as enlivening.

Two important aspects of the atoms pictured in Figure 1 are: (1) the fact that the cloud *is* the electron, and (2) the participation of these patterns in *energy exchange*.

To elaborate the first of these points, remember that when water freezes in the cracks of rocks, it expands, often with enough force to crack the rock. We know indeed that over long periods many huge rocks have been split in this manner. The water exerts such tremendous force as ice because when the water molecules bond to each other in freezing, the bonds, which consist of overlappings of the electron patterns, assume definite shapes and angles. Here is *palpable* shaping at the atomic level! It breaks rocks! This is not a particle "in" a cloud, which could never manifest this strength, but the substance of the electron itself exerting the strength and stability of material stuff, through the shaping of the field.[5]

The second point is that each shape embodies a definite amount of *energy*—we might say in the shaping itself. At least it is clear that if certain definite amounts of energy are added to the pattern, or given up by it, the pattern changes to a different one. The electrons change pattern when they receive or give off energy. In addition, the *merging* of the patterns of atoms to form molecules, or to form the bonds just mentioned which break rocks, releases or absorbs energy, i.e. involves energy *exchange*. Thus, the shaping is dynamic, which is consistent with our concept of spirit-as-such. This elementary shaping is also a model for the restructuring of soul, but of course the latter is much more complex.

In each picture, the electron is bound to a proton, which is the nucleus of the hydrogen atom. It is important to be clear that *each* of the pictures represents a *single* electron, even if it appears to have a number of "lobes." Each picture represents the electron itself: the cloud is *stuff*, and possesses structural strength without which it would not be possible to account for the stiffness and directionality of chemical bonds, as in the breaking of rocks by freezing water.

Another important feature is the fuzziness of the electron when bound in an atom as shown. Only the *innermost* lobes are shown. At much lower intensities, there are ripples in the lobes at greater distances from the center (where the proton is). The atom shows its extended presence in this manner.

In order eventually to give an idea of the ability of spiritual energy to move us, we must continue a bit further in developing simplified *representations* of the quantum state waves. For convenience, chemists usually simplify the electron patterns (which they call "orbitals"). An example of a graphic representation which is intermediate between the pictures of Figure 1 and a line-drawing is the following, which retains some idea of the fuzziness (by means of the dots), and also shows the three-dimensionality more fully:

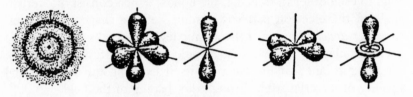

For maximum simplicity, we may represent the electron clouds with line-drawing figures, such as:

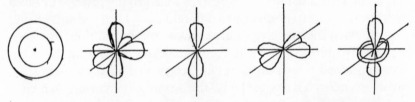

We must remember that these simple drawings represent something which is intrinsically fuzzy, and that there are additional outer lobes or ripples which were not shown in the photographs of models given earlier.

QUANTUM WAVE OVERLAPPING

When atoms join to form molecules, their wave patterns overlap, creating local forces which affect matter in special ways. The moving of water molecules into an appropriate place in a snowflake (Figure 2[6]) by the *weave* of the snowflake's wholeness pattern is a case in point. In *Atoms, Snowflakes & God*, I described the "wholeness pattern" of a snowflake as that which enables water molecules to freeze *symmetrically* onto opposite branches of the growing flake, even though the two freezing points are hundreds of thousands of molecules apart. The snowflake manifests certain possibilities in the

Figure 2.

outer ripples of the hydrogen and oxygen atoms, in several levels of overlapping. The ripples of the atoms overlap to form the outer ripples of water molecules, which again overlap in the particular configuration formed by the freezing of millions of molecules into the snowflake. As the snowflake grows, the wholeness pattern evolves, which also suggests a model for the fact that what *we* do with our lives helps create the possibilities of our growth. When the molecule "fits," we could also say that it "resonates" with the local field created by this overlapping of wave patterns.

For a more visual example, let us look at some *molecules* in which single electrons are shared by two separate atoms:

N_2: CO_2: C_2H_4:

Here, we see the simplest form of the web of the universe. The outer ripples overlap and bond with other atoms. These overlappings are carriers of the energy involved in the bonding process. These bonds must be similar to the patterning of bound electrons in the respect that they also have additional outer "ripples."

My belief is that when the more precise forms or shapes of the bonds are better known, we will see that the following suggestion points to the right *sort* of extension of what we currently know. Here, then, is a speculative picture of outer ripples in a bonded molecule.

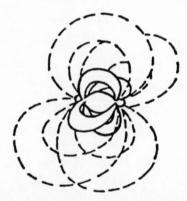

I have merely shown a similar pattern to the bond as presently known, but I have represented it as expanded and fainter. There are undoubtedly more ripples outside these, fatter and fainter still. In fact, the "intensity" of the waves drops off far more rapidly than the impression which I have given, but its effect or effectiveness in influencing the movement of other atoms is still there (witness the snowflake), and the overlap of these outer lobes of atoms and bonds in a large structure or organism would *add up* to the extended wholeness pattern of the structure or organism in question.

We can now picture an animal or a human being as having all these intermolecular bonds, forming a sort of spongy stuff with all these overlapping electron ripples—an intricate web of dynamism, of energy flows and exchanges. Here we have a model from which we can begin to imagine the human psyche. Ultimately, however, who can say what psyche is? Or self-reflexivity, the power of psyche to mirror itself to its own self-aware consciousness? Yet out of this model we can begin to attempt to describe how our intentions, emotions, and thoughts take shape in these flows and exchanges of energy.

PSYCHOLOGICAL RESONANCE

Let us now relate this overlapping symbolically to forces which *move* us in a psychological sense. The term "archetypal nodal point" will be used to designate the overlapping of the patterns in such a way that subtle "ripples" in the field can move things in relationship to each other. It is my speculative view that psyche *consists* of complex patternings of such outer-ripple overlappings as I have described. It arises in the substance of living organisms, and somehow these subtle patternings attain a sort of bonding which gives an integral character to the "soul" (psyche) of the organism. The fitting together of appropriate forms builds a strong foundational structure for the soul because they represent the more subtle effects. When a "major pattern" is formed, we speak psychologically of an archetypal configuration. This phenomenon, by means of the quantity of energy and the centrality of the flow of that energy, is attended by numinosity, beauty, fear, fascination. The dynamism of the local formational event reaches outward, via the ripples in the pattern, to the cosmos. As an example, we might consider something shocking like the human heart sacrifices of the ancient Maya. When the still-beating heart is lifted and offered symbolically to the sun, we can imagine the feelings of the priest and other participants, as containing the energy and other elements just mentioned. Something which can *reflect* back and forth through its own being can *contain* that energy and *resonate* with it.

The case is somewhat similar to the resonance of physical vibrations. The sounding of the strings of musical instruments, and that of organ pipes and wind instruments, all involve resonance. The energy of a violin bow being stroked across the string, and the energy of the air flowing into an organ pipe, all flow into the pitches to which the instrument is tuned at the moment, by resonance. In musical resonance, energy is transferred easily when frequencies match. In our more general view, resonance occurs when *something* matches, as with the pattern of the water molecule and the pattern of the snowflake.

Another simple case is that of "pumping" a swing. You swing your legs forward at an instant which you *sense* kinesthetically. The swing itself has a "natural" frequency of motion back and forth, and the person must *time* the pumping action to the precise point of the cycle. To pump at other times won't get the muscular energy into the motion. We also say that we "tune in" a radio. In so doing, we adjust the frequency of reception to one of the many nearby stations. All of these frequencies are present where the radio is located, but only by matching their specific frequencies can energy be drawn from them by the radio receiver and amplified for us to hear. Again, energy transfer through frequency matching is *resonance*. If one stands alone in a small room with bare walls, such as a typical bathroom, one can also make vocal sounds sliding through a range of pitches until the whole room picks up and holds the tone. Usually several different pitches will be amplified throughout the range of the voice. This is a good resonance experiment. Try it—it's most enlightening.

Psychologically, archetypal nodal points are *situations* where energy transfer occurs easily. Since psychic energy is measured in terms of emotion, any situation in which we typically have our emotions activated can be called an archetypal nodal point. A psychologist would likely say that a "complex" has been touched. This is also the field of operation of psychological "projections," with the additional comment that many real external situations do provide "hooks" for our projections: the person is *really doing* the things which arouse our anger. This only emphasizes and illustrates the situational quality of the energy transfer.

In our human case, *whether or not* excess emotion is aroused, we normally channel much energy every day on the basis of known situations. For example, in meeting people we use established social forms to facilitate the situation, and to avoid tensions which would otherwise cost us a great deal of energy in the form of anxiety. Some archetypal nodal points thus represent established patterns. However, the cases which *do* involve excess emotion give us the clearest concept of resonance at archetypal nodal points.

The process of falling in love provides an excellent model here as well. It is well known to disturb ordinary energy-exchange processes. The field of consciousness is narrowed, the power of symbol is enhanced, and the *sense of Patterning* is heightened: "this is perfect; this is *meant to be*, etc., etc., etc." The mental and physical powers are drawn away from normal pursuits and devoted to the one object. A symbolic field gradient has formed, toward which everything tends. The revenge motive operates in a similar fashion. Both of these intense gradients draw one into psychological disequilibrium.

On the other hand, because of the disequilibrium, we often resist the new, to which we need to be open. The archetypal nodal points represent the means by which the new can break through, yielding deeper human responses.[6]

FORM RESONANCE

When the fundamental patterns of the universe are actualized or fulfilled, "things fit," and the flow of energy is felt with beauty and numinosity. As with the energy of the arm of the violinist converted to glorious sound in accordance with the string patterns which we have seen, and the patterning of the musical composition, we may well speak of a sort of *resonance* with the Patterning. But this is a resonance of form, or of shaping. I call it "form resonance."

Have you ever watched the fat globs change shape on the chicken soup? Of course the soup must be fairly well skimmed, but that's only healthy. Then you stir, to introduce some perturbation, and you will see something like the following:

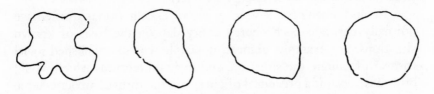

The sequence of forms proceeds from the more complex to the simplest possible form under the circumstances: the circle. As you watch the globs change shape you can think of, and try to visualize, a *shaping force*. This is a concrete case of form resonance. The circular form can be explained in terms of a concrete physical force, "surface tension," along with a principle which says that all stress will seek to minimize itself. A physicist would actually say that the glob "relaxes" into the circular form, and that the *boundary* of the glob seeks a minimum length.

In the case of the electrons bound in atoms, the electrons are patterned in spite of having *no* boundary. This makes for a major conceptual difference between the two cases, the glob and the electron. With the glob we can visualize the forces acting between the fat particles at the boundary of the glob as pulling the glob into shape. But the electron has no boundary, so we cannot visualize forces which "pull it into shape." Thus we must imagine some sort of pure "form field." This should get us closer to the shaping force which spirit is.

The atom, being without a boundary, is *boundless* in the cosmos. As Teilhard[7] put it, each particle in the universe is co-extensive with the universe. So the outer fringes of all the waveforms of the atoms *overlap* each other. Thus *the shaping field subtly shapes the larger forms, especially the living forms, in the cosmos.* Thus, in a sense, the cosmos as a whole shapes us; and thus, in a reciprocal sense, our actions shape the cosmos and its possibilities. As will be seen in Chapter 9, "The Physics of Awakening and Transformation," this shaping can also apply to *process*, as with the transformative restructuring process of daily living which we call death/rebirth.

SELF-REFLEXIVITY

We have said a lot concerning waves and their overlapping, their interrelationship based on their fundamental containment within atoms. Once again, let us move these ideas forward, beginning with an image from ordinary experience.

A rectangular baking pan is ideal for seeing waves reflected from a boundary. I will describe the experiment as if you were actually doing it, but perhaps you can imagine it as you read. With a good layer of water in the pan, make a disturbance on the surface by stabbing it quickly with a fingertip. The familiar circular waves then expand across the surface of the water toward the edges of the pan. These may be easier to see if a ceiling light is being reflected in the water.

Now watch the waves as they are *reflected* at the edges, back across the water surface. You can see that the reflected waves are still circular, and now "inverted" as they expand again toward the center of the pan. Soon the whole surface is vibrating.

The point here is the relationship of *containment* and *reflection*. Without a boundary, the waves would simply continue to expand. Only with reflection does a physical system contain energy. This is also true of, say, a vibrating bell. The waves of energy which produce the tone or sound are reflected back and forth from the boundaries of the bell. The boundaries are determined by the cohesion of the metal molecules, not from some external container.

If we combine this idea with the complex overlapping of quantum waveforms in flexible organisms, and thus picture waves carrying energy from one part to another of the organism, and the organism with various centers sending and receiving, we begin to build a picture of self-reflexivity. The very containment of energy in a system will ensure a new, more dynamic kind of overlapping—that of the waves of energy.

We must remember that as living organisms, we generate energy continually from inside. In Chapter 9, "The Physics of Awakening and Transformation," much more will be said about the flow of energy in various forms. For now it is enough to point out that we generate more than we need for bare existence. Jung[8] defines "will" as "excess energy" which can be liberated from the purely physiological and instinctual functions. At the same time, he defines the border of such liberation as the place where psyche begins. All this fits the present model. It may be that self-awareness or self-reflexivity is the *sensitivity* of an organism to the presence of energy resonating within, in various modes. To the extent that this is a reasonable picture, we have at least a simple way to visualize such a thing. One of the difficulties is the mind-boggling magnitude of the complexity of our own organism.

The model which has been presented is a rudimentary image of the kind of thing which our self-awareness is. We might even say, by analogy with the bell described above, that the tone of the bell is its rudimentary self-reflexivity or self-awareness. We can see that actual self-awareness requires a rather complex container, such as we ourselves are. But when we say that something "rings our bell" emotionally or intellectually, we are using the idea of energy contained and reflected back and forth in a pattern. Moreover, we can see that the cosmos has put itself very much at the service of producing such containers as we are, in the whole evolutionary process.[9]

Since this basic awareness has indeed arisen, it defines a directionality in evolution, an "arrow of time," as physicists now put it. Nobel laureate Ilya Prigogine has gone so far as to define an "internal time" on the basis of the complexity of organisms in the cosmos. With regard to spirituality, the question becomes for us: What *use* can be made of the consciousness which thus comes about?

It should be clear that without at least the elementary self-awareness of which we have just spoken, we would not even have come to a concept of spirituality. It is equally clear that this self-awareness does not *ensure* spirituality. Thus we are led to inquire about the *role* of consciousness in relation to spirituality, which is the topic of the whole of Part II of this book: "Consciousness: The Condition for Spirituality."

The fact that we have a self-awareness which does not lead inevitably to spirituality points toward a consciousness of a different *kind* from mere self-awareness. However, the *direction* of becoming conscious as parallel with becoming spiritual has been established. According to Jung, as we will see, becoming conscious in this newer sense does not occur without the achievement of a new *moral* attitude. This, in turn, links it strongly with spirituality.

SUMMARY OF SPIRITUALITY

With the new visibility of the dimension of spirit in the atom, we can now see that from the point of view of physics, the physicist cannot avoid dealing with spirit, but must take account of the spirit aspect of spirit-matter, its patterning and dynamism. We don't any longer have the *intellectual luxury* of cutting spirit off from "matter" *if* we are a part of the natural realm. A physicist will avoid doing anything intentionally mysterious with "spirit," but we also recognize that our "models" evolve toward greater and greater depth and subtlety. The case, as we now understand it, amounts to a *spiritual imperative*, even for physics itself.

We have been discussing *internal shaping forces* within spirit-matter, by means of which the potentialities of spirit manifest themselves gradually and evolutionarily. Through the forms of atoms and molecules, we have seen how they may be visualized. Earlier, several statements were made mostly concerning what spirituality is not. With all this as a basis, we can now consider specific forms which spirituality may assume. Here is a partial, suggestive grouping:

SPIRITUALITY

The first group consists of a kind of "elevation" within what may be seen as a more "natural" order. The keywords are: 1) Refinement, 2) Subtlety, and 3) Complexification.

The second group follows upon the process of Involution/ Transformation/Opening (Vorticality)/Restructuring. Keywords are: 4) Higher Feeling, 5) Deeper Seeing, and 6) Broader Nourishment.

The third group involves Relation to the Numinous. Keywords are: 7) Inward Awakening, and 8) Focus on Healing.

The last group is miscellaneous/comprehensive, with such ideas as: 9) Going with the Direction of Evolution, 10) Gathering, Raising, Elevating (as in Tai Chi), 11) The Building of Consciousness Itself as Founding the Moral, as in Chapter 3, "Consciousness and the Moral Dimension," 12) Building a

Foundation of *Earth*. Spirit is not "from above." Strengthening the ego to hold the spirit without egocentricity. The milieu is spirit-matter. 13) Transmuting Darkness into Light (anxiety into excitement). 14) Permitting the Emerging Fire (in the above forms of spirituality).

The reconfiguration which we call "insight" is not yet integration of the psyche. It is still to be "worked out" in the moral dimension.

Again, the list is highly tentative in its structure, and only an attempt to express the conclusions from what has been presented. We will just add a few comments on these ideas, to fill them out a bit.

Refinement, subtlety, and complexification are perhaps the easiest representatives of spirituality to grasp. In particular, the fact of the complexification of living forms in evolution is quite obvious. It becomes clear that the whole evolutionary process has a directionality which can be described as spiritualization of spirit-matter. The Patterning manifests ever more of its potentials, and weaves the cosmos into an ever more integral whole. The refinement and sensitivity of sense organs in the same process is particularly noteworthy. Now we take these considerations beyond the merely physical, into the realm of human behavior. We take hold of the process and participate consciously in its progress. Like improved species of grains, its ongoingness now depends upon this care and nurturing. It is no longer merely natural, but, as Jung says, an *opus contra naturam*.

It is said, "The Spirit bloweth where it listeth," which might also be rendered as, "The spirit shapes us according to the Patterning." This is the creation of a truly living form, as figuratively "desired" by the Patterning. In the chapter, "Jung and Transformation," we will encounter Jung's concept of a *co-creative* aspect of our lives. Here I will only comment briefly on what *transformative restructuring* is not, by looking at a quatrain of Omar Khayyam, as rendered by Edward Fitzgerald:[10]

> Ah, Love! could you and I with Him conspire
> To grasp this sorry Scheme of Things entire,
>   Would not we shatter it to bits—and then
> Re-mould it nearer to the Heart's Desire!

The attitude here portrayed shows us just how difficult it is to go with the process I am describing. Certainly we can all feel this immature dissatisfaction, based on an immature "Heart's Desire." Why, indeed, is this a cosmos in which transformative growth comes only with various forms of creative suffering? What is needed is an *opening to the restructuring of soul.* In other words, this is a process which will continue to occur unless we block it, which we can indeed do by protecting ourselves from experience. We actually need to shatter our Heart's Desire (for peace and pleasure), and permit it to be remade nearer to the reality of the Patterning!

Notes

1. Polanyi, Michael. 1958. *Personal Knowledge.* Chicago: The University of Chicago Press. References, in this case p. 398, are to the Harper Torchbook edition of 1964. Polanyi acknowledges Hans Spemann and Paul Weiss as earlier developers of the concept of "morphogenetic fields" from the early 1920s.

2. *Knowledge and Wonder,* Garden City, Doubleday Anchor Books, 1963, pp. 123–141. The section of this book on the quantum state is remarkably lucid and beautiful.

3. The word light can be used in a number of senses. Here it refers to "electromagnetic waves" in general, not all of which comprise *visible* light. They include, starting from the low energy end of the spectrum: radio, microwaves, infra-red light, visible light, ultraviolet light, X-rays, and gamma rays. Rays as energetic as gamma rays behave, in virtually every respect, as particles.

4. Note that these pictures were first published in 1931. They are from White, Harvey E. 1931. Pictorial Representations of the Electron Cloud for Hydrogen-like Atoms. *Physical Review* 37:1416–1434. A rather full description of the qualities of these patterns may be found in my *Atoms, Snowflakes & God.*

5. It is bad physics to picture this as an unreal entity, as has often been done, mainly because the theoretical description makes use of a mathematical device known as "imaginary numbers." It has been incorrectly interpreted in the past as *only* a "probability density" for "finding" "the electron," which implies that "the electron" is something else, usually pictured (incorrectly) as a hard little spherical object, much smaller than the "cloud."

6. The pictures in Figure 2 are from Bentley, W.A. and Humphreys, W.J. 1962. *Snow Crystals.* New York: Dover Publications.

7. It is well to note also that in some cases, particularly those of genius and psychosis, the floodgates open themselves and the individual may or may not be able to handle the material which presents itself.
8. Teilhard de Chardin. 1961. *The Phenomenon of Man*. Translated by Bernard Wade. New York: Harper and Row, Harper Torchbooks, p. 45.
9. Jung, C.G. 1969c. *The Structure and Dynamics of the Psyche*. *CW* vol.8, pars. 179 & 197.
10. This is outlined in Appendix 2, "Cosmic Ecology."
11. *The Rubaiyat of Omar Khayyam*, 5th Ed., XCIX.

PART II

CONSCIOUSNESS: THE CONDITION FOR SPIRITUALITY

In the previous chapter, reference was made to such terms as "seeing" and "self-reflexivity," as leading toward a discussion of "consciousness." Seeing, as an animal sees, is not yet consciousness, though we say "I see" *symbolically* to assert a form of consciousness. Self-reflexivity, or I-awareness, is not yet consciousness, though it is certainly one of the foundations. As I use the term, following Jung, consciousness is the "relation of a psychic content to an ego." In other words, an ego or I is prerequisite to consciousness. The *degree* of our consciousness relates to what *kinds* of contents are so related to our ego, and to what extent.

The fact that most of us live in a mostly unconscious manner is due to our unconsciousness of our cultural determinants, our inner motives, and the effects of others upon us in general. Consciousness, however, is never some disembodied something in the cosmos as its pre-condition or as the goal of evolution. In an earlier book[1] I called the latter something "omniscience," as an aspect of the Patterning of the cosmos, but showed the clear distinction between omniscience, the *unconscious* guiding aspect of the cosmos, and consciousness as such. Consciousness is a potential function of a finite being. These few thoughts on consciousness will be filled in as we go, beginning in the following chapter.

THE TWO CHAPTERS OF PART II

As we add new kinds of awareness to our lives and increase the quantity of psychic contents accessible to our conscious living, we undergo a continuous and open-ended process of waking up. Thus the first chapter of this part is called "The Analogy of Waking as a Gauge of Spirituality." It is central to my whole thesis, that one of the fruits of waking up is spirituality. Mere intellectual knowledge and facility is by no means to be equated with consciousness, nor are theoreticians necessarily competent guides to creative living. *But waking up and seeing reality does lead to creative living and to spirituality, if it is indeed the fullness of reality which is seen.*

Waking up, becoming conscious, is an infinite process. We are indeed partly awake, but there is no potential stopping point for this process, no sort of "complete" awakeness. We can, however, evolve good criteria for awakeness, and outline some steps to be taken by humanity in general, in the next few centuries, perhaps.

The waking process is closely related to the involutions, or transformative in-turnings, which are to be presented in Chapter 9, "The Physics of Awakening and Transformation," which is the real heart of the whole book.

Part of waking up involves awakening a balance of feeling and intellect. We don't merely acquire knowledge, nor is the knowledge we attain merely learned. True knowledge, the self-knowledge which is the stuff of consciousness, costs us dearly if it is really integrated into our lives and being. As we will see, for Jung this emotional integration involves a *moral* confrontation with our own deeper center, the Self. In bringing this out, the chapter "Consciousness and the Moral Dimension" draws from Jung's powerful book, *Answer to Job.* The focus is a description of waking up to the essential and unavoidable moral dimension of living, in spite of the fact that the intellect insists that no connection of morality to living is necessary. The final Jungian conception of a true consciousness is as something which is attained only in a process of struggle with one's own inner moral conflicts.

Chapter 2

The Analogy of Waking as a Gauge of Spirituality

I am awake.
  —*Attributed to Gautama Sakyamuni, called "Buddha"*

How do we *know* when our consciousness has reached a new level? All of us have experienced points in our lives from which we have looked back in amazement at how unconscious we were at an earlier time. One of the most common of these occurs for a college graduate looking back upon the time of high school, but we can also perceive a continuously developing field of awareness by considering our whole life from childhood. The major difference is that it was in high school that we first thought of ourselves as conscious, thinking, deciding individuals, who deeply desired mastery of our own independent existence. Since then, most of us have probably taken that independence for granted, not meditating often on the fact of greater potentials of consciousness, either arising freshly or remaining untried though already present.

We do, however, observe others who are younger, and make mental judgments regarding them, especially in areas where we have learned difficult lessons. We can see where our younger friends are making "mistakes" or being obstinate while we realize that the lessons confronting them will not be learned with our help or "good advice." We also wonder what our wiser, older friends think of *our* choices, while being unable to make our decisions for us. How collective, unindividual, and uncreative our choices must sometimes seem to them! At the same time we may well be "right" and they "wrong" in these cases. At least it is clear that to have others decide for us is our psychological death, whether we are right or wrong, creative or uncreative.

We are also concerned as to the overall quality of our consciousness even as it palpably grows, because it is evident that many of our elders, who have attained great depth of consciousness, also have quite evident blind spots. That is, it is quite clear by our best judgment, in accord with that of others whom we respect and trust. At our level we may be completely incapable of judging those who have attained greater consciousness in some areas, but as we must decide our own paths, so also we must hold to our integrity in judging the development of others, even "sages."

It may well be that our necessity to judge those who are greater than ourselves, and the necessity that they submit to such judgment, is a great moral force uniting humanity. Many great ones, including Jesus, have been killed by the judgment of lesser souls. In Werfel's *Star of the Unborn*, the most conscious person must submit to examination by the youngest learner annually, in order to keep from becoming too detached from the earth.

Our experience with others, then, raises the question with which this section began: how to judge and decide with respect to ourselves when we have reached a new level of consciousness. We know that we can judge ourselves as to the past, and we know that there is a vast field of which we were unaware. What clues can we find as to how conscious we are? This chapter can provide only a few suggestions by way of a chart which is intended to suggest some aspects of consciousness of which we may not at present have a *living* awareness, even though we may possess intellectual knowledge of what that might entail.

AWAKENING

While the concern in the opening paragraphs above has been with the evolution of consciousness in the individual, it is certainly the case that awakening characterizes the whole of evolution: the cosmos is in the process of becoming a *self-aware* cosmos. At an intermediate level, it occurs in cultural evolution as well.

When questioned as to who or what he was, Gautama the Buddha said, "I am awake." From our perspective of more than two thousand years, we can certainly acknowledge that, to an extraordinary degree, he was. It is this statement of his which suggested this analogy as fruitful in assessing our own development, for certainly the Buddha was referring to a change in *his* consciousness with respect to those about him, a change of which he was definitely aware. The Buddha's successors took up this metaphor, especially the branch called Zen Buddhism. Here, the notion of a sudden "awakening" or "satori" is prevalent, indicating a permanent entrance into a new level of general awareness.

However, the same millennial perspective by which we can gauge the awakeness of the Buddha also enables us to become aware of things which those of his time, including the Buddha himself, had no way of knowing. What was not known was intuited on the basis of Buddhist philosophy. Of course, Buddhism is here being used only as an example. The same is necessarily true of any current philosophy or religion. Knowledge of physical reality, in particular, has had a tremendous transformative effect upon Christian thinking in the past few centuries, as illustrated by the destructive impact of then-current theology upon Galileo, whose case is well known, but this is by no means a new phenomenon. Such a case is eternally inevitable as new knowledge is attained, as it *always* is.

Along with the new, which can be dazzling and even confusing, requiring much digestion, it seems wise to pay continual homage to tradition, "ancient wisdom," and perennial philosophy as a check against being carried away. Indeed, as new physical concepts emerge, ancient bells are rung. But our understanding is always consolidated in new ways, at new levels, as on a spiral.

To illustrate by means of Buddhism is then by no means to single out that profound religion for criticism. It is merely convenient, because of the remark attributed to the Buddha. We are here concerned with a general phenomenon: What is learned through physical science must become part of any subsequent philosophy, religious or not. It becomes part of the general awakening of sentient beings.

What the Buddha didn't know can be illustrated in a way which is as definite as was the change in consciousness which he achieved in the first place.

New knowledge of the nature of the physical cosmos provides the ground consciousness from which to critique, for example, the Buddhist doctrine of *anatta* or "no-self." Buddhist doctrine is profound in that it pictures "becoming" in terms of opposites. The short form of the statement of conditioned genesis says:

> When this is, that is
> This arising, that arises
> When this is not, that is not
> This ceasing, that ceases

This echos Anaximander's statement of similar date, on how the opposites arise out of "the Boundless" and disappear again into it. As will be seen in Chapter 6, "The Opposites in Physics as the Web of the Physical Cosmos," this is in deep agreement with a physical account of becoming. However, the doctrine of "no-self" says that all things are "without self." I have elsewhere[2] given a full accounting of "being" and "existence." It is the latter which is characterized by opposites. The level of *being* is known to physics (again, see Chapter 6), and is seen to be a profound formative level, prior to existence as such. This formative worldfield is what I have called the Patterning. It is far from empty of being. There is a beautiful discussion of *anatta* in *What the Buddha Taught*, by Walpola Rahula.[3] At one point he focuses upon three verses of the *Dhammapada*.

> 277. Sabbe samkhara anicca.
> 278. Sabbe samkhara dukka.
> 279. Sabbe *dhamma*[4] anatta.

A reasonable translation would be:

> 277. All conditioned things are impermanent.
> 278. All conditioned things are *suffering*.
> 279. All *essents* are without self.

Rahula comments as follows:

> Why didn't the third verse use the word samkhara 'conditioned things' as the previous two verses. . . . Here is the crux of the whole matter. . . . The term *dhamma* is much wider than *sam-khara*. There is no term in Buddhist terminology wider than *dhamma*. It includes not only the conditioned things and states,

but also the non-conditioned, the Absolute, Nirvana. There is nothing in the universe or outside, good or bad, conditioned or non-conditioned, relative or absolute, which is not included in this term.

Heidegger's famous question[5] "Why are there *essents* rather than nothing?" also includes the level of *being* and does not limit itself to existence. To repeat, the level of being is full and not empty, according to modern physics, and corresponds well with Jung's concept of the Self. The content of this field, as essentially unformed opposites, also corresponds to the "sea of virtual quarks" which is described in Chapter 5.

The doctrine of no-self is the Buddhist foundation for seeing the world as illusion. Nagarjuna, a second century philosopher regarded as the father of Mahayana Buddhism, wrote a treatise called "Fundamentals of the Middle Way," of which a few verses can be given to illustrate his approach to the question of *becoming:*

> There is no origination of that which is destructible, nor of that which is non-destructible. There is no disappearance of that which is destructible, nor of that which is non-destructible.

> Origination and disappearance cannot exist without an existent thing. Without origination and disappearance an existent thing does not exist.

> Origination and disappearance does not obtain for that which is empty. Origination and disappearance does not obtain for that which is non-empty.

> It does not obtain that origination and disappearance are the same thing. It does not obtain that origination and disappearance are different.

These stark words make clear the emptiness of existence, or the reality of no-self for Buddhism. While modern physics admits a varying degree of illusoriness at different levels of physical being, its point of view is that *something is there*, though we may not have an ultimate grip on how to conceptualize it.

The problem of self/no-self cannot be discussed in greater detail here, but it provides a fundamental contrast of Hinduism and Buddhism. In Hindu philosophy *atman*, or "self," is present in every being. That this position squares with modern physics will be brought out in Chapter 5. The notion of *atman* also bears a strong relation to Jung's concept of the Self as the representative of the divine principle within living beings. Jung's statement to this effect is quoted in Chapter 8: "Jung and Transformation."

To repeat, physical knowledge enables us to be aware of needs in other philosophical or religious systems as well: places where such knowledge has a direct impact on the philosophy in question and will engender modifications over time. *Indeed such knowledge will help us eventually to universalize all existing religions.* It may even be that the lack of knowledge of the physical nature of the cosmos is a major source of the blind spots in otherwise highly developed people, which were mentioned in the opening paragraphs.

Science gives us an example of a field in which it is possible to be definite that certain advances have occurred while remaining aware that there will always be new steps to be taken. A concrete example of this situation is the fact that the earth is basically "round," as opposed to the medieval belief that it was "flat." If it ever were found that the earth is flat, we will also know what flattened it! The fundamental roundness of the earth is a fact which will not be superseded, while the *precision* of the knowledge of its roundness *will* be.

To be certain about where knowledge is open, or that something is definitely known, is of great importance to the way we live our lives. This is why it is also important to deal with verification, how we know what we know, in this same chapter. The claims made on behalf of the "new physics" throughout this book fall into a realm of verifiability. They welcome discussion and demonstration.

CONSCIOUSNESS

We will be employing a Jungian definition of consciousness, as distinct from certain eastern ideas of consciousness. Consciousness is always specific: it is always consciousness of this or that, but it can of course be specific awareness of ideas or feelings as well as of things, so long as the objects of consciousness can be named. One may even say "I am aware of a vague feeling of . . ." or just a sense of uneasiness, but still it is the "I" who is aware. As Jung defines it, consciousness is the relationship of a specific content to an ego. Thus our present task is to describe general classes of things at different general levels of which the ego may be or is likely to be aware. The question of the degree of "presence" of an ego is also raised, and is at the heart of the analogy of waking.

When the antenna of a snail is touched, it draws back, but we probably wouldn't describe the snail as "aware" of a hand, because it is not sufficiently complex to have the requisite self-reflexivity. And the universality of the response shows clearly that it is fully automatic, collective, and not individual, as would be characteristic of an alive and creative ego. Yet it is this very stimulus-response exchange which in more complex individuals, in self-aware beings, becomes consciousness. At an intermediate level, many animals are aware of individuals in the sense that they accept or reject the presence or touch of certain members of their own or other species.

As organisms complexify in evolution, they gain what Jung called "disposable energy," which is the foundation of his definition of "will."[6] At the same time, the excess energy increases the possibility of wider applications for that energy, and thus the possibility of individuality of choice with respect to its use. Thus we have a whole range of awareness, in which an amoeba is "awake" with respect to a grain of sand, an ape is awake with respect to a squirrel, a human with respect to a dog or cat, and some humans with respect to others. It may seem arrogant to differentiate among humans with respect to consciousness, but the above evidence makes it necessary to do so.

The foregoing are only examples in a whole continuum of awakeness. That is the analogy of waking: no human is exempt from the continual inner demand for a new level of awakeness. We must always *wake up!* If forced to apply some name to the highest level which I could imagine, perhaps I would call it "manifestation of God." It always feels precarious to use the term "God." Many Jungians might admonish a writer to say "Self" instead, but there are all sorts of manifestations of the Self, some entirely unconscious, and some quite negative in their effects upon the manifesting person as well as on the person's environment. What I am attempting to get at here is a *conscious* manifestation, a bringing to the situation, of that which tips the balance in the favor of Life or Love, both capitalized so as to exclude "lower" conceptions of them. Few persons, indeed, would fall into that category of consciousness, though Jesus of Nazareth has been almost universally felt to have done so, when he is considered as a man.

Naturally, we as individuals also have times of greater and of lesser awakeness, quite apart from the usually distinct states of waking and sleeping. Therefore it would be good to outline these states in humans, as a foundation for discussing higher states of awareness. This is the point of the chart which will appear a few pages hence.

Before presenting the chart, however, one point should be made clearer. One of the pitfalls of awakening is that of mistaking a powerful experience for "revelation." To fail adequately to test such an experience is to "short-circuit" the process which might lead to the knowledge of the true meaning of the experience. The result of such a premature grounding of the energy is often a state of *mistaken certainty*. It is important to note that this does not mean that power and energy are not tapped. Often those in this state manifest charisma and even healing power, which must therefore be dropped as possible criteria of truth.

In *The Way of Zen*, Alan Watts relates a story which is appropriate to this point. He tells of a sage who was so holy that the birds would bring him gifts of flowers. Through a dialogue with a Zen master, the sage received a new level of enlightenment, at which the birds ceased to bring the flowers. Truly, the work of analysis of powerful inner experiences is a down-to-earth task, in which the ego of the individual plays a crucial role. In my opinion, philosophies which intend to get rid of the ego are thus fundamentally mistaken. Only the integrity and commitment of the ego can prevent marvelous fantasies from supplanting the truth.

What needs to be broken down are the protective "walls" of *egocentricity* with which we have learned to protect our egos, but a discussion of this point would lead far afield. Usually, however, if one substitutes "egocentricity" where eastern and other thinkers describe the negative effects of "ego," the whole problem would be cleared up. As one cannot hear music on a radio without the radio itself, there is no manifestation of consciousness apart from ego, its "receiver." On this point Jung was exceedingly clear and definite out of his tremendous wealth of investigations.

LEVELS OF CONSCIOUSNESS

The chart (Figure 3) which follows is a tentative and intuitive presentation of levels of consciousness, or of awakening, from deep sleep to godlikeness.

In the chart I make use of a compact notation for very large or very small numbers. There is not room for the usual breaking down of large numbers by stringing together terms like "a million million million miles." That would be a 1 followed by eighteen zeros. The compact notation for this is a superscript or "power," namely $10.^{18}$ So the figure at the top right of the chart, 10^{30}, represents a 1 followed by thirty zeros, or a moving of the decimal place thirty places to the right of the 1. Likewise, a minus sign in the superscript means moving the decimal point to the *left* by that many places. As an example, 10^{-6} represents 0.000001, or one millionth.

The note on the chart relating the terms "God" and "Self" should be read carefully. A mild controversy arose at the instance of Martin Buber as to whether Jung identified "God" with the whole unconscious, and indeed in his memoirs Jung does say something to that effect.[7] But throughout his writings, it is clear that he regards it as scientifically undecidable whether one can identify or differentiate God and the Self, as the central organizing dynamism in the total individual psyche. I personally feel that it is too limiting to the God-concept to identify it with the Self, or even the whole of the psychic and trans-psychic unconscious, which seems to cut off at least some of the aspect of transcendence. A discussion of other significant aspects of the chart, such as the "integration ratio," follows its presentation.

In the levels chart, as one moves upward all these increase: choice, disposable energy (will), and even psyche itself. The "integration level," like the integration ratio, uses the human as its measure. Since we are accustomed to reserving the word "person" for

Figure 3. A POSSIBLE GENERAL VIEW OF LEVELS OF CONSCIOUSNESS.

In this chart, "higher" levels are presented at the top of the chart. I.e. the more awareness, even in the everyday sense of awareness, the more consciousness. Not every philosopher would agree. The vertical strings of dots merely keep track of the columns. See the note on Integration Ratio in the lower right corner of the chart. These levels are related to the "involutions" which are described in the later chapters of this book.

LEVELS OF AWARENESS	Integration Level	Integration Ratio
Manifestation of God or Manifestation of the Self.	Cosmos	10^{30}
"Self" is Jung's designation for the central organizing activity of the unconscious, as well as its peripheral containment. The depth of the inwardness of Reality in its creative individualization is what we might call "God."		
Relation to God: "Love God" or Relation to the Self.	Planet	10^{10}
Awareness of God: "Know thy Lady/Lord" or Awareness of the Self.		

Figure 3. (Continued)

Relation to Unconscious: "Be thyself"

NEXT GENERAL PLATEAU TO BE ATTAINED

Living awareness of whatever one is aware of.

Community 10^2

Awareness of Unconscious: "Know thyself"

Person 10^0

Presence of Ego: ego fully representative of the personality; personal presence to outer world

Partial being dominates from here on down.

Thought: Directed and Associative

Intellectual awareness of whatever one is aware of. 10^{-2}

Figure 3. (Continued)

LEVELS OF AWARENESS	Integration Level	Integration Ratio
Attention: Threshold of Consciousness-as-such		
Ordinary Waking Life. **PRESENT GENERAL PLATEAU**		10^{-3}
Active Imagination—conscious at lower level, using higher functions, and Charismatic Consciousness; open for tapping primitive healing powers. These "places" accessible from higher levels by lowering of the mental level, or inducing trance.		
Relaxed Fantasy—Primitive Life		10^{-5}
Suggestibility—Hallucination		
Animal Waking (Egolessness) **FIRST PLATEAU**		10^{-7}

The integration ratio uses the human as the "measure of all things," since it has a value of $10^0 = 1$ at the level of the

Figure 3. (Continued)

presence of ego. Above that level it signifies the number of potentially conscious beings (see below) which is included in the feeling-awareness of the individual. Below the level of ego-presence the fragmentation, or partialness ratio, is hard to estimate as yet.

Hypnotic State

.
.
. Sleep Walk

.
.
. Dreaming

. Deep Sleep

humans, I would prefer to find some word which includes other intelligent and loving life forms, i.e. potentially conscious beings. The fact that on the earth not only humans but the cetaceans as well may need to be included complicates the situation. But leaving this problem aside, a "family" may be taken as of the order of ten, or a few tens of "people," a community as of the order of hundreds, a planet as a few billions, and our local cosmos (everything we can see with our telescopes) as 10^{30}, allowing for so-called "alien" life forms. In this way the inclusion levels are intended to match the ratios.

Only at the point of "awareness of the unconscious" can the work begin along the lines of the ancient Greek "know thyself," which is why it is set as a *goal* for those at the level of ordinary waking life. From the level of ordinary waking life, one can make stabs into upper regions on a partial basis. That is, one can become very good at certain types of thought, philosophical, scientific, economic, mathematical, historical, legal, etc., without being good at thinking in general. These kinds of activities certainly don't require that we be aware of the various grounds of our being or of our general unconsciousness. We can do them very well as *partial* humans. Artistic, relational, intuitional, and other less-rational talents also can be developed one-sidedly. In the chart we are generally referring to those qualities on the "spiritual" side rather than those on the material side of living. The question becomes that of the completeness of including the various facets of life.

Our present level is what is ordinarily called "ego-consciousness," but the ego is usually quite fragmented. The ego is built up through those experiences by means of which we learn "who we are." Therefore we must also be concerned with the universality with which we probe the sources of commonly held socio-mythological motifs. A reciprocal relation also exists between the ego-building experiences and ordinary learning. When we have an "aha!" experience, it is as if something "falls into place," and we definitely are stronger in our knowledge, which usually means that we are psychologically stronger as well. Our readiness for certain experiences, including reading certain books, is often, but not always, a matter of waking, but is not waking in itself. It may be that I must study several preliminary subjects and gain the concepts of a field before I can read freely in that field. But I believe most of us have had the experience of not being able to "get into" a given book for reasons we later identified as "not being ready, psychologically." In those cases, the analogy of waking may well be applicable.

THE NEED FOR VERIFICATION

There is another dimension to the levels chart, having to do with inadequate verification procedures, leaving one in a state of mistaken certainty. This was mentioned above as among the pitfalls of a highly developed, but partial, consciousness. In this connection, reference should be made to Appendix 1: "Intellectual and Emotional Integrity," where examples are given of highly intelligent people feeling very "clear" that erroneous positions were correct. Clarity or felt clarity is by no means a decisive criterion, either of correctness or of awakeness. Mistaken certainty as a phenomenon is one of the most direct indications that the analogy of waking is appropriate. Thus we have to say that the lowest level actually achieved by an individual is that of awareness of things in a generally indubitable fashion, e.g. awareness that the earth is round. Such a proposition may indeed be doubted, but not *truthfully*. As noted earlier, the fact the earth is basically "round" will not be superseded, while the current *precision* of the knowledge of its roundness *will* be. The truth in this sense requires adequate relating and communicating with others.

One can assert the truth of the proposition that the world is round on the basis of what I call the "web of verification," which is the fact that we know all that we know in multiple ways—almost never singly. We verify all within our world by means of *multiple paths*, only a few of which are conscious to us in ordinary circumstances. Our brains receive millions of signals per second, sorted by the "reticular formation" in the brain stem as important or not. In this sense we can even say that *we are* multiple channels by our evolutionary structuring. We process much more information than can possibly be in our awareness.

Even everyday reality must be perceived and known in a variety of ways. On the largest scale, science and religion comprise the two major approaches which are both necessary for a comprehension of reality which can be called complete. "Complete," here, means that there are no major gaps in the *kinds* of knowledge appropriate to the subject. Jung understood this with respect to the science of psychology, and stated the need to use both psychological and religious language to describe major moves in personal transformation. This is brought out most effectively by Aniela Jaffé in *The Myth of Meaning.*[8]

Philosopher Ludwig Wittgenstein, in *On Certainty,*[9] asks the philosophical question of what kind of mistake it would be to be uncertain that "here is a hand," while looking at his own hand. Perhaps his attitude can be grasped from just one of his propositions, though they are highly varied:

> Why do I not satisfy myself that I have two feet when I want to get up from a chair? There is no why. I simply don't. This is how I act.

Of course I *do* verify it, but unconsciously! If my feet were not there I would know immediately. I know that, and therefore know that I do indeed verify the fact by means which need not come to consciousness if everything "checks out." If we think about it, we also know that such verification attends us at every moment of our lives.

In his investigation, Wittgenstein overlooks the whole *web of verification.* What if I were to look and my hand could not be seen, though I had experienced no change in internal bodily sense of my physical wholeness or physical status? Why, then I must examine the *stump* for clues as to the hand's disappearance, not just say, "Maybe it will be there next time." There can be no such thing as "just" a hand missing: it is linked to the whole world. If no arm is seen, then where is the *break* which indicates where the hand had been attached to the rest of me, assuming I can still see *some* of me? If a hand is missing, and no "break" is found, then the whole world is missing.

We are supported in our view of reality, insofar as it is valid, by much more than we know. This is the web of verification. We are able also to do several tasks at once, keeping multiple channels open. In part this includes the fact that we depend upon others for much of what we know. One must be open to the educated thought of others, and consider it in coming to a conclusion, but that does not verify the old saying that "the voice of the people is the voice of God!"

SEEING BEYOND THE IMMEDIATE

The web of verification presents us with some facts of which we remain obstinately unaware. We do not *necessarily* see when our lives contradict our beliefs. We remain parochial. We check out what we want to, especially that which relates to our physical well-being, but don't apply the same care to our *lives*. This can give us important clues as to how our philosophy might become *living* philosophy. What *is* it which ultimately gives our lives wholeness? What our living finally rests upon is the nature of reality. We live within it, and it reflects the wholeness and transformative quality of the cosmos.

Since all humans experience this wholeness in some manner, a key question might be that of one's willingness to generalize beyond all world traditions, especially in the area of religion. An inner reality may push outward toward the ego-consciousness of an individual, and take on a specific form which is culturally compatible with the ego—in this sense, the same experience which induces one in the Christian world to say, "I know Jesus Christ." That is, the *same* experience which comes to a Christian in the form of an explicit experience of Jesus Christ will elicit an entirely different interpretation from an easterner, and its "true" meaning, in the sense of the world being round, will be different from the interpretation of either person.[10] Here we need to refer the reader to the Jungian literature for a more complete description of the psychological phenomenon of "projection," but a single example within the experience of most of us is the process of discovering that a person with whom we were in love is a different person from the one we had imagined he or she was. What we had been seeing was truly a projection of our own inner being. Thus it may be clear that many powerful experiences are interpreted by us as other than someone else with better vision would describe them.

CONSCIOUSNESS AND CULTURES

If it seemed arrogant to compare the awakeness of one person to another, what must it seem to attempt to compare *cultures?* If I value cultures for their intellectual development, and their stress on individual choice, while someone else values a culture for its collective mores and family feeling, can a choice be made objectively? Is it not rather that cultures are different, but by definition equal? In view of the existence of levels of awareness in individuals, and also by the nature of consciousness itself as always specific, it seems that we must apply criteria of consciousness to differentiate between cultures. Consciousness yields freedom, and freedom is the exercise of choice. On several occasions I have been told, "You don't understand," when I have attempted to talk with members of other cultures about certain ideas which they hold. The lack of understanding referred to here is based on deeply embedded *unconscious* patterns of experience and behavior which vary from culture to culture. If there were conscious reasons for any given behavior, such reasons could be discussed. "You don't understand" speaks of an irrational obedience to a local pattern, simply because that is the way things are done. In that case, the word "understand" is misused.

I view any individual, regardless of heritage, as an equally valuable human being. I do not regard cultural heritage merely as a collective mode of living which forces the individual to live accordingly. Survival often dictates that one live as a good member of a culture. Conscious comparative valuation of cultures means at the least to observe the differences in their behavioral patterns and to choose on some conscious basis what seems the most valuable and appropriate thing to do. Beyond that, consciousness might involve inventing new behaviors based on conscious values, and especially not being bound to do it in any given way. In at least two different cultures, I have been told, "No [member of this culture] would *ever* get a divorce." Certainly one who feels that way has abdicated all personal responsibility in such a matter.

A number of westerners have "jumped" cultures, say, from Christianity to Hinduism or Buddhism, but all three of these have limitations. One must be able to stand free and look at them all.

Having said all that, I must then stress the real values that are carried for all of us by cultures, and also the fact that no one can ever be entirely free from culture, any more than an individual can achieve full consciousness. While the above chart has a level of "manifestation of God" at its top, that is something that we all now do at some level, and no one can live there all the time.[11] Living at the God-level is the most conscious way in which it might be possible to live. Such living can grow within one as the person develops her or his innate potentials. Further, one does so live only if one *knows* that one does, and has also mastered and applied the arts of verification. Moreover, we all have a structure, a given and evolved form, whether we are earth-humans, or some other intelligent loving species on this or some other planet. But there is a *widest possible* structure which binds all of us in this cosmos, and that is *the way things are,* the ultimate reality mentioned above. This is precisely why the physical knowledge of the way things are is so important to have. Not to be bound to a relatively minor culture, one which, for example, represents only *part* of a planet, is the prerequisite to perceiving the overall binding of finite creatures by the oneness, or unity, or physical consistency of our cosmos. Within that overall framework lies tremendous freedom. For most of us it is sufficient to try to encompass the variety on our planet alone, and to make moral choices (make our choices on a moral basis) in the widest possible arena, in view of global values, rather than on a parochial basis. Certainly cultural plurality can only work on a planet if the leaders of each culture think from a primary commitment to the whole planet.

We must all push beyond the culture we are in, but some of our own cultures do offer a framework of greater established freedom than do others.

Clues as to how we can tell when we have a degree of awakening, and also whether we have a basis for challenging others have been scattered throughout the above. To summarize, it is we as individuals who know, but who are also and always uncertain, especially of the higher levels. It might be said that it is incumbent upon us to be *professionally* uncertain. We gain certainty through the web of verification. Do we always add to that web, and challenge our own certainty? Does what we gain give us deep satisfaction, and an intelligent response for every eventuality? Can our framework be broadened in all its dimensions, but especially those of concept and feeling? Or are we still primarily a member of a partial population of the planet? Does a piercing self-analysis show that we have sacrificed our intellectual or our emotional integrity at any point?

It is much easier to remain unconscious, to accept what those around us think in a general way, than to challenge the basis of our everyday assumptions. Of course this applies to academia as well, and perhaps it applies especially there, because it is there that the responsibility for such challenge might creatively reside. Yet in every discipline, a prevailing "establishment" is formed, which becomes the enemy of the new, even if for the very good reason that the present methods are very powerful and productive.

Certainly the awareness of the unconscious with its negative powers and creative potentials is prerequisite to a modern awakening. Spirituality, as the refinement of spirit-matter and the building of a solid basis for further gains of consciousness, demands all this awareness of us.

Notes

1. *Atoms.*
2. Hitchcock, *Atoms,* and also more technically in Hitchcock, John L. 1976. *A Comparison of 'Complementarity' in Quantum Physics with Analogous Structures in Kierkegaard's Philosophical Writings, from a Jungian Point of View.* Dissertation 76-9150. Ann Arbor: Xerox University Microfilms.
3. Rahula, Walpola. 1959. *What the Buddha Taught.* New York: Grove Press, Evergreen Books, pp. 57–58.
4. *Dhamma* is the Pali form of the Sanskrit *dharma* = teachings, law, truth, elements of existence, here taken in the last meaning.
5. Heidegger, Martin. 1961. *An Introduction to Metaphysics.* Translated by Ralph Manheim. Garden City, NY: Doubleday and Company, Anchor Books, p. 1.
6. *The Structure and Dynamics of the Psyche, CW* 8, pgfs. 179 and 197.
7. *Memories,* pp. 336–337.
8. Jaffé, Aniela. 1970. *The Myth of Meaning.* Translated by R.F.C. Hull. London: Hodder and Stoughton, pp. 112–113.
9. Wittgenstein, Ludwig. 1972. *On Certainty.* Edited by G.E.M. Anscombe and G.H. von Wright. Translated by Denis Paul and G.E.M. Anscombe. New York: Harper and Row, Harper Torchbooks, #148.
10. This phenomenon has been amply demonstrated by Raymond Moody in his studies of the near-death experience. A common near-death experience is that of encountering the "Being of Light," whom Christians often identify with Christ, Jews with Moses or Elijah, Buddhists with Buddha, etc.
11. A psychotic person who thinks that he or she is living at the God-level might be thought a good example of "mistaken certainty." While this *is* an example, the more relevant ones involve non-psychotic persons, and are such as the ones, including Einstein, which I describe in Appendix 1.

Chapter 3

Consciousness and the Moral Dimension

Never sacrifice your intellectual integrity, even for God.
                                    —*Henry Burton Sharman*

One of the clearest of Jung's conclusions, but one most commonly passed over in reading his works, is that no meaningful change occurs in the personality, no significant consciousness arises, except when one takes a new *moral* attitude, both toward the unconscious and its activity, and with respect to living in the world. By "moral," we mean here that the question of right/wrong, or good/evil, is raised and considered, not the application of specific codes of behavior. The question of specific behavior must be individually decided on the basis of "inner necessity," what one can live with emotionally *when one is at the deep personal center.*

Morality, then, always entails the engagement of the *inner depth* by the person. We will work toward the understanding that a higher consciousness is the product of the same engagement. The encounter with one's inner depth uncovers the inner moral conflicts, the reconciliation of which yields new consciousness.

Numerous statements to this effect are found throughout Jung's writings, often under the heading of "conscious realization." In *Psychological Reflections*,[1] Jung is quoted from one of his Eranos lectures:

> The best of truths is of no use—as history has shown a thousand times—unless it has become the individual's most personal inner experience. Every equivocal, so-called "clear" answer mostly remains in the head and only finds its way down to the heart in the very rarest of cases. Our need is not to "know" the truth but to experience it.

71

In *Memories, Dreams, Reflections,*[2] he puts it:

> It is a grave mistake to think that it is enough to gain some understanding of the images [from the unconscious] and that knowledge can here make a halt. Insight into them must be converted into an ethical obligation. Not to do so is to fall prey to the power principle, and this produces dangerous effects which are destructive not only to others, but even to the knower. The images of the unconscious place a great responsibility upon an individual.

Other statements are quoted later in this chapter. See especially one on the opposites in God and the symbol of the cross, which puts the same idea in religious language.

RELIGIOUS AND SECULAR LANGUAGE

The realm of the moral impinges upon both the religious and the secular areas of life, without being absolutely necessary to either. It is possible to function in both of these areas without encountering moral conflict, especially if religion is identified with experience of the numinous. It certainly is possible to have numinous experience without engaging moral considerations. The case is even clearer with the secular, since success in business often seems to require the sequestering of one's moral awareness. But amoral functioning is without consciousness in Jung's sense. From his point of view, most of our day-to-day living is quite unconscious, however professional our work may be, and whatever level of creativity and intelligence is employed.

The division of life into religious and secular areas is one of the major human phenomena of the last two millennia. Mythologist R.T.R. Clark[3] credits the Greeks with the invention of the secular, and thus also of linear time, or developmental history.

> The Greeks were the first to discover spheres of activity which were independent of religious conditions or to be expressed in non-religious terms. Since then—but only intermittently— Western man has been accustomed to set experience into two divisions, Church and State, clerical and lay, religion and science.

Each outlook brings certain different, even contradictory, aspects of life into focus. For this reason, in order to attain a complete picture in dealing with the dimension of morality, it is necessary to formulate the same idea in both religious and secular language. In *The Myth of Meaning* Jaffé speaks of the need for such dual expression of both technical and religious language for psychological phenomena. She says:

> A psychological approach can never quite refrain from reverting to the original religious verbal images. The archetypal contents rising up from the unconscious have an emotional charge, a numinosity, that ought not be lost, but must constantly be called back into memory again. Then only does the reality of the psyche reveal its depth.[4]

As an example, she gives the following: Rather than say

> that the "ego arises out of the Self" or the "Self emerges into consciousness seeking actualization," we would have to say in religious language that "God creates the human" or "God seeks the human and actualizes himself in encountering his creature."[5]

It is an excellent exercise to feel into how these statements say the same thing.

In this chapter these two modes of expression are woven together. In the material about to be presented, Jung speaks freely in religious language. Intermittently, parallels to Jung's thought which are to be found in modern physics are brought in.

JUNG'S *ANSWER TO JOB*[6]

Jung once remarked that of all his books, the only one which he would leave exactly as it is was *Answer to Job*. It is in this book that he makes the strongest connections between consciousness and the moral dimension, as intimated in the opening paragraph above. In the preface to this book, he gives the same reasons as does Jaffé for expressing himself in the religious idiom:

> Although our whole world of religious ideas consists of anthro-
> pomorphic images that could never stand up to rational criticism,
> we should never forget that they are based on numinous arche-
> types, i.e., on an emotional foundation which is unassailable by
> reason. We are dealing with psychic facts which logic can over-
> look but not eliminate.[7]

In the material which follows for the present, then, Jung's own expression is in the religious arena, as he gives us his response to the
book of Job. The story of Job, being such a deep part of western
cultural history, is therefore taken as a precise expression of *psychic
fact.* That is, it is deep inside us, and not a question of historical, but
psychic truth. Therefore, Jung treats it as it is, without undue "scientific caution." For those not familiar with the story of Job, a synopsis
is included in Appendix 2. In addition, since I am aware of many
whose sensitivities are aroused by the use of "God's name," I have
changed Jung's use of "Yahweh" to "YHWH," as suggested to me
by a rabbi with whom I discussed this. He showed me that it was not
awkward to verbalize the four letters, Yod Heh Vav Heh, in any
circumstance.

Jung says:

> The *Book of Job* is a landmark in the long historical development
> of a divine drama. At the time the book was written, there were
> already many testimonies which had given a contradictory pic-
> ture of YHWH. . . . Insight existed along with obtuseness, lov-
> ingkindness along with cruelty, creative power along with de-
> structiveness. Everything was there, and none of these qualities
> was an obstacle to the other. Such a condition is only conceivable
> when no reflecting consciousness is present at all, or when the
> capacity for reflection is very feeble and a more or less adven-
> titious phenomenon. A condition of this sort can only be de-
> scribed as 'amoral.'[8]

With these words, Jung draws an essential connection between
three concepts which are central to this chapter: reflection, consciousness, and morality. Here he makes it clear that *without* a "reflecting consciousness," morality is out of the question. We sometimes say that God is "beyond good and evil," which is equivalent to
saying that God is not encumbered by a discriminating consciousness

as we are. But this is only half the issue. We still need to show that consciousness is *essentially* moral in its nature. That is, there is a *mutual* pre-condition of the one for the other; they grow together. This is hardly a new thought, but I believe that there is a new way to make it abundantly clear. If we begin by accepting the relationship of consciousness and morality which Jung asserts in the above quotation (and other related ones), we can later see that we have preserved the essential meaning which the word "morality" now carries.

It is worth mentioning that the close linkage of consciousness and morality does not mean that if one is conscious, one is "good" in a conventional moral sense, but that morality—the presence of the issues of good/evil, or good/higher good—is the touchstone of consciousness as such.

Answer to Job is certainly not easy to read, since it offers a radical reinterpretation of one of the most loved and studied works in the biblical literature. It seems, therefore, that it is a great risk to excerpt from it, and to present its point of view in relatively few words. But because of the seminal nature of this singular book, it is necessary to attempt it, with the proviso that the reader understands the limited nature of my focus, which is not the story of Job as such, but Jung's explicit and intimated connection of consciousness and morality. I deeply recommend working on the whole of *Answer to Job,* along with the relevant material on *Answer to Job* in *The Myth of Meaning* by Aniela Jaffé. To continue with Jung, each of the following excerpts introduces a specific idea:

> This is perhaps the greatest thing about Job, that, faced with this difficulty [that the God from whom he seeks a hearing is the God who has wounded him], he does not doubt the unity of God. He clearly sees that God is at odds with himself—so totally at odds that he, Job, is quite certain of finding in God a helper and an "advocate" against God. As certain as he is of the evil in YHWH, he is equally certain of the good.[9]

It seems likely that many of us, meditating on this statement, would fall into a "modern" rationalistic conclusion that a non-rational God is simply nonsense. If one can receive evil as well as good from God, it's just as well to say there is no God. If we don't fall off that precipice, then this passage gives a fine sense both of living with conflict, and also therefore what a deep personal integrity might mean.

The next paragraph reinforces the connection of consciousness and morality, but still from the first aspect, not yet saying that consciousness presupposes morality. That will come out in Jung's intimations later.

> If YHWH, as we would expect of a sensible human being, were really conscious of himself, he would, in view of the true facts of the case, at least put an end to the panegyrics on his justice. But he is too unconscious to be moral. Morality presupposes consciousness. By this I do not mean to say that YHWH is imperfect or evil. . . . He is everything in its totality; therefore, among other things, he is total justice, and also its total opposite.[10]

In the next selection, Jung speaks of the "pleromatic state," which he describes in his "Seven Sermons to the Dead" as "a nothingness that is both empty and full," and as "the beginning and end of created beings." "Pleroma" signifies the same state that the early Greek philosopher Anaximander called *apeiron*, or the place of no boundaries, out of which the opposites arise, and in which, by implication, they are mixed without distinction. Jung sometimes uses this word to describe the unconscious, especially in its deeper layers.

The pleroma finds a counterpart in quantum physics in the idea of the subatomic entities (such as electrons) themselves, which can manifest in contradictory modes such as "wave" and "particle," but *in themselves* therefore must "possess" these contradictory properties without any "problem." Note that it is because such non-rational entities are now known by modern physics that we have a more complete basis for the integrity, mentioned above, of not concluding that the holding together of opposites is nonsense: it's there in physical reality. The words could cogently be applied to the *physical* becoming of the building blocks of nature. The second half of this quotation is exceedingly important, for it describes the condition of emerging consciousness.

> In the pleromatic or (as the Tibetans call it) Bardo state, there is a perfect interplay of cosmic forces, but with the Creation—that is, with the division of the world into distinct processes in time and space—events begin to rub and jostle one another.[11]

Here is added an image ("rub and jostle") to one quoted earlier: "None of these [contradictory] qualities was an *obstacle* to the other." I will return often to these images.

TAKING IT INSIDE

It is *we* who, especially as we gain consciousness, are unable either to reconcile or bypass the various conflicts of the so-called good, the moral conflicts which are the stuff of literature. As children, in our relative unconsciousness, we are well able to compartmentalize different forces in life without *feeling* their conflict: e.g. in torturing animals (with no *feeling* obstacle presenting itself) or holding conflicting views in science and religion apart so that their opposition cannot be felt. Their outlook is clearly unconscious and amoral.

I once taught at a school where the students were "born again" Christians and good science students as well. They could cite evidence for scientific theories and could use their knowledge of atomic physics to explain, e.g., the physical properties of two forms of the element carbon, diamond and graphite. They even *knew* that their science conflicted with their fundamentalist Christianity, but they could hold these areas of their lives well apart. The conflict was not *felt* at all, and therefore never became an opportunity for a change in consciousness. Things didn't "rub and jostle." Many unconscious adults have retained this ability in later years. At the same school, a woman in her forties admonished me that I must not be selective or critical about what I use from the Bible. "You must take the *whole* Bible at its face, as inspired and true." Such unawareness of contradiction is truly striking to one who is accustomed to critical thought. Jung says:

It is just by following Christian morality that one gets into the worst collisions of duty. Only those who habitually make five an even number can escape them. The fact that Christian ethics leads to collisions of duty speaks in its favor. By engendering insoluble conflicts and consequently an "affliction of soul," it brings us nearer to a knowledge of God. All opposites are of God, therefore we must bend to this burden; and in so doing we find that God's "oppositeness" has taken possession of us, become embodied in us. We become a vessel filled with divine conflict. We rightly associate the idea of suffering with a state in which the opposites violently collide with one another, but we hesitate to describe such a painful experience as being "redeemed." Yet it cannot be denied that the great symbol of the Christian faith, the Cross, upon which hangs the suffering figure of the Redeemer, has been emphatically held up before the eyes of Christians for nearly two thousand years.[12]

[T]he undoubted lack of reflection in God's consciousness is sufficient to explain his peculiar behavior. It is quite right, therefore, that fear of God should be considered the beginning of all wisdom. On the other hand, the much-vaunted goodness, love, and justice of God should not be regarded as mere propitiation, but should be recognized as a genuine experience, for God is a complex of coincident opposites. Both are justified, the fear of God as well as the love of God.[13]

God has a terrible double aspect: a sea of grace is met by a seething lake of fire, and the light of love glows with a fierce dark heat. . . .[14]

Let any one of us meditate on the circumstances within which we would say of ourselves, "That's when I *really* grew up," or "I learned my most significant life-lesson there," or "That's what has most informed such consciousness as I now have." The existential lesson, if we reflect honestly, will conform to these passages from Jung, or else essential steps in consciousness still lie ahead for us.

Is this the nature of reality? Is suffering the path to consciousness *as such*, or only sometimes, and perhaps not even in the majority of instances? We can derive clues to psychological reality from a scientific view of the outer world.

GROUNDING IN PHYSICAL REALITY

The overwhelming experimental evidence from modern physics says that contradictory concepts are necessary for a complete description of a single entity, such as a photon or an electron. This state of affairs has been under intense discussion and experimental investigation for over sixty years, the most decisive experiments being of quite recent date. Even the most conservative interpretation of this situation says that the contradiction occurs in our consciousness so that (at least) the relationship of contradiction to consciousness is assured. A deeper view, now supported by both theoretical and experimental work, says that the contradictoriness that we perceive in subatomic particles is not limited to our *perception*, but resides in the nature of the reality itself. This view, called "complementarity" in physics, would correspond to Jung's statement that "all opposites are of God." Thus, the oppositeness, the inevitable contradictoriness of our lives, would indeed reflect the nature of reality itself, and is entirely to be expected. The question is then how we have taken so long to discover that fact. To this, the answer is to be found in the turmoils of the psyche which are so well recorded in the book of Job and in the history which has subsequently arisen. Our psyches have gained tremendous scope via rationalism, so we cling to it. Now they may be strong enough to see beyond it.

We don't *want* this collision of opposites to be the way things are. Especially, we don't want such a state to be necessary for the development of consciousness. But just as it has taken a long time for the dual nature of physical reality to come to the consciousness of scientists, the conflicts of life also remain hidden until we pursue, or are *forced* to pursue, the knowledge of them. This process is a continuing one.

FROM PHYSICAL TO PSYCHOLOGICAL INSIGHT

We should try to form an accurate analogy of the contradictions in the physical realm to those in the psychological sphere. The resistance which *we* feel toward the nature of the reality of painful awakening is mirrored in the following excerpt, also from *Answer to Job*. It is a passage that will reward a careful reading:

> The peculiar, unforeseen antics of people arouse YHWH's wrath and thereby involve him in his own creation.[15]

It has already been seen that it takes *obstacles* or stumbling blocks in our path to force us to become conscious of the actual conflict of

opposites which was always present, but unperceived, because un-
felt. But there is a reciprocal action as well. Some deep aspect of
reality is disturbed, even angered, when we begin to become
conscious, and perhaps therefore unpredictable. The wonderful am-
bivalence of the word "provoked" would be good here.

Sometimes Jung speaks of obstacles in God's path and sometimes of obstacles in our own path, as in the passage concerning the
opposites in God and the symbol of the cross, quoted above. This
poses a sort of conundrum which can only be resolved, I believe, if
we consider the "acts of God" which were "done" to Job in the
modern legal sense, that of natural catastrophes which do not take
account of the "moral" status of the recipient or victim. When Job
says "Shall we receive good from YHWH, and shall we not receive
evil as well?" he is, in effect, saying the same thing. I want to make it
clear that I do not see this view as deleting God. The resolution of
the sense of the paradoxicality occurs when we realize the bottom-
lessness of inner depth, i.e. when we "take God inside."

Another step in the process of converting insight into the nature
of physical reality into psychological understanding is parallel to taking the lessons of quantum physics into the everyday world of large
objects. For instance, the concepts of (1) *where* something is and (2)
how it is moving would seem to be quite clear. But even such seemingly clear concepts fall under the purview of complementarity. Until quantum physics came along, they didn't "rub and jostle" at all.
However, it is now generally accepted that the concepts involved in
determining the position and motion of a body *at the same instant* are
contradictory, even in the everyday world. Thus we have a clear case
of the emergence of the awareness of a conflict which was there all
the time, but which required some probing to bring to consciousness.

Here, the nature of physics as an *experimental* science becomes
especially relevant, showing by analogy the open-ended nature of
consciousness. Just as there certainly will always be new physical
facts to discover, so also there will always be inner obstacles to force
us toward a deeper consciousness. This seems very related to the
Moses story,[16] where he asks God's name. The reply is, in some
translations, "I will become what I will become," or "I am what
I am becoming," which conveys the same precise sense in the religious field.

JOB'S NEW CLARITY

That the opposites are from a unitary God appears in the Hebrew scriptures in various places, but the writer of Job takes the understanding of that fact to new depth. The felt conflict here was between the nature of reality as it is, and as it was seen by his contemporary culture. In order to be an obstacle to that culture, to make it aware of conflict, a devastating event must happen to a person who is individually "good," or not guilty of moral breaches. Since that time our cultural view has hardly advanced at all, though some are more aware of the immorality perpetrated in the name of religion. That should suffice to bring the conflict to consciousness, but we largely remain obstinately oblivious.

What Job's certainty of his innocence did for him that no one else could have achieved was that he did not sacrifice his integrity by falsely assuming his guilt in some unknown or unremembered act, which many devout people regularly do as a matter of religious ritual. In refusing to do so, he maintained not only his own integrity, but God's integrity within himself as the bringer of both calamity and healing, and gained consciousness at an entirely new level. He transcended the previous condition of consciousness or unconsciousness in humanity, and thus initiated a new *demand* upon human consciousness in general.

In the end the events "rub and jostle" in *us* and force us, if we can grow, to take a new and deeper view of reality. This is inherent in a universe of a complementary nature. It is helpful to consider this as the way "God" operates in developing consciousness, i.e., self-reflexiveness, in the cosmos.

GOD AS THE CHALLENGE TO BE FREE

How we respond to the opposites which cross our paths constellates and constitutes our value for the evolutionary process. The value *for* Job, i.e. for his consciousness, was his *response* to the events which intervened in his life, and this is also his value for us as a way-shower. I do not refer here to "events" as sent or controlled by conscious powers, but to those occurrences which would seem natural if they did not change our lives *when they are seen by us as meaningful,* such as getting or not getting a job, losing an eye, or getting cancer at a particular time, etc. Jung called such external events which coincide with the inner meaning of the time "synchronous" events. Of course they don't need to be as momentous as those just given. I feel that many more of these sporadic but potentially meaningful events occur than we have learned to perceive. In a letter to M. Leonard,[17] Jung said:

> To this day God is the name by which I designate all things which cross my willful path violently and recklessly, all things which upset my subjective views, plans and intentions and change the course of my life for better or worse.

It is a very helpful exercise to look at such events in this way for a week, or even a day. In order to grow, we must feel the conflict, feel our integrity threatened by events, and hold our integrity in spite of everything which might seem to entitle us to excuse ourselves in one way or another. Indeed, as Jung says:

> Fear is certainly justified up to a point, for to make the conflict complete, there must be doubt and uncertainty as to whether our strength is not being overtaxed.[18]

We are *required* to gain new meaning and new unity in the face of peril, and this constitutes a new definition of the "good," and of a loving God. Those who achieve this in any measure know that it is so, and that the God of opposites, in that very new sense, is indeed a *summum bonum,* but not in any previously held sense of moral goodness. We have imagined that a "good" God would be a "loving" Father, or Father/Mother, who would not let us slip too far, would watch over us with our comfort in mind, would protect us from the reality of our true selves. Instead the reality of love is that we are indeed *free,* which naturally includes the freedom for error and loss. We experience reality as both threatening and benign, but that is from the old, more obvious point of view. In reality, the "threat" is that of being free, alive, and responsible.

It is also important to become conscious of the fact that life is not a "test" against specific criteria. We seem to have absorbed the idea that it *is* such a test very fully into Christianity in our striving (if we do) to be "worthy" of "heaven." Here the idea was that there was some threshold of goodness or faithfulness which would ensure our admission, and/or some equally clear criterion which would prevent it. Neither was Job, nor are we, "tested" *in that sense:* Job *lived*, and so too may we live. If we see that we are tested by and for *Life*, and not for moral perfection under the previous guidelines, and tested continually, then the new picture of reality is at hand.

What makes this view valuable is indeed the deep sense of living that we derive in the process of living itself. This possibility is also what keeps it from being merely a random process, a quixotic windmill. Instead it is indeed a truly awesome conferral of "grace." We might, on some ground, "believe" that this is the nature of things, but "belief" is never effective except as insulation from reality. It is only the *felt conflict* that yields consciousness, and it is purely a matter of courage, moral courage, to face it.

A DEEPER LOOK

Since "Job's day," moreover, the situation has deepened tremendously, for now we must have the courage to affirm that carrying the burden of opposites is valuable to the World Order,[19] in spite of previously held views of morality. As Tillich puts it, "the courage to be is the courage to accept oneself as accepted, in spite of unacceptability."[20] Or, in Job's terms, we must find the courage to say, "my heart does not reproach me for any of my days,"[21] in spite of our consciousness of conventional moral guilt. This does *not* mean that we are *not guilty!* We have indeed hurt others and that entails consequences for us—sometimes grave consequences. But we must affirm the aliveness of our small part of the Process. It is only from an achieved integrity, i.e. acceptance of our own dark side as well as the light, that a modern person can use Job's words with new depth.

This might be a moment in which to remind ourselves, too, of the very real place of humor in the process. The blacks of South Africa say that one of the greatnesses of their people is their ability to laugh in all circumstances, and indeed sickness and death follow them more than most peoples. A sense of celebration is a very real manifestation of aliveness, as is the exuberance of dance and humor. Humor signifies much more than the ability to shake off tragedy or to laugh at our own blindnesses and errors. It is also a very deep ability to perceive the contradictions and to express that fact with extreme efficiency, as well as preparing the feelings for such perceptions. Ideally, humor should grow more acute with greater consciousness, and be, as Kierkegaard saw, the "incognito" of a highly developed spirituality. It is, as the mathematicians say, "a necessary, but not a sufficient condition" for discerning such a spirituality. At least the absence of humor indicates that spirituality has lost its grounding in earthiness. What is "heavier" than the deadly humorlessness of a misused spirituality?[22] To cry fully and to laugh fully are the emblems of the most human. One might call humor "saving" in this respect. Indeed it has saved many lives from psychological perdition. At its greatest, humor is a tremendous humanizing force for stabilizing and for maintaining perspective, but I admit I am stumped when I try to imagine it attending the death of a world. Perhaps I do not yet fully appreciate the power of Life in the cosmos.

Consciousness is the awareness of the conflict of opposites, along with the awareness of the moral dimension of that conflict. In God all opposites are present, essentially *without* conflict. This is a view implied not only in Job, but also in many other places: e.g. in the prayer of God suggested in the Midrash,[23] "May it be My Will that my Love overcome My Wrath." To become conscious, insofar as it is gaining the awareness of conflict, *is* to suffer. Humor is also rooted in conflict. Kierkegaard[24] says, "the tragic is the suffering contradiction, the comical, the painless contradiction." Of course, suffering is not the goal or end. Rather, it is *Life,* and we live our joy more intensely out of suffering rather than in its absence.

The view that things merely progress is blind. At least it is blind now that consciousness has become the manifest goal of evolution. Jung puts it especially powerfully:

> The right way, like the wrong way, must be paid for, and however much [one] may extol "venerable nature," it is in either case an *opus contra naturam* [a "work against nature"]. . . . [Our] instincts are not harmoniously arranged; they are perpetually jostling each other out of the way. . . . Whichever course one takes, nature will be mortified and must suffer. . . . The Christian symbol of the crucifix is therefore a prototype and an "eternal"

truth. . . . Nobody who finds himself on the road to wholeness can escape that characteristic suspension which is the meaning of crucifixion.[25]

Naturally, we may be nailed to the cross equally by our virtues as by our vices.

We *cannot* be aware of all that is present. We must and can *increase* our awareness of it, by increasing the development of our natural abilities to be conscious. We can do so by continually attempting to interpret the world. As Jung said:

Interpretations are only for those who do not understand; it is only the things we don't understand that have any meaning. [We] woke up in a world [we] did not understand, and that is why [we try] to interpret it.[26]

Though, in the story of Job, God, as Jung says, "rides roughshod over him," it is essential to our moral interpretation of the world to realize that *we* do the same every day. Our power moves ride roughshod over innocence and wisdom alike, which is also part of learning the burden of God, if so taken. This becomes the key to our understanding that indeed consciousness presupposes morality. It is only when the moral field is activated that one can see that *we* behave toward innocence, our own as well as that of others, by trotting out our power for display, as God did to Job. Then we can see the point both of the story and of the incarnation of God in the human: to come to realization of our inner darkness, and resolve to bend the thrust of our power to other uses.

APPROPRIATE SOCIAL BEHAVIOR

That which *is* appropriate behavior or action for the help of the world order will now run counter to much of what is *considered* appropriate by any given society, as well as its formal rules and laws. K'ung Fu-tze ("Confucius") made an interesting and important distinction concerning "propriety," saying that it is unlawful to practice it if the "rites" are not also practiced. Translated to our own times, this would mean that there are both formal and informal aspects with regard to our relations with others. He was saying that one ought to guard against a casual appearance of "fitting in," without participating fully. The duality created here between propriety and "the rites" gives one a check upon whether one is fully and sincerely part of present society.

We might identify a modern sense of the "rites" as the most concrete public expression of sincere participation in our society, e.g. if in some location the general (unspoken) rule is, "In this town, *every* decent person goes to church." We can, I think, easily imagine someone who might feel the tension between these "rites" and the most creative individual behavior, or even behavior beneficial to humanity, on a given day. In some places "civil disobedience" might be an example, though in others it might be an outright distancing of one from society. Or the tension might be felt as a conflict of duties, which, as Jung often says, is the sort of "rubbing and jostling" of the contradictory aspects of reality which best engenders a new consciousness.

We are still at a place, as societies, where the Confucian rule must be honored, and one must largely practice the "rites," without which there is little ground for moral reference. But propriety, the more inner and less formal expression of relationship to others, will evolve into something else. It will be a new principle of spirituality which attempts to honor society but is fundamentally responsive to higher values. Such values will not be wholly concerned with the individual, but may well work concretely toward a better society than can be generally envisioned. Propriety, properly embodied and creative, will be "the principle" on its own, equivalent to *alignment* to the "will of God," the creative, innovative will of God, as deeply and morally felt by the individual, and in behalf of which she or he must act or lose all personal integrity. To *that end* one must practice a *judicious* independence of the rites, and be prepared to be "cast into outer darkness" by society. This might be a new creative interpretation of Luke 6:22:

> Blessed are you when others hate you and revile you and cast out your name as evil, on account of the Son of Man!

Here, the "Son of Man" is taken, as Jesus did, as something *in* the human (in general) that can act for God. The case for this interpretation is beautifully and convincingly made by Elizabeth Boyden Howes in "Son of Man: Expression of the Self."[27]

As consciousness enters the domain of embodiment of creativity, the old patterns must be broken so that the new may live. *This is as inevitable as our physical death.*

We seek not an orderly society through ritual and tradition, but an orderly world through conscious choice. Conflicts are our way of becoming aware of the ultimate unity. Or, as W.H. Auden put it, "The distresses of choice are our chance to be blessed."[28] This is certainly a step well beyond Confucian doctrine!

EXISTENTIAL CONFLICT AND EMERGENCE

If I encounter choices, dilemmas, conflicts of duty, imposed upon me culturally, I must ask: Who is split? Me, or society? Is there a difference? And how can I tell? I know that I can easily allow myself to be torn apart when the split values of society present me with a conflict. And yet it is precisely the task of growth to experience fully such rending forces, such as attempting to stay in relationship to others—*all* others—while honoring the individual in myself, my *true being.*

A question occurs here which is of central importance to the whole of Jung's work and to its relationship with modern physics. What is the *point* of the conflict? In a sense, what does *it* want? The point is an *emergent,* something new. There is indeed evolution, and it proceeds by means of conflict. This is, of course, not some statement on the inevitability of physical fighting and war, though in more primitive cultures it has been seen as such, and in some cases still is. In physics we again find some theoreticians talking of an end to physics in the near future. However, physics is *fundamentally experimental* (see p. 80 above), and the discovery of the previously unknown cannot be excluded. This is, if you will, an experimental cosmos, even if you see it as God's experiment. Jung's main point, in breaking from Freud, was identical: The unconscious contains *not only* contents repressed from consciousness, but all that has never yet been discovered as well. There is no reason to suppose that the *conatus* behind evolution has ceased. Eternally, we have to do with an emergent newness. This is why one cannot turn for help to the past alone, though much forgotten wisdom may reside there. I imagine "God" "saying," "Now show me something new and interesting!"

How can we see *new* ways when our cultural expressions, e.g. art and movies, seem to portray heroes molded to existing traditions, or else as anti-heroic, without spiritual development, and so many of us imagine that we have but to turn to the "ancient wisdom" of the east?[29] These ideas fail to raise the real issue. Rather, we are pacified by images of the old ways working. But such qualities as will constitute true morality for the immediate future will declare their own ritual and discipline. If the emergent has any reality, ancient wisdom cannot give us the most needed essence. Instead, we need to hold to the reality of uncertainty as the field in which the expression of our own vitality takes shape, and not give in to the *confidence* which seems so often to attend *ignorance and blindness*. Strangely, it is this experimental attitude, questioning the old ways and holding to our uncertainty, which bestows upon us at last an unshakable security, precisely because it is in this manner that authority is taken inside, and is not dependent upon any exterior approbation. The true heroes of the coming time will not accept coronation at the hands of admiring others, whether many or few.

The feeling of conflict *awakens* the moral. "Obstacles" are required, but they have a strange nature which has been hinted at throughout, a sort of easy invisibility *until* the moral feeling is engaged. In the end, that which is moral is a unification of thought and feeling. It is the feeling which has been systematically repressed by our culture, and left as a *massa confusa*, to pick up the alchemical term for "unworked on." The feelings now flooding our senses in the media are hardly differentiated, but constitute mere intensity. What we need is training in feeling, so that we can come to know those which are deepest and most subtle. Earlier, a Jung quotation referred to these irreducible feelings, calling them "unassailable by reason," which "logic can overlook but not eliminate." As poet May Sarton as said, "we must go down into the dungeons of the heart."[30] An obstacle is that which finally *gets our attention* in a feeling sense, but with the added condition that our moral sense ensures that it does not *dull* our senses. It produces a shock, such as that which led Heinrich Zimmer to use the phrase, "the roar of awakening."[31] It is like walking along a road and coming upon a mirror in the path. Before, one only saw *outward*. The mirror somehow shows your true self, and one gets a hint that it's not as pretty as previously imagined. Not pretty, but somehow more real, and thus intriguing. "Why couldn't I see that before?"

LIGHT IN THE DARKNESS

Consciousness is a form of specific reflection which is based on moral self-awareness, and self-acceptance, *without omitting* unacceptability (see p. 83). The level referred to here is thus deeper than our "everyday" awareness. Each new level of consciousness adds a new "mirror," showing us a new dimension of our being. As Erich Neumann points out in *Depth Psychology and a New Ethic*, what we usually call our moral *conscience* is an in-structure of collective values which protects us from our own moral potential for individual values. We usually have to discover our individual values *in spite of* our "conscience." While conscience is built upon our moral potential, the latter remains unconscious until the new mirror reflects a deeper dimension of the "true self."

Reflection is always representation to the ego. The ego therefore goes through stages of deepening, but retains the sense of the continuity of the "I," as in recollections of the past: "When I was four years old . . ." refers directly to this continuity. What is reflected can be feeling, image, thought. The first product of the awareness of ego or "I" is egocentricity. This cannot be helped; there is no other path to consciousness. Therefore, though the ego's potential egocentricity is indeed a stumbling-block, as perceived in the east, one is *also* looking in the mirror at the potential for the divine manifestation. Thus one encounters the formidable, but central, moral problem for the emergence of consciousness. One must get out of the way, but not, repeat *not*, by means of egolessness. This deprives God of the needed active agent. But once this process is underway, another surprise occurs. God, as described by Jung in *Answer to Job* (see pp. 79–80), *resists* the process, and the question becomes: How can we constellate the "obstacle" (or mirror) which will "force" the self-revelation (or self-reflection) of the nature of God—the new entity felt in the moral field? That is, how can we generate new consciousness? This is the new human task.

One possible key to approaching this task is indicated by the profound note struck by Jung in *Answer to Job*, that the attributes of God to which we appeal for help are *ours*, in our inner depth. "God" desires mercy and justice precisely to the extent which these become actual touchstones of our own concrete actions in the world. If this is correct, then God's *perception* is through *us*. We are beginning to see evidence in art and literature that this is becoming part of our psychic structure. In *Sleepers Awake*[32] Kenneth Patchen constructed a number of prose art pieces which were woven into the text of his surrealistic novel. The following is an edited fragment of one of these verbal pictures:

```
OTHEEYESOFGODWATCHOUTO
FEACHONEOFUSOURPAINFIL
LSHISHEARTEVERYMURDERC
AUSESHIMTODIEALITTLEWE
HAVESTOPPEDHISMOUTHWIT
HTHEGRAYSILTOFDOGSLOSI
NGTOUCHWITHOURSELVESWE
HAVELOSTTOUCHWITHHIMWH
ENTHEEYESOFGODGOBLINDN
OTHINGISSEENOTHEEYESOF
GODWATCHOUTOFEACHONEOF
USANDINTHISDARKNESSTHE
YAREBLINDANDTHEWALLSOF
THECAVECLOSEINUPONUSBE
INGBLINDYEKNOWNOTTHISD
ARKNESSOFGODISWATCHING
OUTOFUSANDHISEYESMIRRO
RTHENOTHINGNESSOFALLTH
```

We want justice, and God wants justice to precisely the extent it comes alive in us. That is what the emergence of God's justice *is*.[33]

If "the eyes of God watch out of each one of us," then the task may not be so huge as *calling upon an external God* has seemed in recent centuries. We need to act "on our own steam" for what to us *is* moral, and to do this simply in our own environment, wherever we are. This requires that we work actively to understand and transform the inner stuff which would shock and does shock us as we become aware of it. For most of us, this yields plenty of immediate material.

It would be wrong, however, to stop with the inner, for the new manifestation of God will be social as well as individual. We need also to constitute a challenge to other humans, to be shocking, but not for its own sake. In *God*,[34] J. Middleton Murry wrote:

> The significance of one's own life depends on the significance of the variations which that person embodies and transmits. That will be judged not in the person's lifetime, or by the minds of other humans. Life itself will ultimately pronounce: this human became a significant variation, or, this human reverted. To strive to become oneself significant variation, by embodying significant variations in a new creative whole, is, we believe, the modern equivalent of doing 'the will of God.'

Alignment to the "will of God" must be a non-attribute of God since God *must always* follow God's nature. God's nature includes all the opposites, and so it is freedom itself, as well as limitation itself. The limitation is seen in that there *is* a nature, as manifest in the existence of laws of physics. Perhaps this means that the nature of *our* search to align with that *will* is the same as willing that will *for God* as in the Midrash prayer. Is the matter of alignment with the will a purely human concern? In this case the human role has been vastly underestimated.

Does God feel conflict, as we do? If not, then Jung's conclusion is right on target that God, seen as external to ourselves, is unconscious. Unless the *moral* opposites mentioned by Jung are *felt by God* as conflicting, then the Love/Wrath prayer has no meaning. Perhaps the fact that this "prayer *of God*" is part of our literature means that the moral conflict is felt by God *in us*. *If* that prayer is a *fact about* God in us, if it takes its place alongside other sacred writings as showing the presence and depth of God in the human, then it may be a *newborn* fact, which might mean that morality is also newborn in God. Perhaps the Midrash prayer is as it is (*may* it be My Will) because God only *vaguely* feels the moral conflict through our rudimentary consciousness, though it is more likely because our choices are always required.

Job's, "My heart does not reproach me for any of my days," is now to be said by us in spite of consciousness of guilt. Feeling the conflict about how we have lived, accepting it and undergoing personal transformation out of the consciousness of guilt, is what is most sorely needed by the world. The picture of "spirituality" which follows from this is very different from the usual, which in the light of the above is mostly a *default* of consciousness. As Jung says,

> The guilty one is eminently suitable and is therefore chosen to become the vessel for continuing incarnation, not the guiltless one who holds aloof from the world and refuses to pay tribute to life, for in such a one the dark God would find no room.[35]

If I retain a deep awareness of moral conflict and of its feeling *and act on it*, it cannot happen that I default consciousness, lose my integrity. It could get lost in Tillich's "You are accepted" unless his "in spite of unacceptability" remains. Acceptance is a rare and great achievement, or else it is a puerile "I'm O.K., you're O.K." If acceptance comes as a result of a tremendous work, then it has value in consciousness.

As an inner experiment, try: "What we feel, God is feeling." This is very different from "God knows my thoughts." How might a piecemeal consciousness such as our own find any sense of participation in the whole? We want justice, mercy, excellence, equality, striving, peace. Only a whole consciousness, one which includes both the dark and the light of the soul, can hope to work to bring these about, but perhaps we are on the verge of patching our pieces together, or "gathering and uplifting the sparks," as the Kabbalists say. We must in any case try at all times.

We may take a new step of freedom in new awareness of the old conflict. Job's statement, "My heart does not reproach me for any of my days," amounts to a new understanding of "knowledge of good and evil." This understanding acknowledges the inevitability of our own actual evil. We would, in essence, know what good and evil are for the first time, as Eliot says in his "Four Quartets":

> We shall not cease from exploration
> And the end of all our exploring
> Will be to arrive where we started
> And know the place for the first time.

Certainly the knowledge that growth is through suffering would be a *clear* step for the world, and a real step in *moral* growth. One then doesn't have conundrums as to why the good and the innocent suffer. This should have been the lesson of the suffering God: God, the *conatus* of moral consciousness, suffers in coming to consciousness. Those who strive to avoid suffering still do not avoid it, for they miss the point of their being.

"Rub and jostle" *is the good*—otherwise life is death. This states the reality, known from modern physics, that existence is contradiction. We try to gain awareness of what *is beyond*, which might be indicated by *definite* concepts *here!* These definite concepts, as we have learned, contradict each other. The reality of both contradictory aspects is *present.* When this becomes clear, then, and only then, do we become aware of a problem! And that's *good!*

One might set forth the proposition that behavior according to one's own deepest (contradictory) nature is moral behavior, so long as it comes from as deep a place as we can reach, and embodies our essential convictions. Certainly *it is immoral not to trust God to that extent.* Then the inward search *is* part of a deeper commitment, and is *essentially* moral. But what if we "make a mistake"? Without that very real, and perhaps consequential, error, we could not have learned *this.* Cultural morality is deep, but must be balanced by individual morality. *Only* by discovering, and aligning with, *our* portion of the Self can we truly serve God and universe.

We must remember that, in Job, God *rejects* the counsels of those (the three "friends") who *do not question God's morality.* Though we now know of Job's greatness in the face of God's power-play, the "unvarnished spectacle of divine savagery,"[36] his comrades did not know it. Job says, "Show me my sin and I will confess it." This is a very great statement, which insists upon consciousness of what one does *in order* to take responsibility.

Do I desire to *appeal* to "divine justice"? No, I appeal to the emergent *will* of God, which is that *love* overcomes *wrath.* There is no way that some unembodied "justice" can *stand above* God. Our course is to embody that will by challenging *humans* to human justice. To honor the beyondness of God, we might pray to the Transcedent for love and *mercy.* May we delve in our depths, ardent for the finding of these divine qualities.

"The right way, like the wrong way, must be paid for." This includes every misalignment *and* every alignment. But *each* path is *wrong* in some concrete moral sense. Even Gandhi's approach was still limited to *race*, "India for the Indians." He said, "The problems will be great, but they will be *ours*." This point of view is not yet global, and thus leaves something moral to be desired. Yet the actions he took embodied the highest human morality consistent with the reality of the time.

What could show us more clearly the open-endedness of the emergence of consciousness?

Notes

1. Jung, C.G. 1961b. *Psychological Reflections*. Selections edited by Jo-lande Jacobi. New York: Harper and Row, Harper Torchbooks, p. 265.
2. Jung. *Memories*, p. 192.
3. Clark, R.T.R. 1960. *Myth and Symbol in Ancient Egypt*. New York: Grove Press, p. 26.
4. Jaffé. *Myth*, p. 113.
5. Ibid. p. 112.
6. In *CW* 11, pars. 553–758. *Answer to Job* was published as a separate book, but for uniformity with the style of Jung quotations, citation by paragraphs in the *CW* is employed.
7. Ibid. Par. 556.
8. Ibid. Par. 560.
9. Ibid. Par. 567.
10. Ibid. Par. 574.
11. Ibid. Par. 620.
12. Ibid. Par. 659.
13. Ibid. Par. 664.
14. Ibid. Par. 733.
15. Ibid. Par. 620.
16. Exodus, Ch. 3.
17. 5 December, 1959. In Jung, C.G. 1975. *Letters, 1951–1961*. Edited by Gerhard Adler. Bollingen Series XCV:2. Princeton: Princeton University Press, p. 525.
18. *CW* 11, par. 659.
19. "World Order," with capitals, is used as a term of definite meaning. Elsewhere I have called it the Patterning, but I also want to bring in the qualities of the ancient Egyptian goddess Maat, or Mayet. As the per-sonification of the World Order, she was the "feather" against which the heart of the deceased was weighed, the ideal being that neither overbalanced the other. The appropriate soul was not disparate from the way things are. See also Neumann, Erich. 1973. *Depth Psychology*

and a New Ethic. Translated by Eugene Rolf. New York: Harper and Row, Harper Torchbooks.

20. "You Are Accepted," in Tillich, Paul. 1948. *The Shaking of the Foundations.* New York: Charles Scribner's Sons.

21. Job 27:6.

22. Up until 1848, Kierkegaard's writings are full of humor, and his section on the subject of humor in his *Concluding Unscientific Postscript* is one of the funniest pieces I have ever read. But, tragically, he was unable to withstand the personal attacks of that year, and turned to bitterness, which is by far the worst enemy of humanity.

23. Jung, C.G. 1959. *Aion.* CW 9_{II}, par. 110.

24. Kierkegaard, S. 1941. *Concluding Unscientific Postscript.* Translated by Walter Lowrie. Princeton: Princeton University Press, p. 459.

25. Jung, C.G. 1966. *The Practice of Psychotherapy.* CW 16, pars. 469, 470.

26. Jung, C.G. 1969a. *The Archetypes and the Collective Unconscious.* CW 9_I, par. 65.

27. In Howes, E.B. 1971. *Intersection and Beyond.* San Francisco: Guild for Psychological Studies Publishing House.

28. "For the Time Being: A Christmas Oratorio." In Auden, W.H. 1969. *Collected Longer Poems.* New York: Random House.

29. In *Shardik*, Richard Adams (1974. New York: Simon and Schuster) has portrayed an exception. His Kelderek learns the "will of God" in the most realistic manner, through apostasy, attempting to imprison God and use the power of possession, and through the "dark night of the soul," falling into the hands of an evil slave trader.

30. "Santos, New Mexico." In Sarton, May. 1974. *Collected Poems, 1930–1973.* New York: W.W. Norton and Company.

31. Chapter title in Zimmer, Heinrich. 1951. *Philosophies of India.* Edited by Joseph Campbell. Bollingen Series XXVI. New York: Pantheon.

32. Patchen, Kenneth. 1969. *Sleepers Awake.* New York: New Directions, pp. 362–363.

33. This would explain God's "patience" in the first fifteen billion years after the "Big Bang," but then the idea that there was a deep-felt need leading to a sudden creative act, the Big Bang itself, would remain unexplained.

34. Murry, J.M. 1930. *God.* New York: Harper and Brothers, p. 245.

35. *CW* 11, par. 746.

36. Jung. *CW* 11, par. 581.

PART III
THE PATH: THE DYNAMICS OF SPIRITUALITY

Chapter 4

Introduction—The Center

In any choice you are centered if you can go either way.
                              —Elizabeth Boyden Howes

It is pointless to speak of spirituality without reference to the Center, the Attractor, that which sets up and empowers the spiritual drive within us. This was shown in Chapter 3, "Consciousness and the Moral Dimension." Here the same condition is approached from a different direction, and in this part several models are explored which tie the material of the psyche to that of physics. The Center, however, is elusive. For this reason the path to it, as the dynamics of spirituality, will be approached by degrees of elaboration. Even so, a warning is needed that in the attempt to clarify aspects of the path, one very real danger will be to make it seem that the clarity is greater than it actually is. Every attempt to clarify requires the cutting away of things which belong to the process but lead off in other directions. This is indeed the elusiveness of the Center. What follows amounts to one formulation, analogous to the rock cairns which mark out a path in the more trackless regions of mountains, or perhaps to some hackings in a jungle which mark one possible course out of many, and where rampant growth will soon reclaim the whole, obliterating whatever waymarkings had been made.

First, then, here is a concise statement of a western path, which will then be elaborated briefly as an introduction to the other chapters of this part.

The Center is hidden, but is present in being felt as an attractor. An attractor signifies tension, or a gradient, which exists between opposites. This tension of opposites gives dynamism to our being. Some of these great opposites, as needed for human wholeness, are: heart and mind (emotion and intellect), light and darkness (including knowing and unknowing), spirit and matter, masculine and feminine, introversion and extroversion, self and other, individual and community, past and future, time and eternality. We experience the tension of these opposites as the pull of value, the various forms of which we attempt to move toward, or to embody. Since there is no direct approach to the elusive center, the most effective movements take two first forms: oscillation between opposites and circumambulation (walking around the center). With regard to the oscillation, the center is "between" the opposites. One does not hit the center more than momentarily before finding oneself clear over on the other side. Circumambulation is experienced often as a deflection from an intended movement, even while maintaining focus upon the Center. It can even be experienced as "going around in circles," which has such a pejorative connotation in the West that we need continual reminders that there is indeed no direct path to the Center. *In the process* of attempting these approaches, we *discover* other phenomena occurring. Through our attending to the Center—giving it energy—a whole process is activated. Something *moves*—is felt or known to be moving. The *new* appears, in at least three forms: as spiral growth, as transformative involution, and as a healing process out of wounds. This is a path of *progression*, which makes it a western way.

This, then, is the outline which will be followed in Chapters 5–9, after some preliminary elaboration.

Tension as Problem and as Value. Human problems of living have a perennial quality. It might be argued that they exist to be worked on, not to be solved. They are part of what Jung called the "rub and jostle" of opposites in *Answer to Job* (see Chapter 3). This is the clash of the "great opposites" mentioned above, and also the aspect of reality which engenders consciousness. Although some cultural and individual "solutions" to the problems posed by the opposites seem to last a good long while, none is permanent. Some forms taken by these problems are: how to find or attain relationship, worldly success, satisfaction, knowledge, self-realization; how to avoid or overcome disease, misfortune, natural disaster, evil, death. These are some of the problems facing individuals. The problems of the larger collective are not the concern at present.

Frustrations abound in the presence of these problems, but they are also sources of attraction, fascination. For most of us it feels *necessary* to solve them, and not to try leads to, or *is*, depression. To make progress yields satisfactions, which can be continual and profound, though never permanent.

We have come to learn that we value another sort of well-being more than mere physical well-being: a mind intact, the experience of a love relationship, clear sight, openness to beauty and other forms of awe. At least these take precedence over loss of limbs or of some senses. The inner light which we value shines through other debilities as well. This that we have learned is *empirical* knowledge, attained through trial and error, through experimentation. It has not been arrived at by means of philosophical thought. Setting these experiences *above* physical wholeness is part of our essential suchness. It is the will-to-spiritualization, or spirituality, though we need also to remember that spiritual well-being entails the care and cultivation of its physical support system.

West and East. The paths of this will-to-spirituality, the approaches to satisfaction in relation to these problems, can be gathered into two: the path of *detachment* and the path of *desire*. To oversimplify for the sake of generality, the path of detachment, freedom from thirst, freedom from *samsara* (conditioned being), has become the basis for many religions in the east. The western way is the desire for, and progressive fulfillment of, greater being, in the western sense of fuller presence and effectiveness in the world. It is said that the way of detachment can be entered with completeness, that one can live in the "world of illusion" completely detached from it, in *nirvana* (the desires "blown out," as a candle is blown out). The other way, being progressive, yields partial but ever greater fulfillments. It is a step-by-step transformation of the desire itself through elevation and refinement, accepting desire as elemental and remaining aware of its roots in a concrete earthiness. As Teilhard de Chardin said it:[1]

> Son of man, bathe yourself in the ocean of matter . . . for it is that
> ocean which will raise you up to God.

Jung's work leads us upon a western path. His wide quotation from eastern sources was sparked by his perception of a "psychological accuracy" in them *in the way they portray the phenomenology of the psyche*. But he also concludes that eastern *methods* are not useful to the western psyche. In the opening section of his "Commentary on 'The

Secret of the Golden Flower,' "[2] he spells this out in some detail. We become "pitiable imitators" because those methods go with that culture, and culture is much more powerful than we believe it to be.

We have come to learn that *we* value—things, ideas, states of being. Value is *desire*, is *thirst*. The thirst for no-thirst is still thirst. The western path is the profound desire for "living water."

Example of Opposites: Inner and Outer. Just as it makes no sense to speak of spirituality without reference to a Center, it is equally nonsense to pretend that value is only external, for the value process is also embedded within us. It is *we* who do the valuing. Unless we admit and work with the fact of that internality, we thwart the process, we "protect" ourselves from its action upon us. One way of visualizing the Center between the inner and the outer as opposites is to find something in our immediate outer situation (as individuals) which grips something in ourselves. We can then find our deepest response to that something out of our developed values. If we desire to include both, we naturally oscillate from one to the other in our consideration. The fact that we look for our deepest values in such a case engages our center in relation to inner and outer.

Another Example: Mind and Heart. We move toward some Value, as it were a Center which attracts. For the intellect, the center is Truth, and our search yields the progression of knowledge, with only occasional glimpses or hints of what we would like to call Truth with the capital T. We know all sorts of facts which are true in a "lower case" sense. Truth as a Center remains elusive, distant, though present in our will to find it. For the heart, or emotions, the center is Love, and here too we find many lower case satisfactions, while the center itself eludes us. We want to pull these together so that Love and Truth coincide. As Middleton Murry puts it:[3]

> The Universe known by the Mind must be, or become, such that the Heart can be satisfied with it.

The problem with this, as expressed by one of Toni Morrison's characters in *Beloved*,[4] is:

> What's fair ain't necessarily right.

Or, to return to Middleton Murry:

> But to know such a Universe is impossible for the Mind. If it had
> been possible, the condition of twofold division would never
> have arisen.[5]

Again, our desire to include both keeps the energy flowing from one focus to the other. Our toward-moving often turns, or turns *us*, deflecting our direction, or reflecting us back toward our point of origin, to retrace our steps once more and learn what we had previously missed.

We move, then, toward some Value, or permit it to move us. There is energy, dynamism. What is the *best* we can conceive? The notion of a *best*, and more practically the notion of a *better*, is inherent in value, though we may not agree upon what that "best" *is*. Again empirically, experimentally, we discover a process of refinement, of elevation: the *substitution* of a higher desire for a lower, or the *transformation* of the lower into a higher (not the *extinction* of desire), and a *choice and effort so to live,* yield for us the experience of satisfaction in progress on the way. Again, this continual transformation of our values is what is here defined as spirituality.

The New. The sort of transformation just discussed is a *restructuring*, which leads of its own nature to new forms for, or combinations of, the elements of living. The more we live the transformative process, the more we value spontaneity and creativity, the hallmarks of the individual at home in suchness. Through spontaneous and creative individuals shines the new, the fresh, the interesting. The continual emergence of the new points to one of the most central of our higher values, the *ever*-new, whose centrality is symbolized as the Divine Child. As with Truth and Love, the New is always now and always beyond. We experience the new in concrete finite suchness as a *this*, which characterizes the concrete situational responses of the Zen masters. Or it might be such a thing as the discovery of a new phenomenon in physics, along with the knowledge that such discoveries will always await us. The finite attainment of the new neither exhausts nor diminishes the *essence* of the new. It awaits actualization—always.

Oscillation and Circumambulation. Physical motions can be used

to visualize the inner psychic movements which comprise the transformative or integrative path: 1. movement around a center, or circumambulation, 2. oscillation back and forth in relation to the great
opposites, 3. the spiral, and 4. the vortex or involution. Each of these
has something to offer us as concrete suggestions for models of living. The first two movements, oscillation and circumambulation, go
together to produce the mandala, which exists in each of us as a
symbol of wholeness:

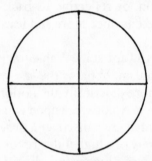

The latter two add progression and energy or dynamism, summed up
as spiral growth or as transformation. Oscillation, circumambulation,
transformation: these are the topics of the chapters of this part. Together they make up the spiral, but the movement is both away from
and toward the Center.

The approach to the center, as the mandala-movement, gives us
the image of stability, the rootedness of the center. The dynamism is
in the movement, and we find that it is mutual: as we move toward
the center by circumambulation and oscillation, it moves toward us
too, giving us more solid inward support.

The sun, as center of the solar system, is so massive that all the
planets (and much else besides) revolve about it as if it were *fixed*, as
indeed Copernicus imagined. This is a very helpful symbol for meditation, with the planets "circumambulating" the central "attractor,"
the sun.

Once we comprehend this system, we can add other symbolism
by taking in the fact that the sun itself is free-floating in space, and
our whole system wanders about the center of our galaxy, 30,000
light years distant, oscillating up and down through the galactic plane
as it does so. These "cosmic" movements can be powerful symbols.
It can be of great value for us to see the attractor-center (Self) in our

lives within this post-Copernican model, by first meditating the solar system as planets circulating around the sun, and then permitting the sun its freedom to wander the galaxy.

The Spiral as Integration in Time. The dynamic progression of the actualization of Self is not a simple process. Given a *present*, within the whole of what was, what is, and what is to come, past and future stand in a sort of opposition; they become problematic opposites of a complementary nature.

The complementarity of past and future produces the spiral nature of development. This complementarity is expressed well by Jung's concept of "regressive renaissance":[6] the fact that we cannot *simply move ahead*, but must, can *only*, do so by finding a symbol from the past to transform. Thus the spiral takes on, in addition to its traditional form, the following aspect:

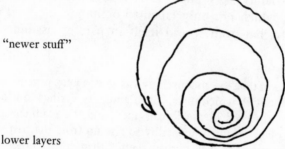

"newer stuff"

lower layers

Jung describes this movement most succinctly in his discussion of Goethe's *Faust*.[7] The use of this material serves an additional purpose, for in the Faust problem is depicted one of our principal needs at this point in our human evolution: the necessity for the assimilation of "evil." Even now, Goethe's solution—the fact that for him Faust is "saved," not "damned"—sticks as it were in our craw, as witness the literature and music which assumes "the damnation of Faust."

We are constantly inclined to forget that what was once good does not remain good eternally. We follow the old ways that once were good long after they have become bad, and only with the greatest sacrifices and untold suffering can we rid ourselves of this delusion and see that what was once good is now perhaps grown old and is good no longer. This is so in great things as in small. . . . A collective attitude is equivalent to a religion, and changes of religion constitute some of the most painful chapters in the world's history. In this respect our age is afflicted with a blindness that has no parallel. We think we have only to declare an accepted article of faith incorrect and invalid, and we shall be psychologically rid of all the traditional effects of Christianity or Judaism. We believe in enlightenment, as if an intellectual change of front somehow had a profounder influence on the emotional processes or even on the unconscious. We entirely forget that the religion of the last two thousand years is a psychological attitude, a definite form and manner of adaptation to the world without and within, that lays down a definite cultural pattern and creates an atmosphere which remains wholly uninfluenced by any intellectual denials.[8]

Even Christianity, says Jung, was a "change of front" for the psyche in general, which not only failed to obliterate the "old attitudes" immediately, but even spread itself in part by assimilating pagan festivals.

Because of this, the unconscious was able to keep paganism alive. The ease with which the spirit of antiquity springs to life again can be observed in the Renaissance, and the readiness of the vastly older primitive mentality to rise up from the past can be seen in our own day, perhaps better than at any other epoch known to history.[9]

It is similar with the individual, and Jung uses the case of Goethe's *Faust* to illustrate. As we will see, Jung considers that Goethe has hit upon the central essence of the present needed transformation.

When we meet a difficult task which we cannot master with the means at our disposal, it typically and regularly occurs that a retrograde movement of libido automatically sets in, i.e., a regression. The libido draws away from the problem of the moment, becomes introverted, and reactivates in the unconscious a more or less primitive analogue of the conscious situation. This law determined Goethe's choice of a symbol: Prometheus, the savior who brought light and fire to humanity languishing in darkness. . . .[10]

But the classical spirit could not simply be recaptured for life in a more modern time either. The image of Prometheus lacked a certain depth. What had occurred in the meantime was a profound development of the "consciousness of sin,"[11] which made impossible the return to the "everlasting natural beauty" of an "undisrupted wholeness" in which "the heights and depths of human nature could still dwell together in complete naiveté without offending moral or aesthetic susceptibilities." Faust, as "the medieval Prometheus," has thus to struggle with Mephistopheles. The new element is the working out of *salvation* within the confines of a pact with the Accuser and Destroyer.

> He is a destroyer but also a savior, and such a figure is preeminently suited to become the symbolic bearer of an attempt to resolve the conflict. Moreover the medieval magician has laid aside the classical naiveté which was no longer possible, and become thoroughly steeped in the Christian atmosphere. The old pagan element must at first drive him into a complete Christian denial and mortification of self, because his longing for redemption is so strong that every avenue has to be explored. But in the end the Christian attempt at a solution fails too, and it then transpires that the possibility of redemption lies precisely in the obstinate persistence of the old pagan element, because the anti-Christian symbol opens the way for an acceptance of evil. Goethe's intuition thus grasped the problem in all its acuteness.[12]

In *Faust, Part II,* the reason for his redemption is spoken by a choir of angels:

> Saved is our spirit-peer, in peace,
> Preserved from evil scheming:
> 'For he whose strivings never cease
> Is ours for his redeeming.'[13]

The greatness of holding together the advocate and the destroyer, prefigured in Job (see Chapter 3), finds here, twenty-four centuries

later, a logical development which, again like Job, leaps beyond
where we presently are, to point out the necessary path.

What, then, is the nature of the spiral? We progress "normally," even to our own tastes, until a problem is encountered which
cannot be solved by "normal" means. The deep inner recognition of
the insoluble nature of the problem draws the psychic energy away
from the direct attack upon the problem toward the layers of the
unconscious containing earlier symbols and adaptations. It is interesting that through the work of Thomas Kuhn[14] this same model has
been applied to the progress of science. Kuhn shows that a mythic
level is activated in the search for new scientific explanations. In the
case of the psychic conflict, fantasies often arise which seem infantile
to the conscious attitude of the person or the culture, as various
"back to nature" movements seem infantile in a technological and
crowded society. The adaptation seemingly called for by these inner
promptings is never the solution in itself, however, so we need not
get stuck there. Some creative transformation of that symbol does,
however, seem to be the nucleus of a new way.

Psychologist Fritz Kunkel[15] has put the matter in a very clear
manner with his image of human development as adding layers, as a
tree adds rings. In the center is the "true heart," which contains the
entelechy of the child:

In the subsequent pictures, various external influences stunt the
growth in directions which are natural but unacceptable in the particular family or cultural environment of the child. Other directions are
encouraged, however, and eventually the child, or youth, begins to
feel that these encouraged areas of growth are indeed what she or he
has desired to do. This builds the facade with which most of us
function on a daily basis, to the great detriment of our individual
meaning. In this model, the cause of the problems experienced by the
person are made exceedingly graphic, as is the solution. Somehow

the "true heart" must be found and revived, and the areas of life which it would have filled out must be given some substance. This necessarily involves some "regression" in the sense of the flow of energy described by Jung.

In this manner we see clearly that the future is not possible without the past, but that the past also speaks for the future. More profoundly than this, by this process linear (historical, progressive) time is bound back (*religio*) to cyclic time, and we learn humility within the circles of the cosmos.

It is this linkage which constitutes the complementarity of the two, and which produces the spiral as well. The images of pots made from coils of clay with the upper layer fused to the lower, or of baskets made from coils of grass tied together with loops, give us a most profound symbolic reminder of this process.

Return to the Center. What is the center? It is a point which cannot be reached with the intellect alone, or through feeling alone, or with *any* half of one of the great pairs of opposites. It cannot be reached by means of ego-consciousness alone, though that is indispensable to the search. It cannot be reached by *any* of our *directed* activities which have produced civilization, with its scientific and social progress. It is a point of transcendence: a surround and a presence. Jung often referred to the ancient dictum that God is "a circle whose center is everywhere and whose circumference is nowhere." He also said the following (referring to a symbolic image in the apocryphal *Acts of John*):[16]

> The definition of the cross or center as the "boundary of all things" is exceedingly original, for it suggests that the limits of the universe are not to be found in a non-existent periphery but in its center. There alone lies the possibility of transcending the world.

Wherever we are, the hidden center is present, to be sought for and experienced by each according to our various levels of consciousness and of devotion to the process.

To that end, descriptions of the "movement toward" are given in the following chapters.

Notes

1. Teilhard de Chardin, Pierre. 1970. *Hymn of the Universe.* Translated by Gerald Vann. New York: Harper and Row, p. 60.
2. In Jung, C.G. 1967. *Alchemical Studies. CW* 13, pars. 1–26.
3. *God*, p. 131.
4. Morrison, Toni. 1987. *Beloved.* New York: New American Library, Plume Fiction, p. 256.
5. *God*, p. 131.
6. Jung, C.G. 1971. *Psychological Types. CW* 6, par. 315.
7. *CW* 6, pars. 313–317. A fuller discussion is to be found in section IIIa of "On Psychic Energy," *CW* 8, pars. 60–76.
8. Ibid. Par. 313.
9. Ibid. Par. 313.
10. Ibid. Par. 314.
11. The essential change from the classical to the modern, brought about by the development of the consciousness of sin, is Kierkegaard's point of departure for his *Philosophical Fragments,* and its massive "sequel," the *Concluding Unscientific Postscript,* which is Kierkegaard's philosophical masterpiece. The beautiful development of this theme at the start of the *Fragments* is highly rewarding to read.
12. *CW* 6, par. 316.
13. Goethe, Johann Wolfgang von. 1959. *Faust/Part Two.* Translated by Philip Wayne. Baltimore: Penguin, p. 282.
14. Kuhn, Thomas. 1970. *The Structure of Scientific Revolutions.* Chicago: The University of Chicago Press.
15. Kunkel, Fritz. 1936. Unpublished lecture notes.
16. *CW* 11, p. 156.

Chapter 5

Oscillation

Without contraries is no progression.
—William Blake (*The Marriage of Heaven and Hell*)

Thus far we have only asserted the elusive quality of the center as the "between" of the pairs of great opposites. From the point of view of logic, there is *nothing* between concepts which stand in logical opposition to each other. The principle in question is explicitly called the "law of the excluded middle."[1] In practice, however, we find that the logical ideal does not hold. In this chapter we will use aspects of a simple physical model of oscillation to demonstrate both what psychological oscillation is and what it isn't. After that, we will discuss the arising of opposites in the psyche, followed by psychological oscillation as working with opposites.

The following model has a very specific purpose: to help visualize a "hidden center," and how the hiddeness of the center gives rise to opposites. The model will evolve from a first to a second version.

In the first version of the model, the center is not hidden. Picture an object suspended between two walls by two springs, and oscillating back and forth horizontally:

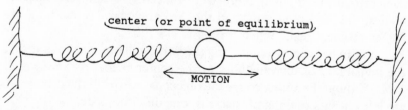

There is a position of equilibrium in the middle where the tension in the two springs would be equal, and where therefore the object could be at rest if it had no energy. We could then give it energy by pulling the object to one side and letting it go. The object would then oscil-

111

late back and forth. In this version of the model, the point of equilibrium or inertia *exists,* is visible to us in our "space and time." We can see the object either as it passes through the center point, or if it is at rest there. The object behaves in all respects as if attracted to that point, but in reality it is pulled from both sides.

Since the object can be seen at the center, this model doesn't yet describe the condition under which we live in a psychological sense. First of all, the center *as a place of rest* eludes us. More than that, the center is not *visible* to us *in our differentiated realm.* As we will see in the second version of the model, the center corresponds to the simultaneous truth of the "opposites," which is indeed the case, but not *logically*—not in a "nuts and bolts" fashion.

Let us therefore look at the second version:

OPPOSITE #1   THE
                              CENTER
                              BEYOND
                               THE
                             OPPOSITES   OPPOSITE #2

Now the center is presented in an invisible "space," even a non-space. The object appears *only* when it is not *at* the center, i.e. when it is beyond the dotted lines, away from the "center." The appearance of Venus as morning or evening star is an interesting symbolic example: we only see it when it is not too close to the sun. Some ancient cultures thought there were indeed two different celestial bodies, the "morning star" and the "evening star." Something becomes visible, "real," when it is *off to one side.*

As can be seen by comparing the two oscillator diagrams above, the invisibility or unavailability of the center *creates the opposites as such.* Without the ability to see the object pass through the center, we are left with its two manifestations, one on either side.

In one sense this is *contextuality:* in a given setting, the real is *this.* How often have we felt ourselves swayed by a context of one opposite or another: the earthy is real, the sublime is real; serving others is real, "looking out for number one" is real; that which can be intellectually grasped is real, that which one *feels* is real; the political left is real, the political right is real; only a black Christ, only a white Christ, only a male Christ, only a woman Christ, etc., etc., etc. This is all *correct*, but none of it is the *Center*. However, if we can oscillate, go either way in a given moment, and thereby experience some of both sides of the great opposites, then we are stretched. We become more flexible and can see at last that no one-sided viewpoint fills out the space surrounding the center—makes us whole, builds our mandala, *finds the center*. At the same time, if we are able to feel the opposites in clash equally, being truly able to go either way, we do also experience the presence of the Reconciling Center, or rather the Center then reveals to us its quality of reconciliation.

The reader may long ago have observed that I speak of *the* Center, whereas *each* pair of opposites should have its *own* center. Teilhard spoke of God as a "center of centers."[2] In addition to this, we have the fact that the *same* transformative process operates along the axis of each and all of the pairs of great opposites, which constitutes an effective visible link between and among them. The following diagram may give us a helpful visualization to take into the discussion of Jung's view of opposites and their operation in our lives. In it, "M" and "F" are abbreviations for *masculine* and *feminine*. Psychologist and mythologist Sheila Moon used these in *Changing Woman and Her Sisters.*[3] She lists about a dozen pairs of attributes or qualities associated with M and F, and ends with this caution: We "are not describing male and female gender, but Feminine and Masculine in god beings and in human beings." The diagram on p. 114 illustrates a sense in which a "center of centers" and a "complex of opposites" are the same. Interestingly enough, the Center of centers corresponds to the eastern concept of the *ekayanam* (one-place = meeting place or center), or the point at which all centers converge. It is found in the *Brihadaranyaka Upanishad,*[4] where it is part of an elucidation of the Self (*atman*) as that which is loved in everything that is loved, and as a wind which unites everything as with a thread, which is a beautiful symbol of spirit-as-such. In these images it clearly is the *attractor*. These attributes all correspond strongly to Jung's description of the Self of the human being. Through such a uniting point, therefore, the eastern and western paths may converge as well.

In the same vein, but even more profoundly, the Center as the

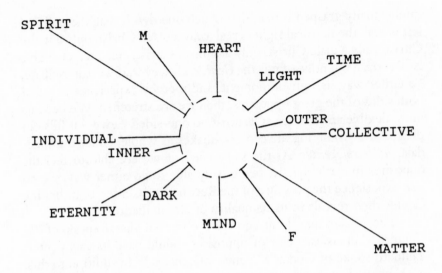

hidden source of opposites is found in the religious philosophy of Shiva and Shakti, in the *Bindu* concept.

In *Structural Depths of Indian Thought*, P.T. Raju[5] describes Shiva and Shakti as M and F personifications of the Godhead. Shiva is the transcendent (at peace) aspect of the Godhead, and as such is called "Lord of Sleep." Daniélou[6] adds to this concept:

> Shiva is himself represented as the perfect ascetic (Great Yogi), in whom is centered the perfection of austerity, penance, and meditation, through which unlimited powers are attained.

Shakti is the activity, energy or creative power of the Godhead. About this, Raju says:

> The world we experience consists of transformations which are . . . vibrations in the being of Shiva.[7] We are all forms of this energy (Shakti).[8] Shakti is this emotive power that creates its objects. Behind all creation, ours or God's, lies emotion that moves. The world is a transformation of the Word. This Word is originally distinct and pure and is the highest Sound. The all-pervading sound of the void . . . is focussed and becomes like a drop (*bindu*). The *bindu* is the whole, about to become world. The evolution of the world of plurality out of the original sound (*nada*, Word, Brahman) . . . is also a mysticism of the Word.[9]

Shiva, Shakti, and the *Bindu* are all also to be found in the great Sri Yantra symbol:

In describing this diagram, Heinrich Zimmer says:

> The Sri Yantra, though apparently no more than a geometrical device . . . is conceived and designed as a support to . . . a concentrated visualization and intimate inner experience of the polar play and logic-shattering paradox of eternity and time.[10] The nine triangles signify the primitive revelation of the Absolute as it differentiates into graduated polarities, the creative activity of the cosmic male and female energies on successive stages of evolution. Most important is the fact that the Absolute itself, the Really Real, is not represented. It cannot be represented; for it is beyond form and space. The Absolute is to be visualized . . . as a vanishing point or dot, "the drop" (*bindu*), amidst the interplay of all the triangles. This *Bindu* is the power-point, the invisible elusive center from which the entire diagram expands.[11] The Sri Yantra symbolizes Life, both universal and individual, as an incessant interaction of cooperating opposites.[12] . . . This is that *Bindu*, which is invisible yet taught through all the visible interdelvings of the triangles. This is that vitality out of which the phenomenon of expanding form proceeds in irrepressible power.[13] It is called "the drop" (*bindu*) the first drop, which spreads, unfolds, expands, and becomes transmuted into the tangible realm of our limited consciousness and the universe.[14]

Since the interplay of Shiva and Shakti *themselves* is also symbolized in the "interdelvings" of the triangles of the Sri Yantra, this symbol

becomes a most complete image of the creative Center. As William
Blake said, "Eternity is in love with the productions of time."[15]

To return to the image of the object oscillating under spring
tension, it also serves as a model for the *origin* of opposites in the
psyche, by means of which we become aware of things. Opposites
arise when a unitary "content" is given sufficient *energy*, so that it
becomes, or can become, conscious. At the point of consciousness,
the content splits in two, and the resulting contrast makes it visible.
In the next chapter we will see how profound this is for the origin of
opposites in physics.

One of the central pairs of opposites by means of which we
perceive our cosmos is that of spirit and matter. Every content which
comes to consciousness partakes of both spirit and matter.[16] Our
whole inner structure for perception and apperception is founded on
a basis of the concrete relationship of *things,* and every abstract or
spiritual concept has some remains of its empirical origin. Or consider the spiritual openings which occurred to Meister Eckhart and
Jacob Boehme when they gazed upon a tree in winter and a pewter
cup, respectively. There was a *concrete object* to act as symbol. Everyone who finds aliveness in symbols in churches or temples, in art, or
in nature experiences the coming together of the material and spiritual dimensions of being. In order for a content to come to consciousness at all, it needs the combination of energy and concreteness. As
Jung says:

> Matter and spirit both appear in the psychic realm as distinctive
> qualities of conscious contents. The ultimate nature of both is
> transcendental, that is, irrepresentable, since the psyche and its
> contents are the only reality which is given to us *without a
> medium.*[17]

So also with the *content* itself which comes to consciousness. Unless
it acquires this distinctiveness by *separating* into its spirit and matter
aspects, it remains below the level of conscious perception. In the
thing itself, as part of the pre-conscious state, spirit and matter are
indistinguishably one.

Note that when we use the term "below," the reference is to the
amount of *psychic energy* which it possesses.

The same mode of thinking can be used in reverse: as psychic energy is needed for the opposites to manifest, so also opposites are needed for the production of psychic energy. There is a mutual implication of opposites and energy. In "On Psychic Energy"[18] Jung describes this situation. We *observe* a rule which Freud called the "principle of equivalence." This rule states that psychic energy is *conserved*, in the sense that if energy disappears from conscious applications, it has gone somewhere, still exists, and will reappear in some other symbolic form. Jung uses this observation to conclude that the psyche is a "relatively closed system."[19] Energy is still energy, and must go somewhere. It can't just disappear.

Jung considers the question of the origin of psychic energy from physical energy premature for the present, primarily because we do indeed observe the conservation of psychic energy. It does not return to a physical form. In Chapter 9 this condition will be dealt with under the concept of *involution*, in which it is seen that more subtle forms of functioning are always available. When the more subtle form comes into play (here: psychic energy) it *controls* the less subtle forms (here: physical energy) but is not identical with them.

For the conservation of psychic energy to hold, the concept of the unconscious becomes necessary, for the energy does retreat from consciousness, but soon returns. In between these times of visibility, it is activating the unconscious.

Given the validity of this interpretation of the observed facts, we then ask what the source is for this energy.

INSTINCT AND SPIRIT

We take a brief excursion here, and note the primitivity, the instinctuality, of the infant, along with the mature, cultured adult which it is the potential of the infant to become. In between, we have the whole range of human development: the cruelty of the child, the sexuality of youth, the drive for security of the pre-middle-age adult. This amounts to a gradual taming of pure instinctuality, so that spirituality emerges, if it is to do so in the individual. As Jung says:

> In the child-psyche the natural condition is already opposed by a "spiritual" one. It is recognized that the human living in the state

of nature is in no sense merely "natural" like an animal, but sees, believes, fears, worships things whose meaning is not at all discoverable from the conditions of the natural environment. Their underlying meaning leads us in fact far away from all that is natural, obvious, and easily intelligible, and quite often contrasts most sharply with the natural instincts.[20]

The inherent conflict of the initial and final conditions of the human is most easily explained as the tension of the opposites of spirit and instinct, confirming the ancient dictum of Heraclitus that "war is the father of all things." We perceive with sufficient force the instinctuality of the merely natural human. In other natures, on the other hand, the power of the spirit can lead to tremendous efforts on the part of the individual. Most of us live in a vague tension of the two, the lack of acute tension corresponding to a lack of energy devoted to these poles as such.[21]

Jung stresses the opposition of spirit and instinct, but notes also the paradoxical fact that if spirit arises in evolution, it was already there!

> The spiritual principle does not, strictly speaking, conflict with instinct as such but only with blind instinctuality, which really amounts to an unjustified preponderance of the instinctual nature over the spiritual. The spiritual appears in the psyche also as an instinct, indeed as a real passion, a "consuming fire," as Nietzsche once expressed it. It is not derived from any other instinct . . . but is a principle *sui generis*, a specific and necessary form of instinctual power.[22]

Thus a study of the nature of psychic energy leads us to recognize a fundamental polarity, the opposites of spirit and instinct, just as God is conceived not only as the final goal, but also the first cause, of that which is. As Jung says, this

> asserts the essential contradictoriness of one and the same being, a being whose innermost nature is a tension of opposites. For this reason the God-concept, in itself impossibly paradoxical, may be so satisfying to human needs that no logic however justified can stand against it. Indeed the subtlest cogitation could scarcely have found a more suitable formula for this fundamental fact of inner experience.[23]

The point has been repeatedly emphasized that the intellect alone cannot grasp the center, which is also to say that *the criteria of the intellect are not the ultimate criteria of truth.* A similar statement would apply to the claims or criteria of the heart to grasp the center.

Unless we consciously undertake oscillation, what then becomes our *fate* (that acted out upon us against our will), as distinct from our *destiny* (a development within constraints in which we consciously participate), is what Jung called an *enantiodromia,* an "enforced" journey into the opposite mode of being. A moving example of enantiodromia is portrayed in Euripides' play *The Bacchae,* in which the paradisal aspect of relationship to Dionysos, the fertile land flowing with wine and beauty, turns into a scene in which Agave and her maidens, under the destructive power of the same god, tears her son's head off and carries it triumphantly, thinking it is a deer that they have dismembered.

OPPOSITES IN THE PSYCHE

Jung's own approach to the universality of opposites is found in his *Psychological Types.*[24] He begins with eastern texts as embodying a superior "psychological accuracy," and then interprets them in terms of the western psyche. It is interesting, and important to the present book, that he wrote this prior to the public appearance of the physics which gives this book its impetus, though at about the same time. Thus the symbolic unity of the material discovered independently in these diverse fields is a remarkable example of the *zeitgeist.*

Jung begins by documenting the mythology of the creative world principle, *Brahman,* then shows that it describes an inherent energy principle in the human, as intuited by the ancient masters, and projected in the mythology.

To sample some texts quoted by Jung:

> Brahman is being and non-being, reality and irreality.... There are two forms of Brahman: the formed and the formless, the mortal and the immortal, the stationary and the moving, the actual and the transcendental.... That Person, the maker of all things, the great Self, seated forever in the human heart, is perceived by the heart, by the thought, by the mind.... That Self,

smaller than small, greater than great, is hidden in the heart of this creature here.[25]

Note, in the second sentence, the use of the term "two" followed by four different pairs of opposites. Here the essence is clearly the two-ness, or, oppositeness, which in itself subsumes all pairs of opposites. This suggests the creative *Bindu* which was mentioned earlier. Jung comments:

> These quotations show that Brahman is the union and dissolution of all opposites, and at the same time stands outside them as an irrational factor.[26]

Following further quotations, Jung adds the conclusion "that Brahman is not only the producer but the produced, the ever-becoming," that which feeds upon itself and grows.[27] The worldview which he discusses fits our physical cosmos (as can be seen in Appendix 2). The eastern mythology contains remarkably accurate psychic representations of physical reality.

He summarizes his introduction:

> The idea of a creative world-principle is a projected perception of the living essence in the human as such. In order to avoid all vitalistic misunderstandings, one would do well to regard this essence in the abstract, as simply *energy*. . . . The concept of energy implies that of polarity, since a current of energy necessarily presupposes two different states, or poles, without which there can be no current. Every energic phenomenon (and there is no phenomenon that is not energic) consists of pairs of opposites. . . .[28]

Finally, he observes that *all energy flows between polar opposites*. That is, the energy concept must not be detached from the condition of its existence, which is the prior formation, or coming into existence, of opposites. On the other hand, as will be seen in the next chapter, the physicist is aware that the cycle of energy and opposites is similar to the conundrum of the priority of the chicken and the egg: with energy we can produce opposites, which then manifest energy. Jung's point is not diminished by this fact, but rather enhanced. Energy and opposites form a unified concept when correctly viewed.

NATURAL REGULATION OF OPPOSITES

In the next section of the text which we are following, Jung draws upon the fact that the cosmic principle of energy and opposites, *Brahman*, is also identified with the world-order, or *rta*. This principle of rightness, regulation and shaping is virtually identical with that which I have called the Patterning. Its imagery is exceedingly rich. Nothing which happens is outside of *rta*, but one is also enjoined to "Bore for the streams of *rta*." Jung interprets this passage:

> In the worship of [the fire god] Agni, the fire obtained by boring is used as a magic symbol of the regeneration of life. Boring for the streams of *rta* obviously has the same significance; the streams of life rise to the surface again, libido is freed from its bonds. . . . The imagery clearly suggests a state of energic tension, a damming up of libido and its release.[29]

This damming up occurs with loss of instinct, i.e. when the presence of a growing store of energy makes available actions of will, and the instinctual is no longer automatic. The energy also makes possible a reflection on the action with respect to the psyche's own purposes. This is a natural consequence of the development of effective adaptations, which make for an increase in available energy. Heinrich Zimmer[30] presents several highly illuminating tales concerning the concept of the "act of truth." In one case a prostitute is able to do what the sages are unable to do, namely to reverse the flow of the Ganges River, by invoking her "act of truth," which is that she treats all her customers equally, from whatever class. In another case, a monk, a father, and a mother are able to drive poison from the body of the couple's son, by admissions of the facades behind which they had been living for years: the monk that he was devout, the father that he gladly gave hospitality to monks, and the mother that she loved the father! All these facades are means of damming up the libido, and the conscious inclusion of the truth which is the opposite of the facade, frees the life energy for continuation in a natural course, i.e. through the health of the offspring. At such a point an increase of consciousness is highly potential, but the will is of course untrained, unaccustomed to choice.

For the purely instinctual human, no "problem" is encountered in a natural flow from one opposite to another, from one form of one-sidedness to another. To employ again the expression from Chapter 3, the opposites don't "rub and jostle" as values. Some of this lack of development naturally persists in modern humans. There will always be such unexplored areas of what Jung terms "untamed libido" in the vastness of available psyche. At present it is reflected, for example, in those who find no problem in their compartmentalization of science and religion, holding beliefs which contradict their own knowledge of physical reality.

The presence of energy for choice raises the value-issues, for choice implies valuation. Value issues therefore arise naturally, as one can see in even the most primitive cultures, whose strict moral codes both recognize, and give good guidance to, the natural increases of energy, up to a point.

If a person or a culture makes a "final" choice between opposites, as distinct from the natural flow of energy from one opposite to the other, it leads to one-sidedness as a phenomenon of a partially developed person or culture. We all know of the western denial of the body these recent centuries. The "conscious" value was given to spirit to the great starvation of matter. This indeed had all the characteristics of a compulsion. The result of all this was the grossest sort of materialistic development—as a phenomenon of psychic *regulation* (!) but *unconsciously*. Thus Jung's trenchant commentary on our western barbarism which appears a few pages hence.

To summarize, let us list the following stages of development of consciousness by means of opposites acquiring energy. This is a general process, occurring in cultures as just intimated, as well as in individuals of all ages.

1. Easy flow, no problem in *knowing* value (primitive).

2. Preliminary awareness of conflict of opposites.

3. Choice of one opposite, with repression of the other. General unconsciousness of the *use* of the other. E.g., the "gentle" person who is unaware of her/his own violence, or the

"anti-science" person who would not give up the fruits of technology.

4. Psychic regulation builds up energy for the opposite.

5. Continual flow between opposites, but without "self-control" ("enantiodromia").

6. Gradual consciousness of the necessity of balance, and consciously bringing both into life activity (pain involved).

Our own fear of the "natural" or of the new is a default of consciousness with respect to the fact that the energy of the psyche is regulated to balance, though in working with the inner world choice is called for in the *way* in which we are going to fulfill the to and fro flow of libido.

> Libido as an energy concept is a quantitative formula for the phenomena of life, which are naturally of varying intensity. Like physical energy, libido passes through every conceivable transformation; we find ample evidence of this in the fantasies of the unconscious and in myths. These fantasies are primarily self-representations of energic transformation processes, which follow their specific laws and keep to a definite "path." This path is the line or curve representing the optimal discharge of energy and the corresponding result in work. . . . It is the path of our destiny and the law of our being.[31]

At present we are witnessing a resurgence of passion for democracy in nations in which it has been long suppressed. This demonstrates the great power for self-regulation of the psyche in the collective. Could we have foreseen this development and trusted our foresight twenty years ago? In the individual, too, *all* of the opposites are potential, and unless the damage to the individual psyche has been too great, we can learn what to expect and how to handle it.

Unfortunately almost none of our educational endeavors has been directed to such ends, and we still largely qualify for Jung's epithet of "barbarian." Even those who feel and respond to the pull to the east usually do so in an unconscious manner, as a headlong plunge and a desperate escape. They forget precisely the power of their western structure, and in a fully western manner believe that it can simply be dropped. Jung often expressed his deep fears for the well-being of those who leap in this manner. It has as well the effect of solidifying the entrenchment of the western for those who witness its effects—results just as barbarous as those of unbridled western rationalism.

> Our western superciliousness in the face of these Indian insights is a mark of our barbarian nature, which has not the remotest inkling of their extraordinary depth and astonishing psychological accuracy. We are still so uneducated that we actually need laws from without, and a task-master of Father above, to show us what is good and the right thing to do. And because we are still such barbarians, any trust in the laws of human nature seems to us a dangerous and unethical naturalism. Why is this? Because under the barbarian's thin veneer of culture the wild beast lurks in readiness, amply justifying his fear. But the beast is not tamed by locking it up in a cage. *There is no morality without freedom.* When the barbarian lets loose the beast within him, that is not freedom but bondage. Barbarism must first be vanquished before freedom can be won. This happens, in principle, when the basic root and driving force of morality are felt by individuals as constituents of their own nature and not as external restrictions. How else are we to attain this realization but through the conflict of opposites?[32]

Faust can be saved only through his contract with Mephistopheles, for the latter represents precisely his own shadow, the scholar's unlived life.[33] Indeed, Faust comes off as barbarian in numerous encounters, until the meaning of this energy is found and given work to do, and Mephistopheles at last yields to him the kernel of truth in his self-definition: "Part of a power which would alone work evil, but engenders good."

WORKING WITH OPPOSITES

Opposites *are* the nature of psychic reality. That they are the nature of *physical* reality as well will be shown in the next chapter. In one sense, then, the work with opposites is "just" learning to live with reality. It does not change itself to accord with our fantasies or convenience. The position of the human in relation to reality is the same as that of the ego, the "I," to the Self, or Greater Thou within, which is also the source of inner "regulation" (*rta*) of our lives. With respect to the opposites, we must attend to them and intentionally follow their flow and direction, must sacrifice the assumed autonomy of the ego.

For Jung, the east has given us a powerful description of the opposites and their source, the hidden center, *Brahman*. The east has been less one-sided than the west, has felt the *power* of the opposites much more fully, and has decided that "salvation" or spiritual fulfillment is to be had by freeing oneself from them completely. Jung quotes the *Ramayana:*

> "This world must suffer under the pairs of opposites for ever." Not to allow oneself to be influenced by the pairs of opposites, but to be *nirdvandva* (free, untouched by the opposites), to raise oneself above them, is an essentially ethical task, because deliverance from opposites leads to redemption.[34]

In the west we have *so far* attempted to free ourselves from them by an irrevocable choice of one opposite over the other, whereas in the east the goal has been to be free of both, or to *endure* both and gradually find freedom from the passion which one feels when attached to the opposites. Here is a brief extract from a longer passage quoted by Jung:

> The one who remains the same in living as in dying, in fortune as in misfortune, whether gaining or losing, loving or hating, will be liberated. The one who covets nothing and despises nothing, who is free from the opposites, whose soul knows no passion, is in every way liberated (*Mahabharata,* 4.19.4) . . . through equanimity and endurance of the opposites, humans will partake of the bliss of Brahman, which is without qualities (*Bhagavata Purana,* 4.22.24).[35]

This overcoming of opposites by means of a transcendence of them is indeed a nonrational union, by becoming as Brahman: beyond them.

> The Indian purpose is therefore clear: it wants to free the individ-
> ual altogether from the opposites inherent in human nature, to
> attain a new life in Brahman, which is the state of redemption and
> at the same time God.[36]

In this view, the world of conditioned things is at best a ladder upon
which to practice a spirituality of transcendence, and the transcendent life can also be lived *in the world* while helping others along the
same path of liberation.

For Jung the west is simply unprepared for this kind of spirituality, having made the irrevocable choices mentioned above, and thus
lacking the experience of *both* sides of the great opposites. At the
same time, as we will see, the western unconscious has become *loaded*
with the unexperienced opposites, and comprises a massive *shadow*.
Of course this has also been the case in the east, for it is precisely the
physical world with its suffering which has become the carrier of the
shadow. One does indeed see the *unconscious* materialism which is
the result, and which contrasts with the *conscious* materialism of
the west.

This merely shows the pervasive reality of the opposites. Even
escape offers no escape! Here we *are*, or as Middleton Murry says,
"Our concern is with the Earth. Here we are bound, and here we are
free."[37] Jung notes (see pp. 119–121 above) that *Brahman* corresponds, among other things, to symbols of vitality, life-force, and
libido, and *rta* corresponds to the regulation of that libido. This
prepares us for the *fact of non-escape*. Being *within* and *between* opposites, we find that the power of being and the regulation of life-force
is *with* us. The question then becomes one of our *attitude* in relation
to it.

Here Jung finds that the west has been uniquely prepared by its
own experience of one-sidedness to move creatively with the opposites, for we have learned the power and danger of living in such a
one-sided fashion. To a great extent we have not yet learned this as
individuals. Still, our *collective* living of it prepares us for going
beyond that one-sided state in a new and creative fashion, if we will
indeed do so. We are largely aware of the dangers of collective
one-sidedness, though not yet well-versed in dealing with them. If
we can learn *as individuals* to do so, we will help the collective. To
repeat a passage quoted earlier:

A *conscious* capacity for one-sidedness is a sign of the highest culture, but *involuntary* one-sidedness, i.e., this inability to be anything but one-sided, is a sign of barbarism.[38]

We may just be coming to the point of consciousness about our economic, social, cultural, and spiritual barbarism as western nations.

Here we focus upon the possibility of individual *conscious* use of one or the other opposite, as distinct from being powerless (as we have been) in the flow of opposites on the one hand, and being completely above them (as it might erroneously seem) on the other. Both of these *unconscious* cases effectively prevent the development of libido. Shortly after, Jung follows the above passage with this:

> Identification with one particular function at once produces a tension of opposites. The more compulsive the one-sidedness, and the more untamed the libido which streams off to one side, the more daemonic it becomes. . . . We see in our patients and can feel in ourselves with what irresistible force the libido streams inwards or outwards, with what unshakable tenacity an introverted or extraverted attitude can take root.[39]

The term "untamed libido" is our major clue to the work with opposites. Every impulse and compulsion signals its presence. The domestication of untamed libido by channeling it into value and use is the western ideal. This is something not for the saint alone to accomplish: the actualization of spiritual value is the promise of every human life. Jung goes on:

> . . . at the instant of its appearance the libido divides into two streams, which as a rule alternate periodically but at times may appear simultaneously in the form of a conflict, as an outward stream opposing an inward stream. The daemonic quality of the two movements lies in their ungovernable nature and overwhelming power. This quality, however, makes itself felt only when . . . culture [is] not sufficiently advanced for us to tame our libido to the point where we can follow its introverting or extraverting movement of our own free will and intention.[40]

To follow the stream of libido with choice and intention is, for Jung, to fulfill the ideas both of creation and of redemption.

Creation or emergence, the mythology of origins, tells universally of the appearance of opposites. In the Brahmanic material, we have seen this clearly. Brahman creates, is the source of, the opposites. What of redemption? Brahman is also identified with Rta, the World-Order, and its functioning is very like the Chinese concept of Tao. For the east, simply to be following Rta or Tao yields for the individual all the meaning of redemption. Precisely through living our barbarism, Jung would say, we have gathered the energy and motivation for a step beyond a detached flow. Having experienced, and often been nearly destroyed by "untamed libido," with its compulsive and daemonic character, we can begin to see that such a way of living is wholly unredeemed. But the idea of the possibility of seeing and doing the "will of God," the idea that our *intention* is actually *needed*, draws us into an *inherently redemptive* schema.

Notes

1. This rule asserts that of any proposition, it can be either truly affirmed or denied. Strangely the usual example is "It is raining." We all know many instances in which we find that proposition without clear resolution.
2. Teilhard de Chardin, Pierre. 1969. *Human Energy*. Translated by T.M. Cohen. New York: Harcourt Brace Jovanovich, p. 68: "God can only be defined as a *centre of centres*."
3. Moon, Sheila. 1984. *Changing Woman and Her Sisters*. San Francisco: Guild for Psychological Studies Publishing House, pp. 24–25.
4. 2,4,11. In Müller, F. Max. 1962. *The Upanishads*. Translated and edited by F. Max Müller. New York: Dover Publications.
5. Raju, P.T. 1985. *Structural Depths of Indian Thought*. Albany: State University of New York Press.
6. Daniélou, Alain. 1964. *Hindu Polytheism*. New York: Bollingen Foundation, p. 202. Distributed by Pantheon Books.
7. *Depths*, p. 510.
8. Ibid. P. 512.
9. Ibid. P. 513.
10. Zimmer, Heinrich. 1962. *Myth and Symbols in Indian Art and Civilization*. Edited by Joseph Campbell. Bollingen Series VI. New York: Harper and Row, Harper Torchbooks, p. 140.
11. Ibid. P. 147.
12. Ibid. Pp. 147–148.
13. Ibid. P. 188.

14. Ibid. P. 202.
15. Blake, William. 1975. *The Marriage of Heaven and Hell*. London: Oxford University Press, plate 7.
16. For a thorough discussion of the mutual dependence of spirit and matter in relation to consciousness in the psyche, including the evolutionary development of our perceptual system, see Hitchcock, *Comparison*, Chapter III.
17. *CW* 8, par. 420.
18. *CW* 8, pars. 1–130.
19. Ibid. Par. 10.
20. Ibid. Par. 98.
21. For those who do devote tremendous energy to the middle ground of physical security, the acquisition of financial power often leads to experimentation in the polar realms of power-oriented sex and a power-oriented relationship to art or religion.
22. Ibid. Par. 108.
23. Ibid. Par. 103.
24. *CW* 6, pars. 327–374.
25. Ibid. Par. 329.
26. Ibid. Par. 330.
27. Ibid. Par. 332.
28. Ibid. Par. 337.
29. Ibid. Pars. 350–351.
30. *Philosophies*, pp. 167–169.
31. *CW* 6, par. 355.
32. Ibid. Par. 357.
33. Faust must honor the dark, fiery element within. An eastern parallel is: "Sacrifice or be devoured." See *CW* 6, par. 338: Prajapati, the cosmic reative principle, begets Agni, who is fire, the devourer. Agni, needing something to feed on, then turns to Prajapati and demands and receives sacrifice. If Prajapati had not sacrificed, Agni would have devoured *him*.
34. Ibid. Par. 327.
35. Ibid. Par. 328.
36. Ibid. Par. 329.
37. *God*, p. 172.
38. *CW* 6, par. 346.
39. Ibid. Par. 347.
40. Ibid.

Chapter 6

The Opposites in Physics as the Web of the Physical Cosmos

This world must suffer under the pairs of opposites forever.
                                    —The *Ramayana*

In the previous chapter we explored the manner in which opposites arise and come to consciousness in the psyche, along with the process of integrating them into our lives as part of the task of spirituality. Opposites are containers of energy, and energy manifests opposites. Presently we will see that quite similar processes of emergence and manifestation occur in the arising of the physical cosmos itself.

The "history" of the cosmos is a story of things *becoming*, where "before that" there was no such thing. This becoming occurs universally in terms of opposites. Some of the opposites which we will encounter are pairs of attributes of the "stuff of the universe." For the sake of convenience we term one of the pair "positive" and the other "negative." This terminology does not imply a value judgment such as "good" or "bad," but simply denotes the oppositeness with which attributes arise. For instance, we will discover positive and negative forms of energy and of electric charge.

In order to look at some of these properties, we will begin with an investigation of things which already possess physical existence.

The "stuff" of palpable objects can be analyzed into some hundred "chemical elements," e.g. hydrogen, carbon, oxygen, iron, gold, and uranium, which are distinguished according to the properties of their atomic nuclei. Because the nuclei consist of fundamental, though not quite elementary particles, namely protons and neutrons, we will focus upon the basic properties of these protons and neutrons, namely "mass," "electric charge," and "spin." Electric charge, or just "charge," is of course the same stuff which flows through our light bulbs and appliances. "Spin" is a property which is not familiar to our everyday experience, but which was discovered by means of an analogy to the quantity of spin which a toy top has. For more recondite nuclear properties (which will not be taken up here) there are no known analogues to our experience at all.

For our purposes, the properties of an atomic nucleus made up of protons and neutrons can be calculated as a sort of sum of the properties of the protons and neutrons of which it is made.

The behavior of the chemical elements in the laboratory, or as substances, depends upon the disposition, around the nucleus, of entities known as electrons. The nuclear properties named above bring about this disposition and so lend identifiable behavior to the elements on a chemical basis. The *nuclear* properties thus determine the visible properties of the elements.

We now are quite certain that the atomic nuclei of virtually all the elements we find on the earth were produced in stellar explosions. Indeed, hydrogen bombs, as mini-stars quite out of place on the earth, replicate the early stages of this process on a minuscule scale of a few kilograms. Though we thus clearly cannot produce elements on a large scale in the laboratory, we are able on a very tiny scale indeed to *construct* representatives of all of these elements in laboratories, using the two known stable "simple" particles: protons and electrons. In the process, some protons are converted to neutrons, which completes the triad of "everyday" nuclear constituents.

It is reasonable to say that after the first second of time of the birth of the cosmos in the "Big Bang," the transformations of matter which occur within the cosmos are limited to the interactions of protons and electrons, for the *results* of all interactions which occur on a large scale may be described in terms of these two.[1] The problem of physical becoming thus resolves itself into the becoming of protons and electrons. From them, all of the elements are produced in known processes in the interior of normal stars, and in stellar "supernova" explosions.

How, then, can we account for the "becoming" of protons and electrons? Physicists have observed that this happens when a sufficiently energetic (or, since Einstein showed the equivalence of mass and energy, we might say sufficiently *massive*) gamma ray, which is a high-energy photon, a blob of "pure" electromagnetic energy (as is visible light), "*becomes*" a pair of particles, or, more precisely, a particle and its "antimatter" mate, or antiparticle.

Pictorially:

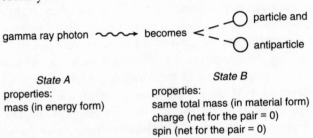

gamma ray photon ~~~→ becomes < particle and / antiparticle

State A
properties:
mass (in energy form)

State B
properties:
same total mass (in material form)
charge (net for the pair = 0)
spin (net for the pair = 0)

A particle and its antiparticle have the same *kind* of mass, which is also the same mass which the gamma ray photon had, but all of their other properties, such as "charge" and "spin," arise in terms of opposites, i.e. positive and negative charge, and positive and negative spin, so that the positives and negatives cancel as to net quantity of each attribute which has become in the process. This is one form of *emptiness*, which we will call emptiness of attributes. Other forms of emptiness are developed in the following subsections.

The role of the gamma rays is stressed here not only because through them the pair-production process was discovered, but mainly because there was a time in the Big Bang when the *typical* electromagnetic photons were gamma rays with quite sufficient energy to produce either particle/antiparticle (proton/antiproton, electron/antielectron) pair. (The antielectron is commonly called a "positron.") Under these conditions, energy can flow easily into material (matter/antimatter) form, on a vast scale. It was at this point in the history of the cosmos that the matter that we see (planets, stars, galaxies) was precipitated out of the primordial energy.[2]

The pair-production process is somewhat reversible. If a particle and its antiparticle come together, they "annihilate" each other, and the particulate stuff with the properties of charge and spin is converted back to energy, but now into two photons, whereas only one photon produced the particle/antiparticle pair. One is then left with the same total mass of the particles which were annihilated, returned to the form of pure energy.

How are we to conceive of this becoming as opposites? Do

these properties exist in some sort of nascent state? In one view this becoming is, or can be visualized as, a *separation* of what was previously a pair of "virtual" particles, or a virtual particle/antiparticle pair, though such virtual particles cannot be detected. The idea is then that the electromagnetic energy "communicates" with what has been called a "sea" of virtual pairs. In this view, the presence of the sea of virtual particles is undetectable, but in the presence of the energy, and depending upon its quantity, various particles from the "sea" can use the energy to make the transition from being virtual particles to being real particles. Or, to put it another way, though the sum of newly appearing quantities or properties is zero, the nascent properties are somehow *there*, or present everywhere. Without the transition from virtuality to reality, we would not have these properties to measure and discuss.

In *A Brief History of Time*[3] Stephen W. Hawking muses that for every type of virtual particle to be available at all points of space, there should be so much mass of such particles that it would curl space up gravitationally and we would be crushed, which, of course, is not observed to occur. This is strong evidence that the mathematical approach which suggests this interpretation is somehow off base. I take this discrepancy as an intuitive indication that we will discover an entirely new approach to thinking about this case, which will yield an entirely new mathematical method. The "sea" of virtual particles is a possible hypothesis, but has the obvious observational shortcomings just noted: space does not curl up! It is thus much simpler, and therefore probably more accurate, to say that the mass of the gamma ray, under a disturbance, *becomes* the particle/antiparticle pair, than to say that the photon's energy *separates* a virtual pair. This requires only that the influence of the *Patterning*, or world-field, which gives the *form* of real occurrences, be present everywhere, not that an enormous mass of virtual particles be present. Thus we have at least two models for becoming: the sea of virtual particles and the world-field.

COMPARISON WITH JUNG

On casual viewing, the theory of a sea of virtual particle pairs might seem to come very close to Jung's concept of the unconscious contents coming to consciousness. One might picture the content as present, hovering around the psyche of the individual, but lacking the energy to cast illumination into the conscious field. Additionally, Jung describes the acquisition of energy by a content as precisely the separation of the content into polar halves, which superficially matches the virtual sea model.

On closer inspection, however, the difference which makes the sea model apply to the psyche, but not to the formation of elementary particles, resides in the *individuality* and *complexity* of the psychic content. The physical particles are exceedingly simple in comparison, and can pop into existence all at once. On the other hand, the content is a complex product of the living organism and its experience. It is already built up of numerous components. The possibilities for different kinds of physical particles are vanishingly few in comparison to the number of possible contents of consciousness. Moreover, the ubiquitous world-field, consisting of the overlapping patterns of all that has come to be, should suffice to shape or form the contents.

It should ultimately be possible to build the world-field model into one of sufficient complexity to account for the virtual sea characteristics of cultural, and even individual, possibilities, which are still more complex than the cultural forms. Such a field may be associated with previously formed aggregates of matter. Perhaps, too, the greater complexity of the individual accounts for the fact that the psychic content gains energy gradually, whereas in the case of elementary particles the transformation of energy into matter form is instantaneous.

In any case, the interaction of these two models of becoming may be very suggestive for our understanding of the foundations of spirituality. To have two models to consider provides some contrast for thinking.

The fact that physicists have tended to favor the virtual sea has an accidental cause in the *interpretation* of the work of P.A.M. Dirac. However, as noted above, Hawking's observation of its shortcoming *for the becoming of elementary particles* is a solid blow to its status.

In returning to the discussion of physical becoming, let us summarize the process we have been describing. The gamma ray photon, depending upon its having enough energy (or mass), can become either a proton/antiproton pair in which the two particles have equal mass, but opposite charge and opposite spin to each other, or an electron/positron pair, again of equal masses, but with opposite charge and spin. In the case of the formation of the electron and the positron, the mass, or energy, involved is 1,840 times less than that of the proton/antiproton pair. Thus, in this case, the gamma ray needs that much less energy.

In high energy accelerator experiments as well, a blob of pure energy can be created by means of the collision of a particle and its antiparticle. Both proton/antiproton and electron/positron collisions are commonly used for this purpose. Because their properties cancel, or have a net of approximately zero, we speak of a *symmetry* of the matter/antimatter creation process which has been described. For many years, physicists have believed that the symmetry was precise, and that what we *see* (rivers, mountains, people, stars, galaxies, etc.) is stuff which somehow became separated from its antimatter counterpart and so was prevented from annihilating. This would mean that some parts of the cosmos are antimatter regions. More recently, this view has been questioned, and a process proposed whereby the fact that the cosmos is in a permanent general disequilibrium introduces a tiny proportion of "symmetry breaking." That is, very rarely the pair-production process produced a matter/matter pair instead of the preponderant matter/antimatter pairs. This would mean that the sum of all properties is *not precisely* zero, but only approximately so—something like 0.00000001. The exact preponderance of matter properties over those of antimatter is not certain.

Though the processes of creation of opposites, matter and antimatter, occur only on a small scale in accelerators (also called "particle factories"), we have solid knowledge that these processes do indeed occur. Since all serious astronomers now agree that we see the remnant of the radiation from the annihilation of pairs in the early cosmos, we have a "standard model" of cosmology in which pair-production processes play a very central role.

This is the account of the creation of matter and "antimatter," and the subsequent annihilation of practically all of the matter by all of the antimatter. We have seen material stuff emerging from pure energy in the "early cosmos," i.e. just after the Big Bang, this emerging occurring by means of becoming in terms of opposites. Again, the mass of the particles and antiparticles is simply the mass of the energy which was converted to particles in the process. The attrib-

utes which have arisen as balanced opposites, apparently from nothing, are "electric charge" and "spin," along with a few others which
have been omitted for simplicity. The net *amount* of each of
these properties which has come into being is approximately zero
when compared to the total quantity of each created in pair-
production, which is in turn infinitesimal compared to the total mass
of the cosmos.

SPACE AND TIME AS OPPOSITES

Another new quality, not previously mentioned, has also appeared, namely the *ability* to come to rest in a definable frame of
reference in space and time. Pure energy, such as light, does not
possess the ability to come to rest in a definable reference frame. We
will see that the space-time framework which defines the possibility
of being "at rest" also comprises a new pair of opposites, for space
and time in modern physics behave as dimensions in a mathematically
identical manner, except for a minus sign. On this basis I am calling
them opposites, though space has three dimensions and time one. It is
clear that something has *become* in the pair-creation process, for we
have three additional attributes, including space-time now along with
charge and spin, but the *net* increase in the *quantity* of these attributes is virtually zero. The net increase of space-time may be precisely zero. We will see shortly the sense in which space and time can
be null.

Einstein's development of Relativity solved many dilemmas by
showing how to construct frames of reference for moving systems,
whereby all observers could understand the necessary discrepancies
in their qualitative and quantitative descriptions of events which
were occurring in these moving systems. A simple analogy can illuminate the meaning of the words "necessary discrepancies," but we
must not expect it to give us a fully precise picture of the relationship
of space and time. Such a picture involves notions which are
counterintuitive (defying common sense). The relevant ideas are not
yet easy to acquire.

If we wanted to measure the "distance" between two "events,"
A and B, say, two flashes of light which are separated both in space
and time, we might display the problem by analogy with the coordi-

nates of ordinary graphs. Space is measured in appropriate units of space, and time is measured in appropriate units of time.[4]

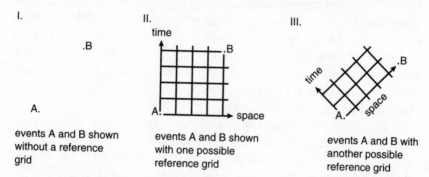

I.

.B

A.

events A and B shown
without a reference
grid

II.

time

.B

A.   space

events A and B shown
with one possible
reference grid

III.

time   .B

space

A.

events A and B with
another possible
reference grid

In the first diagram (I), the two events are merely displayed as separated. With the grid in II, we measure the separation in space as four units and in time also as four units. If another "observer" used a different grid (III), she or he would perhaps measure 5.6 space units and zero time units for the same two events. In experimental physics we find indeed that different observers measure different amounts of space and of time for the same two events, the "rotation" of the reference grid depending on the relative motion of the two observers. It is indeed necessary that two observers in relative motion would accurately measure different numbers of units of each dimension, space and time. They don't "agree" in their measurements, but each clearly understands why the other got different space and time separations for the two events. Each can use the same "laws of physics" for both the measurements and the reconciliation of the "discrepancies."

Conversely, if we insist upon our intuitive notions of space and time, which demand that the passage of time, for instance, be the same between the two events no matter how the observers may be moving, it then seems that the laws of physics must be different for the two observers. We will return to this example.

Actually we should merely say that observers who are moving relative to each other measure distances and times which are different; the feeling of "discrepancy" arises from our "common sense" experience that time and space are unique and uniform, even if our measurements of them may not be precise. We need "merely" to let this archaic and incorrect notion depart.

To repeat, the notion that space and time were uniform and unique yielded results which implied that the laws of physics might be different in different reference frames, *which also could be used to determine which reference frame was in motion and which is at rest.* Conversely, the notion that the laws of physics must be the same in all "inertial" (roughly: uniformly moving, or "coasting") reference frames entails that the speed of light must be a constant of nature which is independent of the motions of the source of light (such as a star) or of any possible observers.

The notion that the laws of physics must be the same in all "inertial" reference frames is called the "principle of relativity." It says that there is no means of analyzing motions in a laboratory which could detect fine differences in the laws of physics. If that could be done, it would tell you whether or not you were at rest. The concept of rest thus becomes a relative, not an absolute, term. Sitting at home in a chair, we seem to be "at rest," while yet we know that the earth is rotating on its axis and revolving in orbit around the sun on a yearly basis, and the sun in turn is in an immensely larger orbit around the center of our galaxy, and our galaxy in motion in the local group of galaxies, etc., etc. For many purposes such as for interplanetary space probes, we take the sun as being at rest. There is no way to determine an absolute framework of rest in the cosmos, though that statement actually goes much deeper than can be seen from the examples given. They may only give some hint of the direction being taken.

The change which solved the problem of cross-referencing measurements in moving systems was the recognition that the speed of light is a constant of nature.[5]

One further hint at the depth of the new Einsteinian view will be attempted. The new outlook provided the scheme, mentioned earlier, by means of which the different observations of space and time could be uniquely *reconciled:* each observer would have the same understanding of what had occurred, and why the measurements were different. In order for this to be so, light takes on a most curious property.

Except for the fact that it is finite, namely 300,000 kilometers per second, the speed of light behaves in every other respect as if it were infinite. The most important aspect of this is that at the speed of light, it takes zero time to get anywhere at all in the cosmos. Viewing the speed of light as infinite would give this result a feeling of rationality, but the speed of light *is* finite. All photons, these "lumps" of pure electromagnetic energy, travel at this speed, but have *no duration* in their own framework. This means that it is impossible to construct a space-time framework for a photon. But space, as that which can be traversed *in* zero time by light,[6] then begins to take on an illusory aspect, or space and time appear somewhat as mutually created illusions, even as opposites arising as if from a virtual pair.

If I see a distant star, I say, in one sense, that the light traveled for a long time at its finite speed to cross the vast space which separates it from me. In an equally "real" sense, the apparently lengthy passage of the light across an apparently vast region of space is an instantaneous, non-spatial transference of energy from the star to me, since it has no duration in its own frame of reference. That is the view which results from seeing the same process from the viewpoint of the light itself. In that framework, space and time simply are not real.

Space and time are made "real" for those entities which possess all of the fundamental attributes of mass, charge, and spin, for only these entities can be brought to "rest." But light lacks charge and spin, and consequently lacks the ability to come to rest in a definable framework, so that when the universe was essentially a hypersphere of photons, essentially devoid of effective[7] charge and spin, there still seems to have been some overall framework relating the interactions of all those photons, none of which possessed such a framework. Under such conditions, what a measurement is can hardly be defined.

With particles, then, space and time also come into being as another pair of opposites, and our whole world of measurability becomes possible.

OPPOSITE FORMS OF ENERGY

Let us now push back the account of becoming to another stage and inquire about the becoming of the photons which precede space and time in being. Cosmologists now describe the "early cosmos," from about one ten-thousandth of a second after the Big Bang until about one hundred thousand years later, as the "radiation era," a time in which the mass in matter form in the cosmos was minuscule compared to the mass in energy or radiation form. It is possible thus to visualize, i.e. to describe physically, the cosmos as an aggregate of photons held together by their mutual gravitational attraction, evolving as a gravitationally unified whole, for the radiation also possesses gravitational mass and does the main job of binding it all together.

The *form* of this whole is that of a self-contained four-dimensional space-time system, a space which is wrapped around itself in such a manner that there is no "outside" in our usual conception of it. It conforms to the ancient conception of a space whose center is everywhere and whose circumference is nowhere, except that it is simultaneously *finite*. At present we have not learned to visualize this "hypersphere" except by the analogy of the surface of a spherical balloon as a two-dimensional space which is finite in spite of the fact that there is no "end" to the surface, no direction "out" while remaining within its two-dimensionality. Let us hold this image for later return.

In order to see the opposite energy forms which give rise to the photons, we need the concept of negative energy, because it will be employed later in a quotation from Marcel Golay. The idea is similar to something, e.g. a large stone, falling down a hole, from which it would have to be carried back up. Some of what we think of as ordinary (positive) energy is lost in the process of falling. We could also call the loss of positive energy the creation of *negative energy*, which would be canceled if we put in positive energy to bring it back up where it had been. That is, the positive energy would cancel the negative energy created when the stone fell into the hole.

The stone and the earth attract each other, so negative energy is created when things which attract each other move closer together, or when things which repel each other move farther apart. But our whole observable cosmos consists of things, such as stars, which attract each other. They form a unified system under the attraction of gravity. While they are not very close to each other by our everyday standards, they are not infinitely far apart. Their very gravitational relationship constitutes negative energy.

But if the sum of energy is zero, the creation of negative energy entails the creation of positive energy. In our example above, we see this positive energy in the fact that the stone gains speed as it falls. Now let's move away from the hole.

Picture the large stone falling through the air under the influence of gravity. It gains speed, and when it hits the earth, its speed represents enough energy to do some work, e.g. to force itself into the ground, or to break something. This energy it obtained from gravity. Now it is "bound" to the earth in a stable fashion, and it reached this stable condition by giving up the energy which it had by reason of its separation from the earth. That energy went into heat and sound and creating a dent in the earth.

Falling *creates* negative energy by creating gravitational relationship. Positive energy, i.e. energy-of-motion, and negative energy, gravitational relationship, were created simultaneously. Once the energy-of-motion is dissipated (after the fall, by conversion to crushing, sound, and heat) the stable, "bound," condition ensues. To visualize the energy of gravitational relationship, we need only to imagine lifting the stone back to the height from which it fell, and picture the energy it would take to do so.

The energy which was released to form the stable condition also has "mass," so the total mass of the system (earth and stone) is now just a bit smaller. The energy has been sent off into the rest of the environment as heat and sound.

A similar case occurs in the building of heavy nuclei from protons in stellar explosions, as mentioned above (p. 131). Here the energy which is released when particles come together to form stable nuclei under the attraction of the "strong nuclear force" is called the "mass defect," again from the equivalence of energy and mass. In order to form a stable combination, any two particles must convert part of their mass into energy and send this energy off into the space. The greater proportion so given away, the greater the stability of the combination which ensues. This is a universal process, though the loss of mass as such is quite noticeable only in the case of building heavy nuclei from protons. In making a helium nucleus from four protons, for example, about three-fourths of one percent of the mass is converted to energy and "lost."

We can visualize this universal process in the following diagram:

State A: ◯ <– mutual attraction –> ◯
State B: ◯ <=> ◯   > energy leaves
          particles closer,
          attraction stronger

In state B, the total weight of the two particles and the departing energy is equal to the weight of the two particles alone in state A. The weight of the energy is known as the "mass defect" of the two particles. But even to get the particles as close together as they are in state A, some energy was given to the cosmos.

This all has a direct bearing on opposite forms of energy. The earliest scientific appreciation of this opposition which I have seen occurs in the following paragraph by M.J.E. Golay, which may well be of vast historical significance in human appreciation of our relationship to the cosmos.[8]

> You may well ask also: Did it [the Big Bang] start with a pinpoint of matter of no size and infinite density? This is an interesting question to think about, for the following reason. When we permit two masses to come together by gravitational attraction, like a mass of water falling toward the earth's center through a hydroelectric plant, we derive useful energy at the expense of the negative gravitational potential energy of the two masses. And when we calculate the gravitational energy for the entire universe, using available astronomical data, we find that it is of the order of magnitude of the total positive energy in the form of masses, radiation, kinetic energy, and so forth. So we are led to ask: Could it be that the total energy of the universe is actually zero, that the positive energy we have in the form of mass and radiation is merely the result of a trade for negative gravitational energy? Then, if this is so, perhaps the Creator did not require the enormous mass of all the stars we see, but required merely the intelligence to trigger the process. . . .

The fact is that the observed negative forms (gravity) and positive forms (mass and radiation) of energy or mass balance to nearly zero in our entire observable cosmos. This fact, Golay suggests, may indicate another level or quality of becoming. To illustrate this, let us return to the image of the falling stone used earlier. We may now suppose that the stone falls an extreme distance into a region of very intense gravity, so that it gains enormously more (positive) energy-of-motion than before. Since we can imagine any amount of gravitational (negative) energy given to the stone, we may as well imagine that enough energy is given to create the stone itself, since its mass represents just so much energy. That is, by falling into a sufficiently deep gravitational hole, and our cosmos *is* sufficiently deep, enough negative energy would be created to provide enough positive energy to create the stone. This is physically equivalent to saying that, *given the present cosmos*, the stone could "pay the price" of its existence simply by *coming into existence*.

The only problem with the analogy of *falling* into the hole is that the positive form of energy which is created is that of motion. However, if the stone pops into existence *at rest*, the form is that of the mass itself. That is, if a large rock were to come into existence, spontaneously appearing in a place, it would represent a tremendous amount of energy needed to produce its mass, but in the process of coming into existence it would at the same time establish a gravitational relationship to the rest of the cosmos, which would *provide* the needed energy.

So why don't we see things popping up all over the place? The physical conditions are not present for the process to occur, and haven't been available since the Big Bang. This process was nonetheless suggested to occur by Fred Hoyle as part of his "steady state" cosmos, which was popular until the remnants of the Big Bang were observed in 1965. Under that theory, Hoyle proposed that about one hydrogen atom per cubic kilometer per century did simply appear. His theory was shown to be untenable, but on other grounds. Undoubtedly the hydrogen atoms do not appear, however. The reason for this is the same as for the stone: the physical conditions are not right. But if the atom or the stone *were* to spontaneously appear, it would cost nothing at all under Golay's hypothesis.[9] In fact, his suggestion is that the whole cosmos, having arisen under the presence of favorable conditions of temperature and density, had no net cost, and may actually have arisen in just this manner. All existent stuff pays for itself by being in gravitational relationship to the rest. The cosmos adds up to *nothing!* A description of how such a cosmos can come into being is given in Appendix 2.

What we are saying, essentially, is that the mass defect of the cosmos seems to be sufficient to create the matter which *comprises* the cosmos, along with the energy stored in the motion of that matter and the energy in the form of electromagnetic radiation (light, etc.). Still another way to say this (for it is an unusual idea) is: If we wished to push all of the galaxies in the cosmos so far apart that they would exert no appreciable force upon each other, the energy required to do this would be so great that it would be necessary to convert all galaxies to pure energy to supply the needed amount. Thus, when the job was completed, there would be no galaxies to interact, an unexpected result. This is consistent with the discussion above to the effect that the total energy of the cosmos is zero. In fact it is a prime illustration.

Another consequence of this condition is that the precipitation of some of the cosmic energy into matter means that there cannot be enough energy in the *motion* of that matter to overcome the gravity of the cosmos. Though the cosmos is now expanding, it must at some time in the future fall back upon itself.

But the point of all of this is that we now have another pair of opposing qualities. Previously we had positive and negative charge, positive and negative spin, and space and time. Now we also have mass (or energy) and mass defect (or negative energy). Physical becoming, then, is the creation of balanced attributes.

STRUCTURAL OPPOSITES: WAVE AND PARTICLE

In all of the above analysis of physical becoming, it is perhaps now clear why the various opposites had to be introduced gradually. Some are highly counter-intuitive. That is, they don't match our culturally developed "common sense." The fact that Jung had to draw upon eastern culture for models of psychic processes had a similar cause. The same is very true of the last attribute of physical becoming and existence in our discussion of opposites.

Wave/particle duality has been the subject of much thought among physicists, especially Einstein and Bohr, who developed two camps of thinking on this issue. The debate survives even now, but perhaps is winding down, as evidence for Bohr's position becomes stronger and stronger. What remains of it may be the portion which follows Planck's rule that physics progresses from funeral to funeral.

Since wave/particle duality is the main topic of my *Atoms, Snowflakes & God*, I will here deal with it only in those aspects which are immediately relevant. It is, however, a tremendously powerful seed of spirituality, worthy of a lengthy study. This immediate relevance is with respect to the predicament of illusoriness of so-called "real" things (breaking down rationalistic materialism), and the inherent dynamism or energy capacity of the psyche as modeled in physical reality.

The presentation of previous opposites of existing qualities, space/time, and positive/negative energy, with a near-zero sum, focused upon particles and bodies, because these are easiest to visualize. Yet there remains the question of the discreteness of such entities, and of photons (gamma rays or light, among others) as well as the traditionally material particles. For instance, the gamma ray which undergoes pair-production was represented by a waveform.

The short of it is that we have definitive experiments which demonstrate that "things" are *neither divisible nor indivisible*, neither discrete (particulate) nor continuous (wave-like). This is especially evident at the "quantum" level, or the level of individual atomic phenomena. In *Knowledge and Wonder*,[10] Victor Weisskopf has an excellent description of the essence of the quantum state and the wave-particle duality. Some of this has been included as Appendix 3. With respect to the point at hand, he says:

> In the quantum state the electron is neither a particle nor a wave in the old senses.[11] The quantum state cannot be described in terms of a mechanical model. It is a new state of matter, different from what we have experienced with large objects.[12]

An interesting aspect of this quotation is that, while we certainly have not *experienced* the characteristics of the quantum conditions of reality, they are nonetheless as true in our everyday macroscopic world as they are for individual atoms. Once we become conscious of the quantum, however, we can indeed see quantum effects in our everyday living. Among these are the fact that objects made of atoms can have physical strength. As physics Nobel laureate Richard Feynman said:

> So now we understand why we do not fall through the floor . . .
> the resistance to atomic compression is a quantum mechanical
> effect, not a classical effect.[13]

We need not go into this in any detail: the purpose of the quotation is only to present the statement of an authority that quantum effects are indeed present in everyday life. We simply never learned to recognize them prior to the present time.

A bit later in the same chapter, Feynman states that "*all* our experiences are with waves and particles." This contrasts with Jung's comment on the same point, that we experience nothing in a pure form, but rather exclusively as "third points," i.e. as entities which unite the opposites. The reconciliation of these views is of paramount interest for our present discussion. What Feynman means is that our experiments without exception force choices between contrasting possibilities. To this, Weisskopf adds:

> Quite generally, all measurements which could be used for a decision between the wave and the particle nature of the electron (or any other entity) have the same property. If one performs these measurements, the object changes its state completely in the performance itself, and the result of the measurement applies not to the original state but to the state into which the object was put by the measurement.[14]

The experiment will not only give an unambiguous result, but a result which fits the experimental apparatus itself. Since such experiments can only decide *against* a theory, rather than to confirm it, we are left with the knowledge that "stuff" is "not this, not that," or *neti-neti* as in the *Brihadaranyaka Upanishad*. The elasticity of "stuff" is so great that it cannot be "tricked" into betraying a definite characteristic unambiguously as wave or particle. On the other hand, that very fact of elasticity indicates that, as Jung has said, the world consists of nothing but "third points," that is, of symbolic stuff which holds the opposites in a non-rational manner.

> What takes place between light and darkness, what unites the opposites, has a share in both sides and can be judged just as well from the left as from the right, without our becoming any the wiser: indeed, we can only open up the opposition again. Here only the symbol helps, for, in accordance with its paradoxical nature, it represents the "tertium" that in logic does not exist, but which in reality is the living truth.[15]

This, then, is indeed the nature of reality. What shows as the case psychologically is also the case with respect to physical "things." To formulate a worldview upon this model of "complementarity" is to subsume the widest possible range of phenomena.

The implication of this worldview for spirituality resides in the principle of the non-rationality of reality, which implies an endless search of discovery of the nature of physical reality. This is a sort of permanent disequilibrium, which involves us choicefully in the evolutionary process in all its aspects, mental, emotional and physical. The universality of the worldview of complementarity ensures that, as Eliot said, "We shall not cease from exploration." We will always be confronted by opposites and the choice between them in specific instances, as well as the necessity to balance our lives by including the "other," whatever pair is active in the moment. By so doing, we build the "center . . . that is created, so to speak, by the circumambulation of the soul."[16]

Notes

1. Because of the extreme stability of protons, it is not necessary to concern ourselves with their internal structure, the theory of which deals with the truly elementary building blocks known as "quarks" and with particles which bind the quarks together, the so-called "gluons." This theoretical field is now known as "Quantum Cosmology," for it requires particle energies which were available only in the first second or so of the "Big Bang" which formed our cosmos. A description of the Big Bang and the early universe may be found in *Cosmology* by Edward R. Harrison. (1981. Cambridge: Cambridge University Press.) For those inclined to philosophy this is undoubtedly the best book around. Steven Weinberg's *The First Three Minutes* (1984. New York: Bantam Books) is also excellent. Either of these is amplified by Stephen Hawking's *A Brief History of Time* (1988. New York: Bantam Books).

2. It is actually quark/antiquark pairs (see note 7) which are produced, rather than proton/antiproton pairs, and the quarks then give rise to the protons. Only a very tiny fraction of the original "precipitate" now remains: one part in many millions. The rest, the vast bulk of it, was "self-annihilated" at an early time in the present cosmos. Our particle accelerators are capable of minor incursions into the energy ranges under discussion, but still far enough to produce copious supplies of antiprotons for the purposes of the experiments. The actual process is somewhat more complex than I am presenting it here. Again, the reader is referred to *A Brief History of Time*.

3. Hawking, Stephen W. 1988. *A Brief History of Time*. New York: Bantam Books, p. 157.

4. Cosmologist John A. Wheeler (*Spacetime Physics*, W.H. Freeman) has suggested measuring both space and time in meters. The notion of measuring time in meters is definitely an acquired taste, but a very sophisticated one to have. At its level it makes eminent sense, and will probably become "common sense" at some time in the future.

5. It is a curious fact that the notion that this speed might be such a constant arose in physics in the 1860s. This was nearly two decades before the birth of Einstein, who was the first to take the implication seriously, and who on that account was himself dismissed for decades more.

6. Particles, massive bodies, moving at speeds *close* to light-speed, can traverse any spatial distance in *nearly* zero time.

7. The hypothetical virtual particle pairs possess charge and spin in their virtual way, and perhaps virtual mass as well. But the case of the mass is different from that of charge and spin, for when real particle/antiparticle pairs come into being, we see sufficient real mass in the photon which ceases to be when the pair becomes, but we see no charge and spin in advance of the becoming.

8. 1961. Reflections of a Communications Engineer. *Analytical Chemistry*. 33:23A–31A.

9. The spontaneous appearance of all sorts of things has recently been suggested by Hawking. I believe that this is a manifestation of the same balance of positive and negative energy forms, but the conditions are provided by Black Holes.

10. Weisskopf, Victor. 1963. New York: Doubleday and Company, Anchor Books.

11. Ibid. P. 137.

12. Ibid. P. 139.

13. Feynman, Richard. 1963. *Lectures on Physics, Volume III*. Edited by Robert B. Leighton and Matthew Sands. Reading, MA: Addison-Wesley, pp. 2–6.

14. *Knowledge*, p. 136.

15. *CW* 13, par. 199.

16. Jung, *CW* 9_{II}, par. 343.

Chapter 7

Circumambulation

Not all who wander are lost.
— *J.R.R. Tolkien (Lord of the Rings)*

Circumambulation, "walking around the center," complements the oscillation described in the previous chapter in several ways. This can be illustrated, first, by means of the circle or cycle of the seasonal year in the temperate climates. There are opposite seasons: winter/summer, and spring/fall. The winter/summer pair embody opposites such as hot/cold, growth/dormancy, and life/death. The spring/fall pair symbolizes birth/dying, or emergence/withdrawal. In addition to the opposites, there is also the cyclic character and continuity of the seasonal year. We know, of course, that the earth revolves around the sun, but seldom, perhaps, think of the fact that the changing attitude or orientation of the polar axis of the earth with respect to the rays of sunlight produces these seasonal changes, now perceived as opposites. Thus, in the case of our example, there is a deep connection between the two motions (oscillation and circumambulation).[1]

Psychically, the same is true. The diagram in the previous chapter which relates opposites to a "center of centers" can be seen to function similarly to the seasonal example, for our concerns move around among the opposites listed there, as well as others.

The image to which Jung returns each time he mentions circumambulation is that of *focus upon the Center* as such. An excellent example is to be found in *Psychology and Alchemy*, in which Jung is discussing a dream wherein occurred a "shapeless life mass."

The "shapeless life mass" immediately recalls the ideas of the alchemical "chaos," the *massa confusa* which has contained the divine seeds of life ever since the Creation. . . . But if the life-

149

mass is to be transformed a *circumambulatio* is necessary, i.e., exclusive concentration on the center, the place of creative change.[2]

In addition, Jung stresses the spiral nature of the process:

The way to the goal seems chaotic and interminable at first, and only gradually do the signs increase that it is leading anywhere. The way is not straight but appears to go round in circles. More accurate knowledge has proved it to go in spirals: the dream-motifs always return after certain intervals to definite forms, whose characteristic it is to define a center. And as a matter of fact the whole process revolves about a central point or some arrangement round a center. . . . As manifestations of uncon-scious processes the dreams rotate or circumambulate round the center, drawing closer to it as the amplifications increase in dis-tinctness and scope.[3]

It is the fact that the same motifs participate in a definite *development* that turns the circular motion into a spiral. In our seasonal example, the endless cycle of seasons also witnesses a development which we call evolution or progress, depending upon our focus. Thus cyclic time is combined with the equally real linearity of time in history. The relationship of cyclic and linear time has been described beauti-fully by Mircea Eliade in his numerous books, especially *The Sacred and the Profane*.[4]

The material of this chapter should be taken with a caution. In contrast to *living* the real "mystical spiral," we have been *fascinated* by the images of Spiral, Wandering, the Labyrinth. The images stir up excitement without producing concrete changes in our lives. What might it mean actually to *live* it in the course of a modern life? This is the issue of actualization in spite of an *essential* uncertainty.[5] Jung stresses that the conscious mind is very prone to deceive itself with regard to the reality of inward processes which really do affect our lives.

An acquaintance of mine once told me a dream in which *he stepped out into space from the top of a mountain.* I explained to him something of the influence of the unconscious and warned him against dangerous mountaineering expeditions, for which he had a regular passion. But he laughed at such ideas. A few months later while climbing a mountain he actually did step off into space and was killed.

Anyone who has seen these things happen over and over again in every conceivable shade of dramatic intensity is bound to ponder. One becomes aware how easy it is to overlook the attention to the unconscious regulation which is so necessary for our mental and physical health. Accordingly one will try to help oneself by practising self-observation and self-criticism. But [these] are entirely inadequate as a means to establishing contact with the unconscious. Although no human being can be spared bad experiences, everyone shrinks from risking them, especially if one sees any way by which they might be circumvented.[6]

In this passage, Jung is stressing the necessity of reckoning with the actual functioning of the unconscious of the individual, which the conscious attitude is usually reluctant to do. The *resulting* "bad experiences" *can* yield such knowledge with appropriate help, but if the knowledge of the unconscious were sought first, many bad experiences could indeed be avoided. Often this requires professional help, but there are awarenesses and attitudes which we can take into account for our own well-being. Among the simple helps which we can keep in mind is the fact, noted repeatedly in the previous chapter, that the Center cannot be gained by conscious intention, unless that intention is to be patient and wait, actively focusing upon what the unconscious might have to say to us, especially through dreams, and unless that intention is to cooperate with the unconscious, giving it its say within the context of the total personality.

The great labyrinth of Chartres Cathedral, shown on the next page, gives us a concrete model for the process which we now approach. If you trace out the path, you will see what is meant by the movement around the Center, but also it is evident that the path moves now nearer, now further away from the Center, as well as in more limited or in wider sweeps. In addition, the path "fills out" all of the space surrounding the Center. I have experienced walking this path laid out on a large enough floor space, and have found it a great focus to meditation. Laying it out is also a marvelous exercise, if one can find the space and perhaps sympathetic friends to share the experience.

This particular "labyrinth" has a sure path to the Center, which corresponds to the intent of its designers, and the outlook of Christianity. Labyrinths were not always so straightforward. In *The Symbolic Quest*, Whitmont says:

> The labyrinth is one of the oldest of symbols; it depicts the way to the unknown center, the mystery of death and rebirth, the risk of the search, the danger of losing the way, the quest, the finding and the ability to return.[7]

The connection of the "return" to rebirth is profound, for one does not *live* at the Center, but rather one lives a new life in the world out of one's encounters at the Center.

Let us recall some of what has been said concerning the Center in the introduction to this part of the book. Finding it is the finding of both God and Self, and it is being both lost and found—lost because the locus is not familiar to us, and found because there we know we are accepted. The lostness can be the deepest distress for the ego, unless the ego can learn to let go of its insistence on *control*.

As an *attractor* the Center grabs hold of us through its fascination and numinosity. Something wants the ego to go through this painful experience of discovering the reality that it is not to be *in control*. Nonetheless, it has an active role in the process, though not as the *prime* actor. Whitmont seems to deny an initiatory role to the ego, though awareness and acceptance may be taken up *actively:*

> Transformation of our personality occurs *in* us, *upon* us, but not *by* us. The unconscious changes itself and us in response to our awareness and acceptance of our station, [i.e.] of our cross.[8]

In *Answer to Job,* Jung gives the ego and the Other more equality of initiation:

> We find ourselves in best agreement with psychological experience if we concede to the unconscious a definite measure of independence, and to consciousness a degree of creative freedom proportionate to its scope. There then arises that reciprocal action between two relatively autonomous factors which compels us, when describing and explaining the processes, to present sometimes the one and sometimes the other factor as the acting subject. . . .[9]

Perhaps enough has now been said to indicate that we are concerned here not with a process of rational understanding, but with *living,* a process in which both the unconscious and the ego have definitely active parts to play. The danger for us, however, is most often to diminish the role of the Other.

DREAM INTERPRETATION AS CIRCUMAMBULATION

By far the easiest source of unconscious material to acquire is that of dreams. Here, unless one has mastered the usually negative art of "lucid dreaming,"[10] one can be certain that the material is not consciously "constructed." This knowledge is essential if one is to take the dream seriously. Usually, once one begins to pay some attention to, and to have a definite interest in, one's dreams, the ability to remember them increases. Once a dream is honestly reported, say, in one's journal, the circumambulatory task of understanding it can be begun. In the first chapter of *Man and His Symbols,* Jung describes both the process of this task and the tendency to avoid facing the dream's meaning.

To understand [the dream] you must examine it from every aspect—just as you may take an unknown object in your hands and turn it over and over until you are familiar with every detail of its shape.[11]

The specific form of the dream itself tells us what belongs to it and what leads away from it. While "free" association lures one away from that material in a kind of zigzag line, the method I have evolved is more like a circumambulation whose center is the dream picture. I work all around the dream picture and disregard every attempt that the dreamer makes to break away from it.[12]

Freud's method of dream analysis involved "free association." The material of the dream became the starting point for a mental wandering from idea to idea, as the mind of the patient associated the next thing with the previous idea. This leads to images and emotions which indicate clearly enough to the doctor the nature of the patient's "problem complex." It is, of course, useful to be aware of one's dominant complex, to know "I have this problem."

Jung tells of his learning of a person who arrived at the same point, not by beginning with a dream, but by musing over the unknown meanings (to him) of the letters of the Russian alphabet. Following up on this, Jung found that other starting points for free association were equally effective; they led to knowledge of the complex. But what then makes for the *transformation* of the complex and the freeing of the energy which is bound to it? It is well known that mere intellectual knowledge doesn't do it.

The discovery that virtually any starting point for associations would reveal the psychic "complexes" was one of the great turning points in Jung's moving beyond Freud. If the dream itself was not needed to discover the problem, then what *did* it do? For Jung, this meant that the dream likely had some other purpose than simply to point out the status of the problem. It might then be the carrier of the transformative solution, but getting at this function required a different attitude. If the dream is the carrier of creative meaning, then, for the sake of the meaning which it bears, it is accorded the place of the Center. Thus the dream is taken very seriously. One then, as Jung says, turns it round and round, or rather walks around it, focusing energy and attention on it. The dream is not the Center as such, but in the process of analysis is its representative or ambassador.

Many dreams will present material which the dreamer simply does not want to face, including the possibly painful changes in attitude which constitute the solution to the psychological problem. Speaking of one such case, Jung says:

> If I, as his doctor, had let him start a process of association, he would inevitably have tried to get as far away as possible from the unpleasant suggestion of his dream. In that case, he would have ended with one of his staple complexes, and we should have learned nothing about the special meaning of this particular dream.[13]

It takes a great deal of work to show that facing and integrating unpleasant dream material is precisely the source of growth. Once this is realized, the person becomes more pliant and willing to treat the dream as a source of healing. Until that time, however, evasion prevails, and for the purpose of this evasion the complex is perfect: unsavory enough to "show" the analyst that the dreamer is "serious" ("I know I have a problem"), but well enough known so that surprises will not occur.

What Jung is pointing out here is one of the most important points in the growth of human consciousness leading to spirituality. Humans still have trouble facing their inner reality, and exceedingly few can do so without external help and guidance of some kind. We all want to stand in judgment of such potential guides to be certain that they are guiding us in the way we desire, so that the part of us which wishes to escape the real heart of the matter of our transformation need not be threatened. We want help but we don't want to face the nature of our problem of unconsciousness. What we fear facing is not always our darkness, but often is a revelation of our potential for success and even greatness. We may fear the responsibility of taking up our strengths. Our fears of both our dark and our shining sides are gathered in this comment by Jung:

> Consciousness naturally resists anything unconscious and unknown. . . . [We] erect psychological barriers to protect ourselves from the shock of facing anything new.[14]

That is, this is a work requiring concentration, and, in particular, a special kind of devotion to a healing process.

Interestingly, this comment very nicely describes what has happened to Jungian psychology since Jung's death! Here, the psychological barrier which has been erected is an intellectual one. The intellect is the tool of choice of academics, as well as others who are embarrassed to have an emotional side, but the unconscious cannot be directly apprehended by the intellect. Thus the failure of the intellect to enter the unconscious has been seen as a failure of Jung to give an adequate description on the one hand; and on the other the intellectual successes of Jung's successors (as distinct from his more immediate younger colleagues) ring hollow as an approximation of truth.

We value "clarity." Students want to be told the facts and procedures in unequivocal terms, and they evaluate their teachers accordingly, inversely to the challenge to work things out on their own initiative. Of course in the aspect of learning known as "instruction" (placing a structure within) as opposed to "education" (leading one out from within), such clarity is entirely appropriate. On the other hand, in many of our finest endeavors, *intellectual* clarity is simply not the point, or else it is a definite diversion from truth.

Perhaps more importantly, it is a barrier to *healing*. In the end we must see living as a work of healing.

THE ROUND DANCE AND THE WORK OF LIFE

The "work of life" has undergone many transformations in, say, the last ten thousand years. This period encompasses both the invention of agriculture and the advent of civilization. We might describe the cumulative process in this period as in some sense an emergence from nature. In *Religion in Essence and Manifestation*[15] van der Leeuw describes how that which "saves" evolves from pure natural phenomena (sexual reproduction, trees, water, animals, the return of spring) to the advent of culture, which envisions a more spiritual sort of saving. In many ancient civilizations the advent of culture is personified in a founder-king who is seen as a god or a god-human, and is the bestower of writing, agriculture, and the arts.

As we will see, Jung uses similar images to describe the emergence of what he calls "work."

Jung says:

> When Nature is left to herself, energy is transformed along the line of its natural "gradient." In this way natural phenomena are produced, but not "work." So also humans, when left to themselves, live as a natural phenomenon, and, in the proper meaning of the word, produce no work. It is culture that provides the machine whereby the natural gradient is exploited for the performance of work.[16]

Let us then look at the transformation of the natural flow of energy into work. We can see in advance that not only the energy, but also the *goal* of the work to be done is simultaneously transformed: the saving work for the primitive is survival and the development of excess energy for expansion of outlook, while for later stages the items of the worklist just below become more relevant. That which saves physically gives way to that which saves spiritually, as physical necessities are provided for more consistently.

Since the word "work" may carry a sense of drudgery with us, here is a more concrete idea of where we are headed. In its highest sense it is the *opus* of spiritual transformation. The following list may be suggestive of possible goals for such psychological work.

WORK

1. Development of Consciousness

2. Refinement

3. Building of Humanity

4. Healing of Wounds (Individual and Social)

5. Facilitating the Self-Consciousness of God

6. Transforming life into Life.

Before presenting a series of four examples leading from primitive fertility rites to the sublime image of the "Round Dance of Christ," we need a good image of the difference between the simply "natural flow" and the *intentional utilization* of energy.

Picture a mountain stream, tumbling among rocks, and meandering across alpine meadows. The flow of water depends upon an overall slope of the ground, so that it can proceed from higher to lower levels. Jung often uses this image of flowing water in a stream or waterfall to visualize the flow of energy in the psyche. The overall slope of the land corresponds to what he calls the psychic "gradient," which is just another word for slope. The stream is a "natural" phenomenon, and one of great beauty.

As humans venture into new territories, they find such streams, and enjoy them for the refreshment of the senses and of the body. If someone builds a place to live near one, the idea might arise to divert some of the water to irrigate nearby fields. Thus the "development" or enhancement of nature is begun. As more people inhabit the region, communal decisions become necessary as to the use of the water, and so forth.

The point here is to distinguish between the nature-cycle of the psyche, its natural flow of energy, and that which would correspond to the *domestication* of the stream or of a river: the construction of containments which will both help prevent floods, and provide a sufficient vertical "drop" to put in a generator to produce energy which can then be distributed and used purposefully.

Jung puts his point of view as follows:

> A waterfall is certainly more beautiful than a power-station, but dire necessity teaches us to value electric light and electrified industry more highly than the superb wastefulness of a waterfall that delights us for a quarter of an hour on a holiday walk.[17]

In view of the widespread destruction of the natural environment, it may take a while for us to take in fully what Jung is getting at here. We need to recognize *that* we do indeed value the physical energy which is placed at our disposal by the power station, though such energy could often be produced and used in a *manner* which is much less destructive than is our current practice. It is precisely our general *greed* for that energy which has let the destruction loose!

Analogous to the development of the stream to do intentional work for the general benefit is the diversion of psychic energy to the *psychic work* which we need to be doing with our lives. We need a positive image for that which will rechannel the natural flow into more spiritual endeavors, will *move* us to devote energy to such goals. The above list of positive psychic "jobs" was introduced early to draw us into the process.

A "work-list" as highly spiritualized as this one already presupposes a tremendous development of humanity as a basis for further work. The examples which follow begin at a much more primitive level, and work toward the possibility of our being moved by the tasks in the list.

A first example is one presented in full by Jung in "On Psychic Energy,"[18] namely the spring ceremony of the Wachandi of Australia. This is a dance in which a pit in the earth is decorated with leafy branches to represent the female sex organ. The men dance round it, thrusting their spears into the pit, chanting, "Not a pit! Not a pit! A c____!" In this dance, the sexual energy of the men is diverted to the seeding of the land.[19] The "natural flow" of energy is harnessed for work which will be of obvious benefit to the community, but which might not be undertaken with the requisite vigor unless the land can be made to take on the symbolic value of the woman. Prior to the agricultural stage, of course, the sexual energy was necessary for the mere survival of the group, but now the group has evolved to the point that the move from a hunter-gatherer culture to agriculture is now possible, though it is clearly somewhat of a risk to divert energy from the hunt.[20]

As much as we like to complain about having to work for a living, we need only compare our living standard to that of more primitive times to see the value of development.

Another example of the symbolic transformation of energy is the specialization of work into a variety of trades and professions, with various levels of prestige and monetary return. The value of work specialization lies in the fact that individuals do not need to know how to do everything which needs doing in a society. Thus, we occupy a much smaller fraction of our mental and physical capacities in earning a living. It is also a product of the development of culture that we *desire* a greater variety of goods and services, that each of these makes life easier and potentially more fulfilling. Here the symbolic shift is much more complex than that from sexual energy to agriculture, but some of the elements of value-shift can indeed be noted. The consciousness to *see* the potential "return" has now been vastly strengthened so that a *decision* often suffices where a *ritual* was needed before, for the diversion of energy to a new form. One can *anticipate* the liberation of time for other pursuits and see the *logic* of specialization. The variety of opportunities for employment in the community ensures that others will do what one cannot. There is some risk in the choice of a specialty, but that element begins subtly and grows stronger as culture evolves. For a very long time it has been solved by father-to-son passage of occupations.

Before going on to the third example, I would like to insert a sort of "interlude" concerning art. Art would constitute a profound example on its own, but is so complex as to defy simple presentation. So here is just a comment or two.

Very early, at least long before the advent of civilization, humans began to devote energy to art, perhaps as symbolic representation of desired power, to channel energy, or perhaps as a purely enjoyable effort. Decoration also symbolizes prestige and refinement. All this, as we know from more recent cultures, is closely tied to religious significance.

It is clear that an attractor was definitely at work, since doing art doesn't plow a field or hunt game. Rather, in art a concrete effort is devoted to something quite abstract: colors on a surface. Such an effort would be made for the sake of symbolic power, or the propitiation of "external" powers. This is a definite transformation of the notion of the Center as a real spiritual presence which might be held or carried in its representation. Jung's preference[21] for the meaning of "religion" as careful observance may be closely related to his ideas of circumambulation as focus upon the Center, the place of creative change, as seen in the "careful observance" shown in ancient art.

The religious drive appears to run parallel to the development of the standard of living through the kinds of symbolic transfer shown in the first examples. In fact, it makes *possible* the transfer of symbolic value from the obvious pleasure of sex to the pleasure of the harvest as bounty of the earth, for its stands behind all ability to shift to a higher value. The perception of, or belief in, a new value to be actualized through changes in behavior which risk the old adaptation is truly a walking around a Value-center. This means that at some level all such changes are religiously motivated. Another way of expressing this would be to say that all gradients ultimately are sloped to the same Center.

The third example of the evolution of psychic work is the emergence of science from magic. Jung uses the word "magic" to characterize a ritual which creates a state of expectancy but in itself does no work, creates no concrete result. Such an expectation may generate all kinds of activity, a kind of "play" with things, which in turn can lead to real discoveries. Jung says:

> Not for nothing is magic called the "mother of science." Until late in the Middle Ages what we today call science was nothing other than magic. A striking example of this is alchemy, whose symbolism shows quite unmistakably the principle of transformation of energy described above. . . . But only through the development of magic into science . . . have we acquired that mastery over the forces of nature of which the age of magic dreamed.[22]

Thus, in the end, we value the very "magical" process of symbol formation, for it draws the energy into an activity which will lead to some form of "mastery."

A most fascinating process to observe is the perception of a spiritual movement out of the newest discoveries in physics. That we should expect such a development follows upon this third example just given, the emergence of science out of magic, and the remarks above it concerning art and the religious center. Witness all the new books which explore spiritual connections of the "new physics," from Capra's *The Tao of Physics* (1975),[23] Zukav's *The Dancing Wu-Li Masters* (1979),[24] and my own *Atoms, Snowflakes & God* (1986, subscription edition 1983), through Ferguson's *The Aquarian Conspiracy* (1980),[25] to what is now a burgeoning field, including Swimme's *The Universe is a Green Dragon* (1984),[26] Weber's *Dialogues with Sages and Scientists* (1986),[27] and Dyson's *Infinite in All Directions* (1988).[28] This situation would argue that science stands as a door to a new realization of spirituality. It clearly has created the expectation of concrete change in the human spiritual condition, but this is not to imply that these changes inevitably occur or that they will be of the kind that we have been envisioning here. That is why I stress going beyond the intellectual apprehension of the material, and finding ways of incorporating the insights into *living*. This incorporation is highly individual, requiring creative work of one who would participate in the process.

But, having noted this, the total movement from magic to science to spirituality shows the widest sweep of a circumambulation around a spiritual Center. More than this, it shows the evolution of the goal of the work of creation.

We come now to the fourth example, a two thousand year old image which is still in process of assimilating energy in the human psyche. This is the "Round Dance" in the apocryphal *Acts of John*, described by Jung in "Transformation Symbolism in the Mass." In the text, this dance is placed between the last supper and the crucifixion of the Christ, the divine-human, or *Anthropos* figure, who has his disciples form a ring around him and move in a circle, while he chants to them. A few verses will be given, for the flavor of the occasion:

> I will be saved and I will save, Amen.
> I will be loosed and I will loose, Amen.
> I will be wounded and I will wound, Amen.
> I will be begotten and I will beget, Amen.
> I will eat and I will be eaten, Amen.
> . . .
> Grace paces the round. I will blow the pipe.
> Dance the round all, Amen.
> . . .
> To each and to all it is given to dance, Amen.
> Who joins not the dance mistakes the event, Amen.
> . . .
> I will be united and I will unite, Amen.
> . . .
> A lamp am I to you that perceive me, Amen.
> A mirror am I to you that know me, Amen.
> A door am I to you that knock on me, Amen.
> A way am I to you the wayfarer.
> . . .
> Now as you respond to my dancing, behold yourself in me who speaks . . . As you dance, ponder what I do, for yours is this human

suffering which I will to suffer. For you would be powerless to understand your suffering had I not been sent to you as the Logos by the Father. . . . Learn to suffer, and you shall understand how not to suffer.[29]

I will not undertake here to reproduce any of Jung's commentary on these lines. The essential elements for the present purpose are, first, the human-but-more-than-human figure in the center. Second, there is the rapt focus upon the center which is so easy to imagine on the part of the disciples as they move around as directed from the center. Third, there is the reflexive quality as summarized by the words, "behold yourself in me." And, fourth, there is the image of creative suffering *which is to be understood by the disciple, so that suffering may become non-suffering.* One might note by implication the *compassion* which the central figure shows. All in all, it is a most gripping image.

When I then comment that this image is still gathering energy, I am referring not so much to this particular text, which is known to few, but to the essential elements which I have just enumerated. The question becomes that of the degree to which we know this central figure within ourselves. In each of us is that regulating center which Jung called the Self. To what extent is our attention drawn inward to the regulatory processes which actually go on perpetually within ourselves, as well as outward to receive those happenings which convey meaning to us? As one reads Jung's *Answer to Job,* one can actually feel him wrestling with his inner *Anthropos* in a circumambulatory manner.

The gathering of this energy can be seen in many ways in many cultures. China actually has had such an image longer than has the western world. It is that of the "superior human," or "true humanhood," *chen-jen.*

It is only the person with the most perfect divine moral nature who is able to combine inwardly quickness of apprehension, intelligence, insight and understanding . . . magnanimity, generosity, benignity and gentleness . . . originality, energy, strength of character and determination.

Thus all-embracing and vast [as Heaven] is the nature of such a person. Profound is it and inexhaustible [as the abyss], like a living spring of water, ever running out with life and vitality.

... Therefore we may say: "Such a one is the equal of God."

It is only such a person in this world who has realized his/her absolute self. . . .

Now, where does such a one derive power and knowledge, except from within? How simple and self-contained this true personhood! . . .[30]

The characteristics which this image shares with the Christ-figure are remarkable. It may be, though, that this figure is so close to the human as to have been premature in the context in which it arose. Or it may be that it lacks the knowledge of *its own* suffering, which may indeed be the element by means of which the *Anthropos* can finally get us actually into the dance.

If it is not too banal, the image of the "power station" may be brought in once again. What *is* it that *catches the flow* of the psychic energy and diverts it from its natural flow, with all its beauty, into the "turbine" which converts the energy to other forms: the building of a conscious humanity, letting the Center act through ourselves? That is, what *moves* us to do the actual *work* of transformation? We should not be surprised that such structures are not automatically in place, nor should we be ashamed of that fact. We are now engaged, humanity as a whole, in the process itself, and whether or not it happens is our deep responsibility.

It should be noted that the two images presented above by no means exhaust the list of such figures. They include the hero-kings of many cultures, as well as innumerable savior images around the world.

As a transition to a brief closing remark concerning circumambulation in physics, the following is appropriate, whether or not we have availed ourselves of professional analytic help in the growth process:

Analytical treatment could be described as a readjustment of psychological attitude achieved with the help of the doctor. . . . There is no change that is unconditionally valid over a long period of time. Life has always to be tackled anew. . . . The new attitude gained in the course of analysis tends sooner or later to become inadequate in one way or another, and necessarily so, because the constant flow of life again and again demands fresh adaptation. Adaptation is never achieved once and for all. One might certainly demand of analysis that it should enable the patient to gain new orientations in later life, too, without undue difficulty, and experience shows that this is true, up to a point. . . . Nevertheless, these difficulties prove to be fairly frequent and may at times be really troublesome. . . . Humans need difficulties; they are necessary for health. What concerns us here is only an excessive amount of them.[31]

THE EVOLUTION OF PHYSICS AS CIRCUMAMBULATION

The fact that physics continually shifts its foundations, as from those of Newton to those of Einstein, and probably always will, constitutes a true circumambulation. The world of the physicist is one of continual discovery: a revelation through the efforts of our search, our attempts to penetrate the surface of things while living in the world of concrete fact. This orientation is a commitment which excludes the possibility that the ultimate nature of things was revealed in the past. All such worldviews abound with errors of fact. We thus anticipate a continual transformation of our ideas as to what the nature of physical reality is.

The new thing which has been added here is the notion that science is a stage in the way in which symbols grip us, following which the energy moves on to the spiritual realm for those who perceive the spiritual imperative in science as such (the topic of Appendix 4).

Not only can the images of physical reality evoke and carry a certain level of human spirituality, but they actually possess the power to move us toward the encounter with the Center as such. They fulfill an essential role in the total circulation of humanity around the Value.

What might appear as the formation of *new* centers or process-goals in succession can thus be seen to be the progressive revelation, through transformation,[32] of the One Center.

Notes

1. This interconnection is provided for in physics in spatial relations which permit circular or elliptical motion to be *sustained* (without a

cost in terms of energy) in a direction roughly perpendicular to the direction of the force of the attractor. In the above example, the earth moves in a near-circle, always approximately at right angles to the force of attraction of the sun, and retains the same total energy in its orbit. In another case, namely the motion of electrically charged particles in magnetic fields, the particle experiences a force which is perpendicular both to the field and to the direction of motion usually giving a spiral path.

2. *CW* 12, pars. 185–186. The same idea occurs on a mirror in a frame painted by a Pueblo Indian, on which have been placed two blobs, each with a sort of "happy day" face. The artist explained that this is to remind us that the face is at first unformed, but is given shape through living.

3. Ibid. Par. 34.

4. Eliade, Mircea. 1961. *The Sacred and the Profane*. New York: Harper and Row, Harper Torchbooks.

5. Parallel to this is the statement of a prominent physicist that the relation of the opposites in specific circumstances is "by no means obvious." What has the potential of obviousness is the rational, whereby figure and ground are clearly distinct. The hard-won discovery of non-rationality in modern physics at once corroborates and clarifies the psychological condition of humanity and consciousness.

6. *CW* 8, par. 164.

7. Whitmont, Edward. 1978. *The Symbolic Quest*. Princeton: Princeton University Press, pp. 306–307.

8. Ibid. Pp. 307–308.

9. *CW* 11, par. 758. The uncertainty as to which factor is primarily active is reminiscent, of course, of the wave-particle duality and "complementarity" in physics, with its principle that the manner of reconciling the opposites is by no means obvious *in principle,* and calls for choice on the part of the "observer."

10. Under proper supervision, lucid dreaming has been used effectively to depotentiate nightmares, and other fears as well. To others it is a mere curiosity, a source of power to manipulate the unconscious, or even an outlet for sexual power fantasies. These latter attitudes deprive the dream of precisely the autonomy it needs to be an effective messenger of the unconscious.

11. Jung, C.G. 1964b. With Marie-Louise von Franz, Joseph L. Henderson, Jolande Jacobi, and Aniela Jaffé. *Man and His Symbols*. Edited by C.G. Jung. New York: Doubleday, p. 28.

12. Ibid. P. 29.

13. Ibid.

14. Ibid. P. 31.
15. van der Leeuw, G. 1963. *Religion in Essence and Manifestation*. New York: Harper and Row, Harper Torchbooks, Chapter 12.
16. *CW* 8, par. 80.
17. Ibid. Par. 90.
18. *CW* 8, pars. 83–85.
19. The resemblance of this ritual to various "team chant" forms of "psyching up" for sporting events is obvious. One wants to channel the maximum energy into the "work" at hand through symbolic rituals.
20. The potency of agriculture can be seen in the theory of language migration (Renfrew, Colin. The Origins of Indo-European Languages. *Scientific American*, October, 1989, pp. 106–114). It is now believed that the spread of the Indo-European language group from its original home in Anatolia followed the development of agriculture as such. With cultivation of the land, the land supports more people, the population grows more rapidly, and groups break off seeking more land. Their greater numbers and stronger physical health give them the power to conquer new territories, and their language, too, dominates the new area.
21. *CW* 11, pars. 6–8.
22. *CW* 8, par. 90.
23. Capra, F. 1975. *The Tao of Physics*. Berkeley: Shambala.
24. Zukav, Gary. 1979. *The Dancing Wu-Li Masters*. New York: William Morrow.
25. Ferguson, Marilyn. 1980. *The Aquarian Conspiracy*. Los Angeles: J.P. Tarcher.
26. Swimme, Brian. 1984. *The Universe is a Green Dragon*. Santa Fe: Bear & Company.
27. Weber, Renee. 1986. *Dialogues with Sages and Scientists*. London: Routledge and Kegan Paul.
28. Dyson, Freeman. 1988. *Infinite in All Directions*. New York: Harper & Row, Perennial Library.
29. *CW* 11, pars. 414–427.
30. Yutang, Lin. 1938. *The Wisdom of Confucius*. New York: Carlton House, pp. 130–131.
31. Jung, *CW* 8, pars. 142–143.
32. See Chapters 8 and 9.

Chapter 8

Jung and Transformation

Die and Become! Until you possess this truth,
You are only a dreary guest on the dark Earth.
                    —*Goethe ("Blessed Longing")*

As we think about spirituality in all its aspects: a deep inner life or aliveness, refinement and elevation of our outward expression of ourselves, concern for higher values and for seeing earth and humanity as a whole, and so much more, we usually feel that spirituality is something which we may arrive at by cultivation. Find, plant, and water the seeds, and in the generous sunlight our spirits will simply grow. We seldom take account of the possibility of a necessary pain in the process.

But the reality, as described by Jung, is quite different from these preconceptions. It is nothing less than a *transformation of the personality*, which means a generally painful breakup of old psychic structures, so that they may be replaced by more authentic ones. Here, "authentic" means true to our unique inner natures, and objective in the sense of integrating our inner being to outer reality *as it is*.

The word "transformation" is not unfamiliar, but the *process* of transformation, as described by Jung throughout his writings, is sufficiently rare to necessitate a fairly full discussion. We tend to hope that our hidden parts, or our "shadow side," can remain undisturbed in such a process, which is indeed the case if we seek mere intellectual understanding of it.

It is to be hoped that adding the weight of evidence from modern physics will so bring the unity of reality to view that readers will be supported in the difficult choices which facilitate the transformative process. The parallels from physics to the processes described in this chapter will be brought out in the next.

It should be obvious to the intellect that an *effective* transforma-

168

tion must touch and restructure that which *concerns us most deeply*. In modern terms, this is our "religious formation," which we each possess, shaped by our culture as well as by our formal childhood religion. For many, though, the humanistic academic studies now occupy the place of this formation in the psyche, and the concern with them is virtually as deep as if it were consciously religious. Others are equally absorbed in ideologies. In all these cases, in order for transformation to occur, that formation must somehow come to a *conflict* which will require of us some central sacrifice.

Chapter 3, "Consciousness and the Moral Dimension," provided some essential preparatory work for our present considerations. Without reiterating the full argument of that chapter, its essence may be recalled through the following.

The essential connection between consciousness and the moral dimension is made by Jung in his book *Answer to Job*. There Jung describes God's treatment of Job (in the book of Job) in the following terms:

> ... his faithful servant Job is now to be exposed to a rigorous moral test, quite gratuitously and to no purpose, although YHWH is convinced of Job's faithfulness and constancy, and could moreover have assured himself beyond all doubt on this point had he taken counsel with his own omniscience. Why, then, is the experiment made at all, and a bet with the unscrupulous slanderer settled, without a stake, on the back of a powerless creature? It is indeed no edifying spectacle to see how quickly YHWH abandons his faithful servant to the evil spirit and lets him fall without compunction or pity into the abyss of physical and moral suffering. From the human point of view YHWH's behavior is so revolting that one has to ask oneself whether there is not a deeper motive hidden behind it.[1]

Jung concludes that the motive lies in the fact that God lacks, while suspecting that Job possesses, a "superior consciousness based on self-reflection."

It can hardly be doubted that such a consciousness has arisen because of its evolutionary "survival value." We have developed it because of the needs of our concrete physical forebears, as the species evolved. As Jung points out,

> God has no need of this circumspection, for nowhere does he
> come up against an insuperable obstacle that would force him to
> hesitate and hence make him reflect on himself.[2]

Here, in a most modest compass, is a compelling statement of the role
of *obstacles*, painful conflicts, in the transformation of unconsciousness into consciousness. And, as the story hints, the transformation
of God is at stake as well as that of the creature.

It often is the case that we become aware of a conflict long
before we permit or force ourselves to experience its depth. But
actually to *feel* conflict makes more specific demands upon us. While
sustaining the moral stress of the conflict, we must also use our
capacity for reason, our "consciousness based on self-reflection," to
evaluate that which impinges upon us via factuality. This is a *bringing
together* of our emotional and reasoning sides and, if lived to the full,
is equivalent to a symbolic death by crucifixion. Emotion and reason
are always at "cross purposes" and to hold and honor both kills each
to some degree. Out of such a death, however, comes a solution in
the form of a new life different from any which might have been
envisioned before.

THE RELIGIOUS FORMATION

That which concerns us most deeply, and is to be transformed,
is the religious formation. Again, this formation often assumes forms
which are apparently non-religious, and we often repress the awareness that it is indeed a religious center. Nonetheless, the etymologi-
cal root of "religion" is just the "binding back together" of that
which has become separated in the development of our modern consciousness, here represented by our split-apart emotional and reasoning sides, but by no means limited to that. We have also lost
whole areas of our personalities by splitting them off, as our lives
were shaped in childhood. Some of these may well have been creative
thrusts which were unacceptable at the time.

Whether consciously religious or not, we all need binding together of our fragmented selves. It is in this sense that I speak of our
religious center as a deep place within ourselves where our whole-

ness remains. This wholeness-center gathers about itself the relics of the psychological world or cosmos built by and for the young human being, in a specific culture with its dominant values—those things which were *substituted* for our own thrust to being, and which represented our means of enjoying the acceptance of our elders. Not possessing ourselves, these bits of structure were all we had to hang on to. And so we do!

At the center of this formation, protected and hidden from cultural attack by the cultural relics just mentioned, is what Fritz Kunkel called the "true heart" of the child, which needs to be matured by use into the true heart of the adult.

Tillich called the center of the formation our Ultimate Concern —that which concerns us in an ultimate manner—and identified it with God, the Ground of Being from which we live. A specifically Christian formation is collective in nature. Even an atheist in a Christian culture has basically a Christian religious formation, for what occurs in the culture may well be more dominant than what happens in churches. At least it pervades the life and thought at a much deeper level, as that which automatically "is done." The same would be true in the environments of all the great world religions. The linkage of cultural and religious formations is still quite secure in the world, but we may be at the brink of rapid shifts.

THE ALCHEMICAL ANALOGY

To *meet* the human world, even to be *in* the human world, we need to let our religious formations be touched and transformed by something which *breaks down* and rebuilds. It is here that Jung's study of medieval alchemy as a model for transformation comes to our aid. In those mysterious alchemical treatises, the process of breaking down existing structures was emphasized at all times. Without going into this material in any detail, but simply by listing a few of the descriptive terms for the stages of the alchemical process, we can see how vividly this is true.

The matter to be transformed, the *prima materia,* or sometimes the *massa confusa,* here stands for the psyche as such, as it comes to the process. This must undergo "dissolution in its own water," which we might interpret as "stewing in one's own juices," "calcination," or purgation by fire, "mortification," and even "putrefaction." And, of course, the rebuilding was often symbolized by the transmutation of "base metal" into gold, which to the alchemical "adepts" meant not the physical metal, but a "philosophical gold" of the soul.

Edinger has described the alchemical symbolism of the transformative process beautifully in his *Anatomy of the Psyche.*[3] A study of his work is greatly rewarding. The advantage of using alchemical symbolism lies in the wealth of imagery which carries feeling value. The complementary advantage of describing the same processes using the symbolism of modern physics, as is being done in this book, lies in the concreteness of the facts as facts, which can convince one that the nature of the process is written into the very nature of our everyday physical reality. This can engender a different level of conviction, or operate on a different temperament.

Among the ways in which our rigid inner structures can be broken down are: factuality, which dissolves boundaries, and the action of the great opposites as they are encountered in a religious context. In a later chapter I will gather these together into the process which I refer to as "seeing." That which builds new structures in place of the old is *symbolic resonance*, which will be the topic of a later section of this chapter. Let us speak first of factuality.

THE IMPACT OF FACT

Mythologically and alchemically, the image of an old king who is ill, or who is king of a diseased kingdom, represents our existing structures when they no longer function and are in need of transformation. The alchemical processes mentioned above are mirrored in Jeremiah 23:29:

> Is not my word like fire, says YHWH, and like a hammer which breaks the rocks in pieces?

It is consistent with my point of view, which sees physical reality as a form of the "word of God," to make the same claim for factuality. In

Memories, Jung says:

> I came to see that a new idea, or even just an unusual aspect of an
> old one, can be communicated only by facts. Facts remain, and
> cannot be brushed aside; sooner or later someone will come upon
> them and [recognize what is there].[4]

As a first example, we have one of Jung's own. Later in *Memories* he
points out that consciousness is newly formed, and not pre-existent.
It is an evolutionary development. He goes on:

> It is time this obvious fact were grasped at last. Just as the body
> has an anatomical history of millions of years, so does the psychic
> system.[5]

He calls the fact that consciousness is secondary, or new, or an
evolved function "obvious," yet the whole of the eastern world and
much of the western would deny it outright. They would say not
only that consciousness is pre-existent because it is transcendent, or
an attribute of God, but that physical creation was a conscious act on
God's part. Both of these views would insist that consciousness pre-
ceded physical creation.

Here is an exercise in meditation: Can you discern whether or
not you have an internal conflict involved with the idea of God's
unconsciousness? As you take it inside, does an emotional response
come up? If your immediate response is to think, "Obviously God is
conscious," then this counts as *not* being a conflict! You have a clear
unconflicted position. But, then, how does one account for not only
the evolution of consciousness in its nature as we know it, but also
for all the material discussed around the book of Job in Chapter 3?
There is indeed a lot to sort out here, at a deep emotional level. The
meditative inner search can be used to listen for clues from the
depths as to what has been repressed. Attempting to portray the
situation pictorially is also useful.

Insofar as the religious formation, as supplied by the culture and
family, is neither specific to the individual nor global in its scope, the
individual may, as she or he perceives more and more alternative
worldviews, come to question precisely that which was formed to

preserve the primordial wholeness. This is the impact of factuality upon the religious formation.

In Paddy Chayefsky's *Gideon*, the following is a bit of dialogue between Gideon and the Angel of the Lord, who is asking Gideon why he listens to human advisors, when he can talk directly to God:

A: I watched you sit there just now, greedily believing all of Hezekiah's claptrap about socio-economic conditions—you who have seen the Lord face-to-face and beheld his wonders.

G: Well, Hezekiah is well thought of as a scholar. He knows all about the ecliptic of the sun as it revolves around the Earth.

A: The sun does not revolve around the Earth, you imbecile; the Earth revolves about the sun.

G: Oh, that is patent nonsense, my Lord. The sun obviously revolves around the Earth.[6]

In the play, Gideon receives information from God which *we* know scientifically to be the case: the earth goes around the sun, rather than the reverse. But Gideon is stuck with *appearances* which form a deep prejudice. Gideon is merely expressing the general view of that ancient time: *everyone* believed that the sun circles the earth. We could say that those people had a strong but false *formation*, which determined how they saw things, and that this formation would eventually require transformation, via scientific investigation.

This scene precisely reflects the position of Galileo historically, when the church authorities took a position corresponding to Gideon's, namely that the earth is stationary. Though in the play Gideon is given the correct scientific information from God, that path is not available to us. Galileo conducted a reasoned investigation, which gave the factual view that in the solar system it makes sense only to say that the earth orbits the sun, and not vice versa. In Galileo's day, the church held the power, but it was *wrong*. Galileo was weak, but *correct*. Yet the scientific truth, unimportant as it may seem to us theologically, was able to *transform* the view of the church in the past few centuries, with much additional impact on attitudes toward scripture. For the most part, views which contradict the facts have been allowed to expire. I believe that this is a permanent situation. Where official theological views are in opposition to the facts of physical reality (whether or not these facts are yet known), these views will have to be relinquished by the religious authorities (of whatever religion) at some time.

Yet even at our own scientifically advanced time, there are numerous holdover manifestations of a *symbolic* geocentric viewpoint in the way we live. There is quite a nice analogy between our attitudes and the fact that the earth "woke up" to find itself revolving around the sun. By this I refer to the fact that life evolved, which eventually became self-reflexive. Earth woke up in a *basic* sense. We are now (potentially) in the process of waking up individually, but have we even yet discovered that we are not the "prime inhabitant" of our own bodies? When we as individuals eventually *have* an experience of fuller awakening, we are forced to ask what was going on all those previous decades, when *we* were not present, but our body and its ego were in a semi-automatic mode of functioning. We *wake up* when we really discover what Jung calls the Self, which I am here referring to as the Prime Inhabitant. Indeed, the Self was at work in the life all along.

In the present analogy, of course, the Earth is where we live, and (except for nuclear fission) the sun is the *source* of all our forms of energy, and thus symbolizes God. We tend simply to accept the appearance that *we* are the centers. We can feel the difference for ourselves personally, if we can permit the external facts of the earth-sun system to penetrate our psyches. As an experiment, silently imagine for a moment the two cases: the sun circling the earth, and the earth circling the sun, and then ask yourself what *inner* shift might be prefigured *for us*, to go from living as if the sun (our energy source) goes around *us* as a center, to living according to the fact that *we* circle the sun.

In Part II of *Faust*, Goethe described the deepest level of being, the "deep of deeps" as: "Formation, transformation—Eternal Mind's eternal recreation."[7] The transformation of any of our formations touches the very depths of being.

Psychologically, we know this process as death and rebirth,

which is the *only* means by which our lives—from physical birth to physical death—gain substance. It is a constant necessity to die and be reborn. Whether or not we succeed each day in living it, or even in seeing where sacrifice on our part is required, we must be working at it.

Of course the transformation of our physical being occurs continually, and our inward life often makes opportunities for growth from sicknesses, accidents, loss of physical ease, and other seeming adversities. Eventually, our atoms will be recycled decisively. We will die. There is not enough room on earth for us to continue our physical existence indefinitely. Undoubtedly most of our present atoms have been through life previously at at least the animal level—in formations and transformations—and perhaps that has some effect upon what we are able to do with those atoms.

Scientific theories, too, are formations, all of which remain to be transformed, as in the overwhelming transformation from Newton's physics to that of Einstein. If all this is so, and if we include the previous evidence from the case of Galileo, then religious formations are dependent to some extent on those of science. We should therefore learn to *expect* our spiritual worldviews to evolve continually and endlessly. If God is not to be seen as running out of creative possibilities, the emergence of the new is eternally available and *demanded*, requiring the sacrifice of old forms.

Facts are transformative, and therefore we usually do our best to avoid them. How often have we watched friends, and wondered how it is that they can't seem to see what is staring them right in the face? But, then, how often do we apply *this* insight to ourselves, by asking ourselves where *we* might be blind to some obvious need for transformation? As Jung said, facts remain, but we don't see them. Something must *occur* which will set them apart as figure from their ground for us. But our world remains unbroken, and therefore we remain unconscious. In the light of this situation, the role of making *errors* cannot be overemphasized, for they are prime actors in breaking the seamless unity of our unconsciousness.

When our inner contradictions become conscious to us, we can begin a journey—a journey which includes all the major symbols of our religious heritage: suffering, sin, wounds, healing, forgiveness, the cross. For us to move toward consciousness, the cross must be our *own* cross: our own inner contradictions, which *we* must bear, toward expiation and grace.

Consciousness grows by contrasts within ourselves, of which we become aware. How do we do this—become aware? The game of Charades gives a very applicable analogy. It is as if some power is trying to make us aware of something, some central point about ourselves, but it is so hard to see that point. The world, as actor, or God acting in a given situation, gestures various clues for us. And when the "actor" sees that the point is not being taken, different ways of presentation are tried, and thus many different things happen to us in a life. If only we "get the point," we, and the situation, can be transformed. The analogy suffers from the fact that the actor is conscious, in the game, and conscious of a definite something to be conveyed. But something about our life is as if this were so; some purposiveness for the maximization of life attempts to be grasped. We must try *listening* more.

The point of including little inward experiments in the text is just to help the listening process. One way of encountering something which might transform our *given* formation would be to take seriously that which is at the heart of each of the great religions, with their great cultures: the unique vision which each has of the face of the Mystery and of the way in which things consequently are to be done. When we are moved to explore rapprochement with other cultures, we usually attempt to get together on the basis of what we have in common, rather than trying to receive what is unique from the other. This may require a talent for empathy which we do not yet possess. In this process, motivated by the desire to let the other into our being, we simply see that the way we always assumed was "right" is a matter of convention, and that the other cultures take the same attitude toward their habits that we do toward ours. But the point is that these conventions are arbitrary. Once we see that, the field of the application of values becomes something entirely other than what it was. We are drawn into the process of choicemaking, of discovering and exercising an *inner* authority, and the formation of values which integrate fact and reason.

It is a question of facts, and the use to which we put those facts. Facts have moral implications—*all of them*. Facts *unearth* conflict, and facing conflict to become conscious is the essential moral act.

THE ROLE OF OPPOSITES

If factuality is a "hammer which breaks the rocks in pieces," we still need to see what the hammer is made of, and how it holds the rocks for cracking. Perhaps the image of hammer *and anvil* is better, for our aging formations are actually crushed between "opposites." These present to us ineluctable choices when contrary values are encountered. The effectiveness of what have been called the "great opposites" is a consequence of the fundamental non-rationality of the cosmos. The fact that such opposites cannot be "resolved" is behind our undoubted *thrust to consciousness*, for contrast is our only mode of awareness. The central and moving element of the Oedipus story is his passionate need to search out the truth, no matter what it is or how painful the consequences.

Some of these great opposites, as needed for human wholeness, are heart and mind, darkness and light, spirit and matter, masculine and feminine, introversion and extroversion, self and other, individual and community, to name those which come immediately to mind.

Many great thinkers have given much effort to discover the most fundamental of these great opposites. Of these, I will present only the briefest sampling.

For J. Middleton Murry, as for Nikos Kazantzakis,[8] the most fundamental pair were heart/mind, or emotion/reason. In *God*, Murry wrote: "The world known by the intellect must become such that the heart can be satisfied."[9]

The great German poet Hölderlin made a different choice:

[I] had struggled to the point of exhaustion to fix my faith and my vision upon that which is supreme in life . . . what is more important, the eternal fountainhead of life or the temporal . . . but I continued to struggle till I found out the truth . . . there is only one quarrel in this world: which is more important, the whole or the individual part.[10]

But he found this quarrel "invalid in action," for the one "who truly acts out of a sense of the whole . . . is more disposed to honor every individual person and thing. . . ." Thus Hölderlin anticipated the discovery of complementarity in modern physics in the intimate relationship of opposites.

The struggles of Murry, Hölderlin, and others to find the *prime opposites* take on the same role as the struggle of the ancient Greeks to discern the *prime element*, but the great opposites have an evanescent quality. We have a sense of disappearance beyond a gateless gate, and reemergence in other forms elsewhere.

It is virtually by definition that we cannot see the overall unity of things if we see by means of opposites, by means of rational distinctions. In this sense it is an advance to seek out the prime *opposites*. But as there are many elements, the case with the opposites is also more complex than that a single pair would subsume all others.

THE ARCHETYPE OF WHOLENESS

There is that which patterns our lives in such a way as to see to it that the opposites which we need for wholeness will be encountered by us in our lifetime, if we can be open to them, and not egocentrically "render God ineffective within ourselves."[11] Jung called this Patterner in the life of each human "the Self." For Christians it is related to what some call "the Christ within," though Jung points out that the usual Christ-image lacks "the nocturnal element" of the psyche, and the feminine as well. Jung writes:

> It was this archetype of the Self in the soul of each human that responded to the Christian message, with the result that the concrete Rabbi Jesus was rapidly assimilated by the constellated archetype.... But as one can never distinguish empirically between a symbol of the Self and a God-image, the two ideas, however much we try to differentiate them, always appear blended together, so that the Self appears synonymous with the inner Christ of the Johannine and Pauline writings, and Christ with God, just as [in the east] the atman appears as the individualized self and at the same time as the animating principle of the cosmos, the Tao as a condition of the mind and at the same time as the correct behavior of cosmic events.[12]

If the term "the Christ" could be broadened to refer to that internal divine image *in its totality*, as it has appeared in the totality of world-religious symbolism (as evidenced in the above passage), it would be a tremendous step forward. This would add to all of that the very moving image of "the anointed one of God."

The point of the above passage is not yet the transformation of the Self *as such*, though a major shift in its mode of functioning has been occurring over the past two millennia. Rather, the present focus is upon the transformation of the way in which we *perceive and relate* to the true Self. The very fact that the human religious dimension is so much more vast than any one of the major religions paints it shows it as the ultimate source of opposites for our transformation processes.

The motif of these processes is that of death and rebirth, which was brought in earlier in connection with Goethe's *Faust*, and which can occur for each of us, even daily. This is the *essence* of transformation, the necessity of sacrifice by the ego, the necessity of pain. This is Life. As Goethe also said:

> Die and become! Until you possess this truth,
> You are only a dreary guest on the dark Earth.[13]

Jung related the process of death and rebirth through moral conflict symbolically to that of crucifixion. Though the following passage refers specifically to Christianity, the process is by no means limited to a specific religion. He says:

> The fact that Christian ethics leads to collisions of duty speaks in its favor. By engendering insoluble conflicts and a consequent affliction of soul, it brings humans nearer to a knowledge of God. All opposites are of God, therefore we must bend to this burden; and in so doing we find that God's oppositeness has taken possession of us, become incarnated in us. We become a vessel filled with divine conflict. We rightly associate the idea of suffering with a state in which the opposites violently collide with one another, yet we hesitate to describe such a painful experience as being "redeemed." Still it cannot be denied that the great symbol of the Christian faith, the Cross upon which hangs the suffering figure of the Redeemer, has been emphatically held up before the eyes of Christians for nearly two thousand years.[14]

In another place, he says:

> No one on the road to wholeness can escape that characteristic suspension [between opposites] which is the meaning of crucifixion.[15]

SYMBOLIC RESONANCE

Our cultural religious formation is generally much stronger than our ego, which is one of the reasons why the emergence of ego-consciousness results in such disastrous egocentricity. The ego is in a very tough situation being so weak, and it would be even tougher for it to sacrifice the little it has: its sense-of-light and the pleasurability which was so necessary for its very development. Jung sometimes describes consciousness as a blend of the operation of ego and Self. The only way for this to be possible is for the ego to gain in strength via a commitment to a greater process and the exercise of real choice for value. Then a true partnership can ensue, with the ego sacrificing its dominant role, but not being taken over by the Self either. This sacrifice is precisely what is required for the sake of a new seeing. Indeed, our cultural-religious formation was created by the collective psyche precisely for the purpose of protecting the ego from such sacrifice, and also for preventing the ego-strengthening. The collective demands that we be *satisfied* with its values.

How can we learn that higher feeling and deeper seeing are infinitely *more* satisfying than either collective satisfaction or ego-gratification? When such an inner move occurs, individuals call it the "grace of God," but there *is* a way of building to the point at which one can let it happen—building to the point of involution, transformation, opening, awakening. In Luke 17:22 Jesus specifically enjoins us to destroy those protective barriers which we have "done about" (Gk: *peripoieo*) our psyches in an effort to "save our lives." This active breaking down has been weakly translated as "losing one's life," which has tended to permit people to put off the transformative process by projecting it beyond physical death.

But it requires conscious activity to become open to the infinite life which flows in consequence of this opening. Jung described this in psychological language as the formation of a "gradient" through symbols which can motivate the person to such action, by arousing the desire for greater life. This is symbolic resonance. It is experienced as a new coming together of elements in a way which manifests a new, more purposive life-direction, and which could not previously have been seen. It is experienced as rebirth.

The more this death/rebirth process is lived, the more the person assimilates of total humanity, becoming more accepting of the full range, dark and light, of human potentials. One "takes in" more humanity, is more deeply connected to humanity, and becomes "more human." This process is always painful, because of the self-identity of the ego and its desire to be the only resident in the body.

Notes

1. *CW* 11, par. 579.
2. Ibid.
3. Edinger, Edward F. 1985. *Anatomy of the Psyche*. La Salle, IL: Open Court.
4. *Memories*, p. 104.
5. Ibid. P. 348.
6. Chayefsky, Paddy. 1962. *Gideon*. New York: Random House, p. 126.
7. *Faust/II*, p. 79.
8. See especially Kazantzakis, Nikos. 1960. *Saviors of God: Spiritual Exercises*. Translated by Kimon Friar. New York: Simon and Schuster.
9. *God*, p. 131.
10. Hölderlin, Friedrich. 1980. *Poems and Fragments*. Edited and translated by Michael Hamburger. Cambridge: Cambridge University Press, p. 11.
11. Charlene McCarthy, Hebrew scriptures scholar at the University of San Francisco.
12. *CW* 11, pars. 155–156.
13. Goethe, Johann Wolfgang von. 1958. "Selige Sehnsucht." *Wërke, Band II*. Edited by Erich Trunz. Hamburg: Christian Wegner, p. 19 (my rendering).
14. *CW* 11, par. 659.
15. *CW* 16, par. 470.

Chapter 9

The Physics of Awakening and Transformation

It is a terrifying thing to have been born.
 —*Pierre Teilhard de Chardin (Hymn of the Universe)*

By now it will be abundantly clear to the reader that the spiritu-
alizing process involves the total person and is not something which
can be achieved merely by taking in ideas and insights. The total
engagement of the person is required, which includes, on the one
hand, facing inner darknesses and potentials, and, on the other, gaining an ever wider field outwardly, with ever greater objectivity. The
latter involves really taking inside other cultures, so that one is open
to the fullness of humanity.

In the above paragraph I have deliberately used the word "involves" and the idea of "taking in" several times, along with support-
ing concepts. We *speak the language* of involution and opening,
which must become the model for our living toward spirituality.

In this chapter physical models will be presented which can be
held as symbols for the *psychological process* of involution and opening. The models have their beauty. This always presents the danger
that we will hold them outside ourselves in fascination, as with an
elegant piece of art which we might buy just to hang on the wall, or
which we visit in a museum. The step to employing them as concrete
patterns for our actual dance of living is indeed a great one. Let us
therefore keep that end in mind.

Whatever we do with them, it is necessary to get the ideas
before us. We will see immediately that they deal with concepts from
the field of religion. This is inevitable, since one of the goals of
religion is the spirituality of the individual. It was seen earlier that a
duality of expression is needed; we want, then, to provide a more
secular basis for these terms.

I would like to begin anecdotally by positing a view of the "problem of sin," as it occurred to me while teaching a physics class. I was pointing out that the Second Law of Thermodynamics explains the fact that no thermal source of energy, such as food, can be fully utilized to do mechanical work. It must dissipate or "waste" heat to the environment in the form of thermal pollution. I said: "So if you want to minimize your pollution of the environment by waste energy, you should simply lie upon your bed all day and not move." Hoping that the students would see the absurdity of such a philosophy, and being in a whimsical mood, I added a well-known biblical passage (Romans 3:23): "For all have sinned and fall short of the glory of God." By this I mean that no one is exempt from this wasting of energy (since our energy is indeed from a heat source), and our approach to life must include its effects.

What I failed to foresee is the fact that this quotation raises the question as to whether *even God* can act without some sort of polluting effect, assuming that God acts *through* the finite, through *creatura*. My little book offers no solution to this last problem, but in raising it a number of ideas are brought to view. In addition, it illustrates the kinds of questions and images which arise in juxtaposing science and religion. *We,* at least, need to face the fact that every action of ours is in some way subject to this law of pollution. In the term of Nobel laureate Ilya Prigogine, we are "dissipative structures."

The category of dissipative structures includes living entities such as ourselves. Dissipative structures take in energy and channel its flow, but can never use *all* of it. In our case we take in food and employ the energy derived from it in activities on various levels, some directed at mere personal survival, but some dedicated to the survival of larger entities, such as families, businesses, groups of common interest, nations, or even humanity as a whole. Some of us channel energy also in the service of ideas, entertainment, and other intangibles. In order to employ any energy for purposes beyond mere survival, for spirituality, we must possess an *excess* energy beyond the "equilibrium" amount for mere continuance of existence, and even more so, since some is inevitably lost. On this account, the phrase with which Prigogine characterizes life is "far from equilibrium."

We will see that not only does physics require the consideration of "sinfulness" in the form of pollution, but it also addresses the universality of encroachment or, in the term of the central Christian prayer, "trespass."

THE NEED FOR CONSCIOUSNESS

There is an apocryphal logion of Jesus which appears in the very ancient *Codex Bezae* at Luke 6:4 with regard to the question of keeping the law of the sabbath: "Man, if indeed thou knowest what thou doest, thou art blessed; but if thou knowest not, thou art cursed and a transgressor of the law." This saying offers some hope in the face of the hopelessness of avoiding pollution and trespass altogether. Our transgressions may be redeemed if we truly know what it is we are doing. It is also echoed by Teilhard de Chardin when he says: "To see or to perish is the very condition laid upon everything that makes up the universe."[1]

The centrality of the need for ever more consciousness gives importance to the fact that through the work of Prigogine we finally have a physics of awakening and transformation. Prigogine's most accessible book is *Order out of Chaos*,[2] which contains many gems. In view of the positions of Jesus, Teilhard and Jung, claiming a physics of awakening and transformation is virtually the same as claiming a physics of a process which can be said to embody a very deep meaning of "saving." In this case, the saving element is constituted by the reality and availability of the transformative awakening process.

In the following, several of Prigogine's keywords are introduced, beyond the notion of "dissipative structures," already mentioned. These keywords will be italicized.

FROM THE IDEAL TO THE REAL

Since Galileo's time the goal of physics has been to describe an ideal world, free from what he called "external and artificial impediments" such as friction. In all real mechanical devices, of course, friction operates to "sap" the energy of the system to render it less than our assumed ideal. But rather than calling it a "sapping," Prigogine would put it that energy is *exchanged* with the environment; the object is in *communication* with the world. One of the clearest examples of a situation close to the erstwhile ideal of physics is that of the orbits of the planets, which are so stable that we can calculate an eclipse of the moon for thousands of years in the past or the future. When there is no net exchange of energy, we say that the system is in *equilibrium*. If the planets exchanged any significant amounts of energy with the environment as, for example, if a "stray" star passed by and gravitationally upset the system, the so-called "ideal" condition, that is, the equilibrium, would be broken and the system would *forget* where the planets had been in the past. In general such an exchange is an *irreversible* process. After an encounter in which energy is irreversibly exchanged, the system is *new*. Sometimes, when some irreversible event has occurred in our lives, we exclaim, "It's a whole new ballgame!" One also recalls here a verse from the *Rubaiyat of Omar Khayyam:*

> The Moving Finger writes, and having writ,
> Moves on: nor all your Piety nor Wit
> Shall lure it back to cancel half a Line,
> Nor all your Tears wash out a Word of it![3]

Here, the moving finger is the finger of action (creativity or loss) whether ours or God's. In fact, according to Prigogine, the irreversible exchange of energy is the very source of newness and creativity. He says, "We . . . speak of entities *formed* by their irreversible interaction with the world."[4] Certainly those choices which we make whose consequences cannot be called back are best seen as our opportunity for creative response. Really to live such a view would transform most of us into beings much more fully alive. It would indeed be a profound *awakening*.

INVOLUTION AND AWAKENING

In order to see the relationship of equilibrium and awakening, we might start with a stone. Except for assuming whatever temperature its environment possesses, a stone does not take in energy. It doesn't eat anything, and therefore is not required to find food for its survival. It needs no awareness of its surroundings. Simple life-forms survive as long as they are located where food is, or where food comes to them, and their energy is used for their own survival and for reproduction. They are fairly close to equilibrium, and have few choices. The farther from equilibrium an entity is, the more precarious its life with regard to its intentionality. To survive, and to ensure survival of its intentions, it must be more and more aware of larger and larger environmental conditions. Mere survival is not usually the issue for such as ourselves, though this is not to deny that for some it *is*. I could probably survive as a handyman, but I don't *want* to do that. Therefore I put myself far from equilibrium. I have a family, and also a contribution to make to the community in the form of teaching and communicating original ideas. I believe that some such distinction applies to most of us: we live at the most complex level which our circumstances permit us to maintain. I am not arguing the justice or injustice of this situation, but merely observing its factuality. In order to fulfill our "calling," our lives' meaning, we push ourselves farther and farther from equilibrium and from mere survival: we take risks.

From this point of view we can see evolution and growth as processes which tend to take us farther and farther from equilibrium toward "points of instability" or of choice. At these points of instability, or "singular points," the entity is as far as it can go from equilibrium in its present mode of existence. While it is true that *energy* is stored in the "environment" which can become available, the dominant environmental influences are in balance, so that a very small force from a more subtle patterning can decide which course it will take. In this regard, Prigogine quotes the great nineteenth century theoretical physicist James Clerk Maxwell:

> In all such cases there is one common circumstance—the system [environment] has a quantity of potential energy, which is capable of being transformed into motion, but which cannot begin to be so transformed till the system has reached a certain configuration, to attain which requires an expenditure of work, which in certain cases may be infinitesimally small, and in general bears no definite proportion to the energy developed in consequence thereof. For example, the rock loosed by frost and balanced on a singular point of the mountain-side, the little spark which kindles

the great forest, the little word which sets the world a-fighting, the little scruple which prevents one from doing his will, the little spore which blights all the potatoes, the little gemmule which makes us philosophers or idiots. Every existence above a certain rank has its singular points: the higher the rank, the more of them. At these points, influences whose physical magnitude is too small to be taken account of by a finite being, may produce results of the greatest importance. All great results produced by human endeavor depend on taking advantage of these singular states when they occur.[5]

As we as individuals reach new points of development, we move away from some previous equilibrium, i.e. a place where we can function easily and comfortably, and which might be called our "stable equilibrium." If something "catches us up," to get us involved in something which moves us out of our comfortable place, then of course we are *already* deriving energy from the symbolic value of this new undertaking. Perhaps we see it already as a present nourishment, perhaps as a potential. We then approach a singular point, a balance which is akin to crossing a ridge into a new territory.

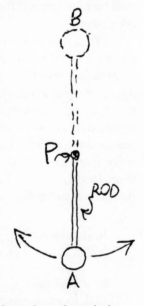

This balance involves a different *sort* of equilibrium from our usual conception of equilibrium as stasis. It can be nicely illustrated by means of a physical model, a pendulum which consists of a rigid rod with a weight on one end, and freely pivoted at the other end, shown here as point P. The pendulum can of course just hang there at point A. This is analogous to the point of comfortable living. If we were to hold the pendulum at point B, we could probably *almost* get it to "balance" there, but the slightest push in either direction, or the tiniest vibration of the earth, would cause it to swing back down.

Point B is then also a point of equilibrium, but since it is so easily disturbed, it is called an "unstable equilibrium." At such a point, very subtle forces can determine what will follow, as Maxwell so eloquently pointed out. This is one very useful analogy of the model, as will be seen.

Getting to the point of unstable equilibrium requires having more energy than one has at stable equilibrium. As energy is gathered, there comes a point at which one becomes, or can become, sensitive or open to delicate nuances, the subtle forces, which might move one in one direction or another.

If we gave the pendulum a big push, we could set it "spinning." Let us denote "spinning" and "swinging" as the two possible modes of its motion. If we use a *lot* of excess energy with respect to point A, we can be in the "spinning" mode, and still not be at the place of sensitivity to the subtle forces which are effective if the pendulum is almost stopped at point B.

By analogy, then, the trick is to live in such a way that one is always near a point of unstable equilibrium. One limitation of the model is that it does not show what can then happen: a transformation which can bring us to a *new source of life*, which is not symbolically equivalent *either* to spinning or to swinging! For this we need more complex images or models.

The model for involution which follows has *just the right* complexity to show a turning-inside-out as virtually a *molecular* process. The forces which were visualized in Chapter 1 as being present in the overlap of the outer ripples of the quantum-state wave forms of molecules can be pictured as a "pulling into shape" of something "even this large," or "even this small," depending on our focus. The evolving entity is large enough to have sufficient complexity, but small enough so that we may see that it is not too complex for us to grasp what is going on. If we are to benefit from the analogy, *we* must, as even more complex organisms, see that as large as we are, we may be *moved*, may put ourselves at the disposal of even more subtle influences so that we may consciously participate in the unfolding of the Patterning.

Here, then, is our example of a transformation to a new level of interaction with the environment, which occurs in every animal embryo (Figure 4). In this "gastrulation" process, the overall outcome is that part of what was the exterior of the entity is taken inside to become the gastro-intestinal tract, the cells of which, originally similar to those which remain on the exterior, take on quite a different function. The embryo is able to obtain food from the outside and to *contain* it for processing. Energy becomes available to it not only at a

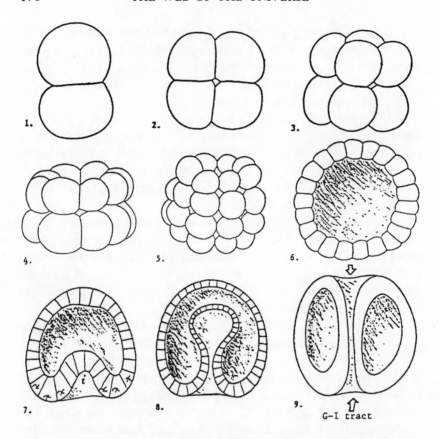

Figure 4. DEVELOPMENT OF FERTILIZED OVUM THROUGH GASTRULATION

In the first stages of cell division the cells simply get smaller, and the process is "running" on internally stored energy, using a small amount of oxygen from the environment. At the eight-cell stage (3), the "blastula" is now fully three-dimensional, and thereafter develops into a hollow sphere (4, 5, 6). After the fifth picture, two or three cell-division stages occur between pictures, the entire depicted process requiring about a day. Pictures 6, 7, 8, and 9 are cross-sections. In 7, certain cells' outer parts (x) expand, forcing a dimple or indentation (i) inward (8) until it meets the opposite wall and opens into a full gastro-intestinal tract (9). What is shown as the upper opening (arrow) will become the mouth, and the lower opening (arrow) will be the anus. At this new stage, the blastula becomes a "gastrula," and begins utilizing energy (food) from the environment. This is a classic case of moving far from equilibrium to a point of instability (pictures 6 & 7, the formation of the indentation), followed by a reconfiguration which utilizes energy much more rapidly, which in turn begins a new move even further from equilibrium. The living entity is now much more engaged with its environment.

much greater rate, but from a different source. Previously it lived like a seed, on food stored within, but now it has gained a new relationship to a much greater whole, along with the need *and ability* to sustain itself at the new source.

With involution processes such as gastrulation, a living entity is produced which feeds on the latent energy sources of the environment. A human gastrula has the potential to use energy to grow into an organic whole of the highest order. But to survive and continue to grow, it must find new kinds of energy sources throughout the various stages of its life. To be alive, there must be a continual increase of energy processing. This need expresses the essence of disequilibrium. As Prigogine says, *life itself* is being "far-from-equilibrium," and moving ever away from equilibrium conditions. Prigogine equates moving farther from equilibrium with "waking up." In order to find the energy to sustain and increase aliveness, an organism must *continually* wake up.[6]

This awakening requires consumption of energy in an increasing spiral. Hence the interlocking of awakening with the problem of encroachment or trespass. Do I have a right to consume energy to increase my consciousness and aliveness when someone else needs energy to actualize mere subsistence? One conclusion which can be drawn from the above views is that the consumption of energy, a high standard of living, can only be moral *as* a vehicle for awakening. This certainly has not been our image of the value of a high living standard. It has been called "the good life," as if it were a value in itself. In an earlier stage of human development, we saw the need for security in relation to the unpredictable forces of nature. For many this is no longer a threat which obtrudes upon effective daily living. The "goal" has moved on beyond such security needs, and we need to follow.

Some of the spiritual projects of individual humans now require, however, a high level of income and expenditure, and a kind of security which will sustain a new kind of risk. It is indeed moral to undertake such projects solely upon the authority of the individual in cooperation with the Self within and in the situation.

Part of the solution to the dilemma of having and using a great deal, but by no means the entire solution, is the fact that the energy source becomes more spiritual in nature, as does the energy "wasted" back to the environment.[7] The whole project becomes more spiritually encompassing for everyone concerned if undertaken from the Self. The mere application of money or material goods is one form of maintaining separation from humanity.

Prigogine says:

> At equilibrium, molecules behave as essentially independent entities; they ignore one another. [No exchange takes place.] We would like to call them "hypnons," "sleepwalkers." Though each of them may be as complex as we like, they ignore one another. However, nonequilibrium wakes them up and introduces a coherence quite foreign to equilibrium.[8]

Here we have a new idea: that a *coherence* arises as entities and groups of entities move away from equilibrium. The additions of energy which move a system away from equilibrium always move it toward some sort of "point of instability," at which very small forces, which Prigogine calls "long-range correlations," can introduce this new coherence, can organize the activity on a new level, as we can see in the next figure. In other words, such tiny forces as can push a pendulum either way may actually have something coherent and meaningful to say *on behalf of the whole.*

Figure 5[9] shows a chemical solution in which energy is being released at its point of instability. Instead of a chaotic result, which happens when energy release is not at the singular point of instability, an overall pattern emerges, which shows that organizational forces are at work over distances which are long when compared to the separations of the molecules in the solution. Just imagine for a moment what might be different if, at the numerous points of instability in our lives, we might stop to realize that just because of instability we have become susceptible to subtle forces acting for a new coherence! These are crucial times for attentive listening in meditation for the "new gradient" which can redirect our lives.

I have selected five illustrative points of involution, representing evolutionary steps to greater spirituality. Undoubtedly there are more, but these are intended to indicate a full range of spiritual development as we might be able to see it now.

Involution I: Blastula → Gastrula.
First "within": Physical processing of food.

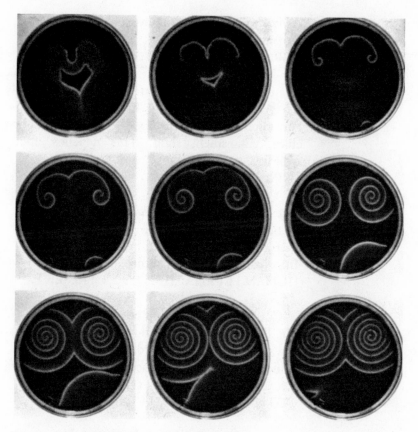

Figure 5. THE BELOUSOV-ZHABOTINSKII REACTION: CHEMICAL SCROLL WAVES

Spiral chemical waves develop when the Belousov-Zhabotinskii reagent is allowed to stand in a shallow dish. The waves can appear spontaneously or be initiated by touching the surface with a hot filament, as in the photographs above. The small circles are bubbles of carbon dioxide evolved by the reaction (see the section on coherent structures in chemistry and biology in chapter 5). After the initial photograph was taken, subsequent ones were taken at 0.5, 1.0, 1.5, 3.5, 4.5, 5.5, 6.5, and 8.0 seconds.

"Awake" I: *Response* to 2nd order stimulus: Cell specialization,
environmentally driven.
EMBRYOLOGICAL LEVEL.

Involution II: Matching of symbolic patterns.
Second "within": Awareness in organic function.
"Awake" II: Pattern *seeking:* finding food through symbolic
clues, e.g. smell, sight. This depends upon
mobility.
ANIMAL LEVEL.

Involution III: Residence of person *inside* ego. Subjectivity.
Third "within": Self-reflexivity.
"Awake" III: Self-awareness, Thought, Feeling.
Information storage, Culture, Technology.
HUMAN LEVEL ACHIEVED AT PRESENT.

Involution IV: "Consciousness": living beyond ego.
Fourth "within": The whole inner world of the unconscious.
"Awake" IV: Awareness of a supra-ordinate inner authority
which is not ego, and concomitant awareness of
external world with new clarity.
POTENTIAL HUMAN LEVEL AT PRESENT.

Involution V: Communication as bonding of a world community of individuals.
FUTURE LEVEL.

The third involution, the development of ego or individual "I-
ness," is the last *involuntary* involution, the last one which "just
occurs" in the patterning of evolution. The fourth can only be ef-
fected with the consent and committed action of an ego, a person, an
"I." My friend and teacher, poet, mythologist, and psychotherapist
Sheila Moon, described the process in one of her poems as "turning," as learning "to wrestle our desire another way, to face it around
to see its eyes."[10]
I will say more concerning the fourth involution at the end of
the chapter, for it ties together Prigogine's ideas of transformation

with Jung, the "new physics," and the needed spiritual transformation for our time.

Each involution is a kind of turning inside-out to form a container for a new process. To each involution also corresponds a kind of awakening, and the establishment of a new *kind* of relationship with the environment. At each succeeding stage, also, more and more subtle influences can control greater and greater amounts of applied physical energy for purposeful activities. An example of this at the animal level is their food-seeking activity. How *little* energy is involved in the smell itself, but how *much* energy is galvanized when the scent is recognized! This is also what symbols do for us at our own level, and they organize very long-term efforts.

In later stages the person assimilates more and more of total humanity. This is really most remarkable from the standpoint of physics: a deep inner connectedness of all personal "Selves" is revealed in the *collective* aspect of the Self. This inner connection must always have been there, though not recognized until the stages of this level of consciousness have begun. The implication is that the physical stuff out of which the organism was woven, each single subatomic particle, always was connected to every other particle. The complex-ification has revealed a single overarching entity coming to self-awareness (potentially) within every living organism. Another implication is that autonomy is precisely unconsciousness, in spite of the fact that consciousness never develops without separation from the collective.

INVOLUTION AND OPENING

Not only is each involution the creation of a new "within," and a new level of awakening, but it also is an *opening*. The organism exhibits a new form of permeability. Prigogine says that at equilibrium (absence of exchange) structures are "immortal," that is, inert or repetitive.

> However, when we examine a biological cell or a city, the situation is quite different: not only are these systems open, but also they exist only because they are open. They feed on the flux of

matter and energy coming to them from the outside world. We can isolate a crystal, but cities and cells die when cut off from their environment. They form an integral part of the world from which they draw sustenance, and they cannot be separated from the fluxes which they incessantly transform.[11]

The words of Teilhard quoted earlier: "To see or to perish is the very condition laid upon everything that makes up the universe," might now be paraphrased as: To awaken or to perish is the very condition laid upon all living being.

To be alive, then, we must be energy processors, open systems, transformational vortices, and open in ever new, ever more spiritualized dimensions. But do not get the impression that this means "sweetness and light." Openness is vulnerability, and when the wound occurs, as it will, openness is the same as rawness. We seldom spontaneously associate rawness with being alive, but if you think about it, that's what works.

Prigogine's "thermodynamic" approach to the development of living organisms heads in the opposite direction from the usual references to thermodynamics in this area. The usual assertion is that the "universe tends to run down," and that highly evolved entities are merely improbable. Thus it is clear that this new approach involves a whole new way of seeing reality.[12]

As I have worked with this model of life, it has been my experience that the model has illuminated and brought together many situations which previously seemed unrelated. Above all, it has explained to me my impatience with people who seek equilibrium in their lives and why I associate an unliving quality with such an attitude. Yet, many of us have this tendency, myself included. The model can help us to see that the processes of life and growth are *naturally directed* away from equilibrium, and to affirm that this is what we really do want. In *seeing* this situation as natural and right, we may be enabled to *go with it* much more readily than we otherwise could. That is, we may be able to assign to it the *reality value* which it possessed all along.

The fourth involution is that of becoming aware of the Self as what Jung called a "supraordinate inner authority," and of submitting to that authority. Jung documented case after case of this religious need in his clients, along with the activity of the Self which moved people toward this transformation.

Each succeeding involution enables the application of specific energies to the facilitation of previous involutions. Jesus was a full involution ahead of his contemporaries, and his perception of reality enabled him to help others toward similar transitions through images which would appeal to them at their own level. Then the task is to live it fully. Deep inside, we still know that the aliveness is in the risking of ourselves in some real way with an irreversible outcome. Only out of the risking comes the joy.

Notes

1. *Phenomenon,* p. 31.
2. Prigogine, Ilya and Isabelle Stengers. 1984. New York, Bantam Books.
3. Fitzgerald, Edward. 1956. "The Rubaiyat of Omar Khayyam." *The Pocket Book of Verse.* Edited by M.E. Speare. New York: Pocket Books, Quatrain LXXI.
4. *Order,* p. 95.
5. In Prigogine. *Order,* p. 73.
6. *Order,* p. 181. The cosmos is in *fundamental disequilibrium* as is shown in Appendix 2.
7. If all energy can't be "used," then the greater "brightness," the greater *dissipation,* shows, or *can* show, the locus of the process of becoming.
8. *Order,* pp. 180–181.
9. Prigogine, Ilya. 1980. *From Being to Becoming.* New York: W.H. Freeman. Photographs by Fritz Goro.
10. Moon, Sheila. 1972. Prolog. *Joseph's Son,* Francestown NH: Golden Quill Press.
11. *Order,* p. 127.
12. Prigogine asserts that the path to the place at which he has arrived begins with Einstein's work in the foundations of statistical mechanics, the third of his great revolutionary papers of 1905. Many of us are aware that Einstein's work in quantum physics and in relativity has forced us to see physical reality radically differently, and that may well be true of the third paper of the "miracle year" as well.

PART IV
PROSPECT

Chapter 10

Theonomy—The Self-Integration of Freedom and Consciousness in the Cosmos

The will of God, known in advance, ceases to be the will of God.
—J. Middleton Murry (*God*)

In all that has been said in Part III on the dynamics of spirituality, an attempt has been made to express the material in a language appropriate either to psychology or to physics. The reason for this has been to let the symbols speak as purely as they can on their own.

However, it has also been clear that something much deeper is available from these sciences than has been seen in the past. In order to honor that depth, some sort of God-language is needed. The merging of "God-language" with that of science honors the ultimate convergence of science and religion, and the necessity, noted before, to employ opposites in the description of reality. More importantly, however, the use of God-language gives a different sort of *life* to the "prospect" for spirituality, in a world in which science and spirituality will no longer be split apart.

It is indeed appropriate to see all that has been said as pointing to the fulfillment of *divine* ends, even though some of the ideas of those ends are radically different from previous conceptions.

In what follows, then, that shift of language will be employed, but with some preparation. In particular, the transition will be made from *teleonomy* to *theonomy*, i.e. from viewing the *telos* abstractly as *internal goal*, to the *recognition* of that internal goal and regulator as the *divine activity within*. In the process, it will also be necessary to say what has become of the perhaps more familiar concept of *teleology*.

Ernst Mayr coined the term "teleonomy" to rescue values threatened by the demise of teleology in evolutionary biology. Teleology envisions the evolutionary process as being shaped by external design and final causes which function as fixed goals. In contrast, teleonomy recognizes *internal* goals in organisms, the prime example of which is that the embryo develops into an adult. Teleonomy also accounts for the fact that *theoretically unpredictable* properties arise in evolution. If there were an external goal, it might be possible to think out in advance what it *must* be. At least it is the case that many physicists have thought that the laws of physics must have such a *necessary* nature that arriving at them by cogitation should be possible. Teleonomy recognizes tendencies and fulfillments, but these are not of a nature knowable in advance.

The move from teleology to teleonomy in biology suggests that we explore the question of whether there is any analogous ground for urging a parallel consideration of "theonomy" in relation to theology. Is there, e.g., any precedent for a concept of an *internal* Other, or for an Unknown *Telos?* What might it mean to see humanity as presently embryonic with regard to the embodiment of God? What kind of vision of "saving" follows from such a view?[1] Here are a few thoughts, based on all that has been said in this book, *bearing toward* answers to these questions.

The word "theonomy" was first employed by Tillich. It has been presented by others as "religion of the concrete spirit," and as "the Ultimate *in* every creative human function." In Tillich's own words it is

> a culture in which the ultimate meaning of existence shines through all finite forms of thought and action.[2]

And, more technically, it is:

> autonomous reason united with its own depth . . . and actualized in obedience to its structural laws and in the power of its inexhaustible ground.[3]

While "theonomy" is Tillich's term, the point of view of this book is entirely consistent with his thinking. In making my own offering, I am not distorting his meaning, but adding another possible dimension along similar lines. Even apart from the consideration of precedence, the present use which I am making of the word-ending "-nomy" in relation to "-logy" has a sufficient number of parallels with other accepted usages of the same word-endings to merit consideration in its own right. In what follows, the proposition will be developed of the *Internal and Unknown Telos* (capitalized to signify the divine) which might be called the "Theonomic Proposition." From the above quotations, the *internal* aspect is clearly central to Tillich in the expression "its own depth," and his "inexhaustible ground" certainly implies the *unknown*. For Tillich, all such grounds converge in an "Ultimate Ground of Being," one of his expressions for "God."

Some time ago I attended a lecture by one of our leading cosmologists, John Archibald Wheeler, of Princeton and the University of Texas. His title was: "World as System Self-Synthesized Quantum Mechanically." Since I had already formulated the title to this chapter, I was struck by the similarity of our emphases. To me, the import of the emphasis on such ideas as self-synthesis and self-integration by scientists is that God has opened up a whole new front of self-revelation in an area where many disdain to see such a thing appear: science itself. Since science is often seen as the source of such ills as the loss of purposiveness, fostering rationalism, birthing technology, and materialism, this new development is of great interest. God is, to use a biblical image, "eating with sinners": us scientists. And as the "sinners" in the story responded to the message, so are the scientists responding to the Mystery which they are encountering. Science is undergoing *metanoia*, a change of attitude.

In particular, the attitudes are crumbling which underlie rationalism, determinism, things as hard objects (including atoms), and action at a distance, which were mainstays of physics from the time of Newton until the end of the nineteenth century. As we will see, scientists are bringing the new, while many theologians stick to the old.

FROM NEWTON TO A NEW PHYSICS

The physics of this twentieth century is indeed a new physics, in that the above attitudes are no longer foundations of physical thought. In *Spacetime Physics,* the shift from the Newtonian view to that of Einstein is characterized in the following epigrammatic way. The authors are picturing how an earth satellite "knows" how to follow its orbit.

> Where does the satellite get its moving orders?
> From a distance, answers Newton.
> Locally, answers Einstein.[4]

Put in this way, it is easy to see that this shift of worldview is from external shaping to a local shaping because the satellite simply follows the local "curvature of space." For Newton, the gravity which holds the satellite in orbit was "action at a distance," something mysterious, implying that God was involved in seeing that physical order was maintained, even though God was external to that order. Einstein's view is much more "physical," and the gravitational field is not a mystery superimposed on a rigidly "flat"[5] space, but is simply a *name (nomos)* for the curvature of space itself. It is quite parallel to the shift from teleology to teleonomy.[6] Newton himself used "action at a distance" as a proof of God. Later science rejected this idea, but still kept the fundamental tenets of the worldview as just listed.

In spite of the discoveries of Einstein and others, the Newtonian attitudes linger, even among physicists, for the psyche readjusts itself only slowly. In the world of non-scientists, the adjustment time is even longer.

We need to shake off the Newtonian hangover. Part of the evidence of this hangover is a perceived need to refute Newtonian science. Even Whitehead's attacks on Newton, early in the century, were too late, were unnecessary. *As a viable worldview,* that science had already crumbled into useless shards. It would be much more profitable for humans to take up the dialogue with God, *where God is now in process of self-revelation,* a significant part of which is occurring in science.

In *Foolishness to the Greeks,*[7] Lesslie Newbegin has renewed the attack upon the same imagined Newtonian bastions. Newbegin is quite correct to assert that *Newtonian* science splits the world into public and private spheres. The public sphere includes that which can be agreed upon generally, as with scientific consensus and international law. Since religious differences cannot in general be reconciled *globally*, between all individuals and among all peoples, they form part of the private sphere, which is held back and held onto inwardly when venturing into "public." Newbegin is also correct to assert that what he calls the "modern western worldview," based on Newtonian science, has ejected the dimension of *purpose* altogether from the public field. This is essentially what forced the religious life into the private realm. This ejection of purpose is the same as saying that as an outgrowth of Newtonian science, it has become untenable to assert teleology in scientific theory, though the process by which this occurred was not simple. Thus, the private, non-scientific world becomes the repository of teleology, as the intervention of God in human affairs from without, to enforce the unfolding of a "divine plan." With this division between purpose and non-purpose, the world is split apart.[8] Note that this only holds as long as *both* sides remain Newtonian. Once we move from externally fixed purposes to internally guided evolution, the two "sides" need not remain apart. One who *accepts* this split must be classified as Newtonian in attitude.

In view of Newbegin's attempt to confute Newton, it is ironic that when he comes to some of the newer developments in physics, such as quantum realities with their implications of a non-rational cosmos, and Prigogine's concept of life as "far from equilibrium," he says[9] only that their possible validity must be left to others to discuss. The irony lies in the fact that it is precisely with *these* sorts of developments that the Newtonian foundations have fallen, leaving the new ideas of physical reality free to diffuse into other interested fields. Indeed, physics *as such* is the *only* arena in which the refutation of Newton could have been successfully undertaken, and the manner in which it has come about is of particular interest.

It was the *rationalistic* thrust of the science of the past few centuries which uncovered the *non*-rational nature of the physical cosmos. One might even say that rationalism has finally encountered the Mystery. Intuition has "known" of the Mystery all along, but when *intuition* encounters the Mystery, the world is not necessarily healed, for that level of knowledge lacks the transformative factuality and concreteness of science. Now we can assert that the world is no longer split, nor will it split again in the same sense. We have crossed a threshold, or, better, gone through a death-rebirth process, which never would have been discovered except for seriousness about rigorous thought and factuality. We accepted this form of the death of a certain hope, and have discovered not only that God was there, but that it was absolutely necessary to take that step into darkness. In thus encountering the unity of spirit and matter, we have taken a major step toward a unified worldview and a unified God-image.

The arguments which have been presented in this book are not subject to the *sort* of criticism which has been directed at Newtonian science, for science is not replacing the Newtonian fortress with a similarly made structure. The new factuality has no resemblance to eighteenth and nineteenth century science, where *things* are hard objects, where space, time, and location are well-defined, and where the Second Law of Thermodynamics[10] projects a cosmos dissolving into randomness. The foundation is *factual*, not theoretical. Theoretical foundations based upon so-called "first principles" have no staying power. The new factuality employs a much more gentle *logic*, while losing nothing with regard to its factuality. It thus provides a foundation for a new edifice of thought which can be expected to be habitable for some time. In any case, the base of fact will remain: the world will not go from round to flat. It is time for theologians to *assimilate* modern physics and respond to it, for they are in a position to have a positive effect upon the consciousness of the general public.

TELEONOMY IN BIOLOGY AND PSYCHOLOGY

In an article in *Science* entitled "Biology is not Postage Stamp Collecting," Ernst Mayr states:

> Before Darwin, scientists and philosophers believed in a direction of purpose in nature and its processes. The theory of natural selection removed teleology from nature, but nevertheless leaves the special property of teleonomy in the developing organism. The genetic instructions packaged in an embryo direct the formation of an adult, whether it be a tree, a fish, or a human. The process is goal-directed, but from the instructions in the genetic program, not from outside.[11]

Later in the article, he includes the aspect of evolutionary open-endedness of the internal *telos* when he says:

> New properties turn up in systems that could not have been predicted from the components, which means you have to study things hierarchically. Reductionism can be vacuous at best, and in the face of emergence, misleading and futile.[12]

In other words, there always remain unknown capabilities of the present genetic makeup. Let me emphasize Mayr's statement that the new properties *could* not have been predicted. If the *telos* embedded in *physical* systems is evolutionarily unknown, we should be extremely cautious in any assertions as to our knowledge of the *spiritual telos*. We are reasonably knowledgeable about the spiritual qualities of a mature human adult, but can hardly extrapolate the potentials of the species. We have been here as *homo* for a mere two million years, and as *homo sapiens* for a trifling hundred thousand, whereas our sun has a good five billion years' worth of nuclear fuel remaining. God, as seen by theonomy, would fill all of that time with creative newness and with consciousness infinitely beyond present human consciousness, so that it would be entirely futile to attempt to imagine what will have emerged evolutionarily by the end of the sun's lifetime.

Jung's empirical depth-psychology also encountered the necessity of considering something teleonomical in the human psyche. He felt the need to distance himself from teleology, because the "goal," for teleology, was assumed to be known. We see this distancing in his essay "On Psychic Energy," where he writes:

> I use the word "final" rather than teleological in order to avoid the misunderstanding that attaches to the common conception of teleology, namely that it contains the idea of an *anticipated* end or goal.[13]

Though Jung chose another word to carry that which could be saved from teleology, his concern was clearly in the same direction as that which we are calling teleonomic.

In the words quoted is a clear reflection upon the fact that the spiritual, in this case psychological, *telos* is unknown. Jung also frequently mentioned his empiricism, the fact that we are engaged in the *naming* (-nomy) of what we see and experience, rather than in *knowledge* (-logy) of what is to be. I have presented the same idea earlier, in the fact that physics is *descriptive*, rather than a theory deduced from "first principles."

Besides the naming aspect, the Greek *nomos* carries a connotation of *inner law*, which is deeply resonant with all which has been presented. The wisdom of such a matter-of-fact approach to emergence within the divine experiment—of an approach which doesn't claim esoteric "knowledge"—might be developed more strongly than it has been.

The very real convergence of science and religion, which has been shown in the parallel chapters on Jung and on the New Physics, can thus be seen to have its ground, or to have found a common ground for the two, in the theonomic proposition. We see indications and implications of the divine from within the fields of physical and psychological science. The empirical material developed by Jung and his associates demonstrates the God-image in each human being, as well as the unknown character of the psychological *telos*. This was shown in Chapter 8, "Jung and Transformation."

The term "theonomy" is very apt for inner working out of the divine, with inherently unknown outcome, which manifests a creative newness in the deepest sense. In so naming the evolutionary thrust in spirit-matter, we are merely giving voice to the other side of a reality which we ordinarily prefer to address in more secular terms. In particular, freedom and consciousness have been seen as attributes of God, of the divine. We have, however, not really faced the implications of the fact that they are developing attributes of the human. Let us then move that view forward.

THE INTEGRATION OF FREEDOM AND CONSCIOUSNESS

It has been customary for both physicists and philosophers to assume the human, with its mental faculties, as *given*, as a creation as it were from above, whereas these faculties, along with psyche itself, have developed evolutionarily. Jung's concurrence with this view was shown in Chapter 8. A correct assessment as to the nature both of consciousness and of reality must account explicitly for *human nature* in terms of the facts of evolution and the nature of the evolving "stuff of the universe." It must account for the in-betweenness of psyche with respect to both spirit and matter and its separation from both, though it retains a form of connection to each.

The fact is that *consciousness has evolved out of that which is not conscious.* There is a parallel of this in our own lives: each of us has experienced becoming more conscious as we grow older. But the case is most clearly seen in the fact that from a primordial universe of elementary particles which are *not* conscious, conscious entities have indeed evolved. There is a physical continuity in spite of the logically contradictory terms "conscious" and "not-conscious." Obviously, the *potential* for consciousness is inherent in unconscious stuff. The evolution of consciousness in the cosmos exemplifies both of the previously mentioned qualities of bi-polarity (conscious/not-conscious) and non-rationality (unity in spite of logical opposition of attributes).

With some justification we attribute consciousness to humans. In *every* case this consciousness is associated with a person, an ego, an "I." The ego has a sense of distinctness from what is *not-I*, along with a form of connection to the *not-I* which it calls "knowing," not to mention its indubitable *dependence* upon both the spirit and matter aspects of physical stuff. The realms of spirit and of matter both present themselves as *other* to the ego, as forms of the *not-I*. That is, for normal human individuals, the connectedness of *knowing* falls into two classes of objects, one of which, *matter*, is very concrete, involving the five senses, and the other of which, *spirit*, seems much more nebulous, but can be very compelling indeed. About the relationship of spirit, matter, and psyche, Jung says the following:

> Matter and spirit both appear in the psychic realm as distinctive qualities of conscious contents. The ultimate nature of both is transcendental, that is, irrepresentable, since the psyche and its contents are the only reality which is given to us *without a medium.*[14]

If we think of spirit as "above" ego-consciousness and matter as "below," then psyche is in-between. Jung often likens this relationship to that of light frequencies, the *visible* range (corresponding to the conscious ego) being "above" those of infra-red, and "below" those of the ultra-violet.

Here is a brief evolutionary scheme using the representations of atoms and snowflakes which were shown in the first chapter "What Is Spirituality?" along with another diagram which shows cross-sections of the human brain, to indicate briefly how the internal aspects of our psyches might come to attain spiritual qualities evolutionarily. Only one spiritual quality will be traced from the atomic level, namely freedom, but love, consciousness, and meaning could be followed symbolically, and others as well.[15]

In Chapter 1, Figure 1 shows representations of some of the various forms which a hydrogen atom can assume in accordance with its energy content. As Victor Weisskopf says:

> The patterns of the atoms, and their inherent symmetries . . . are the basis of their orderly arrangement in molecules, and also of the symmetric arrangement of atoms and molecules in crystals. . . . Ultimately the regularities of form and structure that we see in nature, ranging from the hexagonal shape of a snowflake to the intricate symmetries of living forms in flowers and animals, are based upon the symmetries of these atomic patterns.[16]

One symbol of freedom discernible through these pictures is simply the multiplicity of form of the simplest form of spirit-matter, namely hydrogen. Another is the fact that the paths by which the atom can change from one pattern to another, by giving or receiving energy, are not fixed or unique. In fact, as was also noted in Chapter 1, Teilhard de Chardin was moved to refer to atoms as "elementary freedoms," as distinct from being elementary determinisms. In our lives, freedom is related fundamentally to the number of options in a situation, and to the multiplicity of paths by means of which we might act. At the very simple level shown in the pictures, the hydrogen atom does not exhibit what we might call *will* to choose paths, for the probabilities of what path it will take are well known, but without the options, will is meaningless.

A third symbol of freedom which shows up at the atomic or quantum level is the freedom to manifest as either of two logically contradictory modes, wave or particle, which corresponds to the oscillation between opposites discussed in Chapter 5. The inherent non-rationality of nature which is implied by this oscillation is a central source of freedom of all entities made up of atoms, at whatever evolutionary level.

In snowflakes (Chapter 1, Figure 2), the multiplication of the possibilities of freedom is symbolized in the fantastically increased "repertoire" of possible patterns.

An interesting *new* form of freedom also becomes discernible if we consider how the symmetry is propagated as the crystal grows. As can be seen from the pictures, the symmetry is a general one rather than precise, molecule for molecule. Here, freedom can be seen in the *margin of error* which can be overcome by the wholeness pattern.[17] If we take this symbolically at our own level, one possible implication is that our errors are not absolute, but to some degree our own wholeness patterns can be fulfilled in spite of them. The wholeness pattern can even do a certain amount of healing or restoration in the entity if damage occurs. I find this symbol most comforting.

In higher forms, this same freedom gains complexity in the mobility of an organism to respond to the wholeness pattern, and in actual organic healing. An example of the mobility of the response is given by Edmund Sinnott in *The Biology of the Spirit:*

> A pine tree is as simple an organism as one can find, save among the lowliest of living things. It has few of the complexities of an animal—no stomach, no heart, no muscles, no nerves, no sense organs, and certainly no brain. Despite this it possesses a bodily pattern to which it stubbornly adheres, maltreat it as you will. . . . First bind a cluster of terminal growing branches with a loop around the whole about halfway down, so that the umbrella cannot fully open. Though the lower portions of each branch are thus held vertical, the free upper portions act like typical branches and spread out until they reach the normal angle of about seventy degrees to the main axis or trunk. They have come as close as they can to restoring the typical growth pattern of the tree.[18]

The same mobility of the wholeness pattern is evident in the healing of wounds on a tree as the wood "flows" out over cut places over a period of years, and also in the much more efficient healing processes

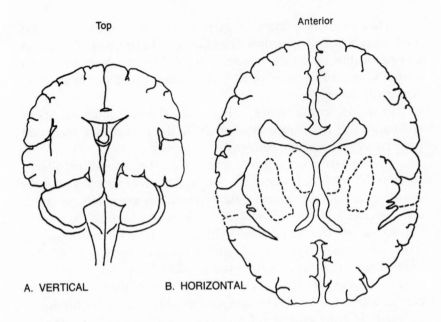

Figure 6. CROSS-SECTIONS OF THE HUMAN BRAIN.

in the animal realm. Ultimately, in social situations for healing of human wounds, this mobility is maximized and its significance extended beyond individuals. Even more important is the fact that the perception of the wound in the social fabric becomes conscious, and the movement toward healing becomes choiceful, even when it involves sacrifice.

All this is *theonomic* in the sense that healing forces are developing *internally* in the organism, which is a precursor to an internal *transformative* power.

With respect to the brain (Figure 6), first note the power of elementary patterning of small whole numbers, for in spite of the tremendous increase in complexity, the number six still shows in the lobes of the cross-sections, whether vertical or horizontal. This gives a sense of the continuity of the evolutionary process.

Along with more highly evolved forms of the freedoms already mentioned, another new one appears. This is symbolized by the breaking of the rigidity of previous symmetries, and the doubling of lobes which nonetheless are known to fulfill complementary functions, rational and associative, for the left and right hemispheres respectively. It was the conflict of these functions and its manifestation in epilepsy that led to the research which first began to show the differences in the hemispheres. Here, freedom lies in the conflict of opposites, which is the evolutionary expression of the wave/particle duality mentioned earlier. Again, reflection upon what the role of conflicts, emotional, intellectual, or with respect to social values, has been in our lives would probably leave us in agreement that such freedom as we have achieved is attributable to our having had to deal with such problems.

Consciousness depends first upon the development of *psyche,* which Jung defines as the sphere within which the will can exercise its empirical freedom, consisting of those human functions which have been emancipated from physiological necessity. Psyche, in turn, rests upon the increasing mobility of the wholeness pattern just described. I have shown elsewhere the inverse relation of bond strengths and this mobility. Again in Chapter 1, a model was developed by means of which to visualize the most subtle bonds as a sort of overlapping of outer fringe lobes of the atomic patterns, since each pattern is actually of indefinite extension. Since psyche is between spirit and matter, this actual physical enclosingness of the overlapping outer lobes is quite suggestive of the arising of the "within" (Teilhard). An example of the within is that which responds to the most subtle fields, as with the impingement upon ourselves of psychic fields in the vicinity, such as the mood of a group. This is now to be seen as a consequence of the wave-aspect of electron patterns and the overlap in the bonding, through which complexity builds.

At the human level of complexity we have self-reflexivity, but the emergence of consciousness has been strongly shown by Jung to involve work on internal conflict and can only be said to be underway in the human arena, and not very far along at that.

IMPLICATIONS I: THEONOMY, MONOTHEISM, AND THE "DIVINE PLAN"

In what follows, I use the word "God" for God *as seen by theonomy:* a commonly rooted *ground* which functions in individuals and in situations. One of the foundations of my work is the proposition that we do not want to live in a split world, for that prevents us from being whole persons. Therefore, what are seen as the disparate worlds of science and religion, of fact and value, are really one. To express it in the singular, the world which we examine as scientists, and the world through which we are addressed by God with an ultimate demand upon our lives, is one and the same world. This is an ultimate sort of extension of the Anthropic Principle: since we are so addressed if we perceive the subtle field, the nature of reality is attuned to that end internally, from the beginning.

Again and again in the diversity of our lives, we return to the quest for oneness: Reality is One: *Uni*verse. This may be called the Ultimate Monotheistic Hypothesis. The Theonomic Proposition, which entails the Ultimate Monotheistic Hypothesis, implies that if the spirit-matter cosmos is *one*, and God is *One* and one with it, then the cosmos and its physical laws offer clues to the nature of God.

Perhaps the most fundamental property of the cosmos thus indicated is that since consciousness is increasing, having begun from zero in the "Big Bang," it follows that God is self-revelatory *from within*. Our realization of this fact then constitutes a new opening to the knowledge of God for humanity.

There is a mutual implication of the permanence of the general nature of the cosmos and the self-revelation of God. If God is in process of self-revelation, we *must* assume that the fundamental laws of the cosmos *have* not changed and *will* not.[19] This does not refer to physical laws *as presently known*, for they definitely will change as we discover more penetrating modes of describing and understanding physical reality. This is *also* part of the self-revelation of God within the scheme which I am presenting. But, one might say, a God who "really is" God, who *designed* the Universe, *could* redesign it differently and change it *now*. But if God were a *good* designer, a designer of the good, then God *could have* no desire to change it, or rather *couldn't* do so. The monotheistic hypothesis also implies that the *good* entails the integration of opposites, for this process is palpably one of the fundamental attributes of the cosmos (see Chapters 5 and 6).

If these things follow, we need not speak of "design" at all. It is *such as it is*, reflecting the nature of God. It is patterned, evolutionary, integrative.

If the self-revelation of God is a permanent feature of the cosmos, then our understanding is incomplete, *permanently and in prin-*

ciple! The *telos*, or, to use Teilhard's term, the "Omega," is infinitely far off, permanently and in principle, or we would have to say that God could "run out of ideas for the new." This, I believe, is the true application of what astronomers call the "Perfect Cosmological Principle." The "Cosmological Principle" states that it is wholly unlikely that we are living at a special place in the cosmos, such as at its center. The "Perfect Cosmological Principle" states this but adds that we are not likely living at a special time. The application of the "Perfect Cosmological Principle" would imply that perpetual embodiment of God *is* the World Order.

If the Omega is permanently distant, its nature does not *exist* as *knowledge* to be *imparted*, or as some sort of Divine Secret. The *internalization* of the *telos* prevents certainty as well as it prevents there being such a "secret." God "imparts" knowledge as *we* grasp it, whether it be intuition or the interpretation of physical fact, for it is God's world.[20] The evolution of the cosmos is guided through its *internal patterning*, but this happens neither mechanistically, nor with a knowable *telos*. In the "bootstrap" language of modern physics, it "manifests its own nature," and this continually, through its inherent tendency to self-reflexivity and consciousness.

Within this view, with its radical uncertainty, *our* struggle has high purpose, and is a risky experiment, for the intellect can "bypass" wisdom and consciousness as a motorcycle can a walker. It does so daily in every university.

If God is self-revelatory, *permanently and in principle*, it also follows that all the gradients to knowledge and consciousness are *in* the cosmos because they are *in-God*. They direct a flow of potential contents toward the psyche as psyche develops, and as consciousness grows. They release energy, confer life. We are led perpetually to *satisfaction*. Our *knowledge* exceeds that of our ancestors and will be exceeded by that of our progeny. *In this sense* each one does live at a *special* time, but has access to all the satisfaction which she or he can stand, as well as the freedom to forfeit that joy. What is *my* consciousness? It can only be a step in evolution and will seem minuscule in the future. But we *feel alive*, we *can live*, we *can participate*, and we will have a place in the development.

It also follows that God's "interest" is alive in, and with regard to, every moment in time. Creation completes God eternally. But finally every finite thing dies; good kings and tyrants, cities, civilizations, nations, sages . . . even stars and galaxies die. The only question is "personal," concerned with the role of the individual entity at every level of evolution: What was left undone which could have been accomplished, and what was the legacy? The cosmic interest is *local* in time and space.

IMPLICATIONS II: THEONOMY AND SAVING

In *Puer Aeternus*, von Franz beautifully described the *mutual* sacrifice of the Self and the ego in the concretization of consciousness. One might also see it as the mutual sacrifice of the *internal Christ* (see Chapter 8, "Jung and Transformation") and of the ego. Von Franz writes:

> When the Self and the ego come together ... both are wounded. . . . These two entities cannot meet without damaging each other. For the Self you could say that instead of being a potential *wholeness* it becomes a *partial* reality; part of it becomes real within the individuated person. . . . That is a restriction for the Self and its possibilities. The ego, however, is wounded because something *greater* breaks into its life . . . which is why Dr. Jung says that it means tremendous suffering to get in touch with the process of individuation . . . because, put simply, we are robbed of the capacity for arranging our own lives according to our own wishes.[21]

And Jung, on several occasions in his treatises on the symbolic meaning of alchemy, and in his *Answer to Job*, describes as *crucifixion* the process which occurs to *both* parties of the great meeting: the Self and the ego. The participation in the process of divine self-realization *entails* the sacrifice of egocentric defenses and ego-bound intentions. Jesus transmitted to us his discovery that this sacrifice releases an eternal quality of livingness (Greek: *zoogonesai*) into our daily lives. This is the Great Paradox, given in its purest form at Luke 17:32 (my rendering):

> One who seeks to save life by walling about the psyche will destroy the life of the psyche, but one who destroys the walls of the psyche will experience the eternal quality of life.

This is a glimpse at a theonomic view of "being saved."

As Jesus implied when he refused to cast himself from the pinnacle of the temple (Matthew 4:5–7), *the laws of nature are God's laws*. Thus they are the ripe field for the discovery of God's nature, and scientific knowledge, with all its limitations, becomes a fertile arena of theonomy.

Behind all of what I have said is my assumption that we want integrity for the split world of mind and heart; we want to use the intellect without sacrificing the wonder, and without tearing ourselves apart to do so. We also want the gifts and the demands of God: we want to be held accountable, and thus also to be forgiven for the reality of our sins. When our heart is weighed against the truth, the World Order, we hope to be accepted. I believe that these ideas, of which I am a transmitter, not an originator, represent a significant step in that direction.

Notes

1. This issue was raised in the previous chapter.
2. Tillich, Paul. 1957. *The Protestant Era*. Chicago, University of Chicago Press, p. xvi.
3. Tillich, Paul. 1973. *Systematic Theology*. Chicago: University of Chicago Press, p. 85.
4. Taylor, Edwin, and John Archibald Wheeler. 1966. *Spacetime Physics*. New York: W.H. Freeman, p. 180.
5. "Flat" simply means uncurved. In the Cartesian-Newtonian view, the word "straight line" invokes an absolute, non-physical standard of straightness, against which the non-straightness of curved lines could somehow be measured. It was also *assumed* that light rays travel in straight lines. Once it was shown that light rays also bend, following the curvature of space, it became clear that the absolute standard really didn't have a representative in the physical realm.
6. In theological terms, the Einsteinian worldview is much more "incarnational."
7. Newbegin, Lesslie. 1986. *Foolishness to the Greeks*. Grand Rapids: Eerdmans.
8. It is one of the false beauties of some theological perspectives that they create an abyss between God and humans, which requires that we invoke the sheer power of an infinitely distant God to *bridge that abyss!*
9. *Foolishness*, p. 93.
10. This law states that in every practical process some energy is "lost."

11. Mayr, Ernst. 1982. Biology is not Postage Stamp Collecting. *Science*. 216:719.
12. Ibid. P. 721.
13. *CW* 8, par. 3n.
14. *CW* 8, par. 420.
15. The others are traced in my *Atoms, Snowflakes & God*.
16. *Knowledge*, p. 126.
17. As individual water molecules freeze onto one of the six lobes, others are freezing onto each of the others, a tremendous distance away when measured in terms of the number of intervening molecules, which is hundreds of thousands or millions. The clear implication is that there is an internal "wholeness pattern" of the entire snowflake, which is able to move the freezing molecules into corresponding positions on each of the six lobes.
18. Sinnott, Edmund. 1955. *The Biology of the Spirit*. New York: Viking, pp. 18–19.
19. It would be a split (Gr: *diabolikos*) God who would create with one set of laws and then would transform the cosmos to a different set apocalyptically. And, of course, the observed unity of the physical laws of the cosmos means that to transform the *earth* would entail transforming the whole universe.
20. A more concrete reason for saying it is God's world will be discussed in the next section, namely the essential role of ego-sacrifice in the process.
21. von Franz, Marie-Louise. 1970. *Puer Aeternus*. New York: Spring Publications, p. V-17.

Intellectual and Emotional Integrity

Truth, by itself, never *forces* one to change an opinion. The truth cannot be in danger from our self-deception. Only *we* can be. The degree to which we perceive that which is, *as it is,* clearly depends on the appropriateness of our questions. Some items are such that they demand and obtain unequivocal decision between two alternatives, such as that the earth is fundamentally "round" or "flat." Some are matters of approximation, for instance that the earth is "spherical," and some require deeper penetration and redefinition, as in the case of the statement that light is a "wave phenomenon," and perhaps also require whole new modes of thought. Statements which have attained unequivocal decision (the world is round), or are stated with sufficient caution (the earth is spherical within 3%), are regarded as *true* facts.

In all that has been said, a certain *attitude* has been implicit. Intellectual integrity is required, and behind that is emotional integrity. Henry Burton Sharman, a biblical scholar, once said, "Never sacrifice your intellectual integrity, even for God." In the context in which this statement was made, the intellectual aspect of integrity was Dr. Sharman's prime concern: that the critical study of the synoptic gospels which he was conducting be done in an atmosphere of scientific openness. Inspired by this saying, I have added what I feel certain was not far from his thought, namely that emotional integrity be included as well.

Integrity, or unity, implies wholeness as an *attitude,* and therefore implies *expanding* boundaries of self-knowledge. Emotional integrity stands at a deeper place than intellectual integrity, because only a *feeling* conflict will bring about a change in consciousness. It is well known that many persons who are employed in scientific pursuits can easily "compartmentalize" their science, isolating it from their religious or cultural beliefs. Thus *intellectual* conflict is not effective to produce a change. We might say in this case that one has identified an emotional pocket *as the whole* of one's own personality. Though it is just a part, it anchors the personality and limits its movement. This implies that philosophy cannot be done apart from a commitment to wholeness in one's life. One *truly* can do philosophy *only* in the way that one *lives*. I have dealt with this whole issue much more fully in Chapter 3: "Consciousness and the Moral Dimension."

One of the beauties of the term "spirit-matter" is that it combines the languages of both "ways of knowing," religion and science, as the *facts* indicate that it should. Seeking the origin of "spirit-matter" is a very different quest from seeking the origin of "matter." In some respects it may call for a different sort of verification.

Is it possible that I am being deceived? Yes, always, not only about the object of my search, but also about the search itself. The question of the objectivity of my subjective commitment forces me, in Kierkegaard's image, to "dance" back and forth between objectivity and subjectivity.

LIVING WITH INTEGRITY

In the end we return to our involvement in daily living, for philosophy has no other goal. Here is an actual incident which occurred to me bearing upon this claim.

An acquaintance, reporting on a book about Kierkegaard, said that Kierkegaard advocated an "approximation process" for reaching the truth. My immediate reaction was: that is *not* Kierkegaard. I checked the book, and found that it did indeed say "approximation" but I still knew that Kierkegaard's point of view was that one must *appropriate* the truth by means of a *leap*, and that one could *never* reach the truth by an *approximation* process. My acquaintance was quite doubtful that I was correct, though he knew that I had used Kierkegaard as a major figure in my doctoral dissertation.

Then I got out my Kierkegaard books and found the places where he explicitly discusses appropriation versus approximation, and produced from them quite a sufficiency of evidence to support my contention that the book first mentioned contained a misprint, but more likely a psychological slip, in substituting "approximation" for "appropriation." The response of my acquaintance was, "But it *makes sense* to me as approximation." Upon this, I naturally dropped my pursuit of the question.

My acquaintance possesses credentials, and has achieved a great deal. His intelligence is quite superior, and in all other respects he lives up to this impression. But it is clear that intelligence and honesty have difficulty prevailing when an erroneous idea "makes sense." Such has often been the case, even with physicists of such undoubted character as Einstein, to whom a mechanistic view of nature "made sense" to such a degree that as evidence to the contrary accumulated, he said that he could only call upon his "little finger" to testify on his behalf. The idea *made sense!*

If a person's self-valuation is bound up with an issue in which one is essentially wrong, then that value is misplaced, even though that person makes a tremendous contribution to the advance of human consciousness. Whether Kierkegaard was right or wrong, it is clear that he was presenting a view which was unacceptable to my acquaintance. The same is true with respect to Einstein's view of physical reality. Again, Einstein was of inestimable value to humanity, though he was "stuck" on mechanism. It seems to me that it is only when one has a clear realization that erroneous ideas can "make sense" that one is on the threshold of intellectual integrity, and can thence be open to a real change of opinion based upon evidence.

Erroneous ideas can even be beautiful, as the history of physics shows. Probably every false theory which has been pursued by some investigator was thought beautiful by that person. Truth and beauty are definitely not identical.

In assessing the degree to which the testimony of another is trustworthy, it is always necessary to gather evidence in some way, as to such a person's susceptibility to erroneous ideas which "make sense." But this often requires that one be beyond where he or she now stands as a person. One must indeed be close to the truth. It seems likely to me that another's experience will be similar to my own: one learns which areas of response one can trust in another. As I stated earlier, I know of people with profoundly developed consciousness who are quite blind in certain areas, and undoubtedly this blindness applies to me as well.

One value of using the Kierkegaard illustration is that the question involved (unlike that of Einstein's case) was essentially clear-cut and factual: what *Kierkegaard's position is* with respect to approximation versus appropriation. It does not yet raise the question of how one *actually does* approach life or truth. I also do not intend to analyze all of the psychological reasons for a person getting off the track of the truth. The main reasons certainly *are* psychological, but I am only concerned with the fact that such derailings do indeed occur, and do so within intelligent, honest individuals. It is in part the presence of all of these psychological forces which makes a true scientific pursuit so arduous.

So in the end we do want to deal with the deeper question of how to find truth and life. If "making sense" can so easily sidetrack an intelligent and truth-committed person, how are we to assume we might be able to gain any assurance at all with respect to the truth itself?

It seems that only a much wider commitment can give us any confidence at all. We see people with impressive minds holding different views on every central issue. It is a good guess that some of these are in a state of mistaken certainty. In many cases, these great ones will say of themselves that their guiding experience of "making sense" occurred at a youthful age, and that their lives have essentially been an unfolding of these early discoveries. At the same time, others with less powerful mental capacities will easily (and truthfully) see that the great ones have great blind spots, and even have spent their prodigious talents and energies in endeavors which will survive neither as truth, nor as errors which led others to lasting values and knowledge. It should be clear that while such great persons as Kierkegaard and Einstein had points of error, even their errors have been tremendously productive for the rest of us, but there are those not blessed by that happy fault.

Another central and allied question is how we know or judge that others know when the *relevant* facts to a question are being pursued, or that the central question itself is being pursued rather than lesser issues. Anyone who approaches these questions is ultimately humbled by them. It is impossible to predict which paths will be fruitful and which unfruitful. It *is* often possible to exclude *silly* pursuits, such as the case of the man who spent a lifetime documenting each resident of San Francisco at the time of the 1906 earthquake. He was bitterly disappointed when it didn't make him a millionaire. (But he is remembered as this example, so even his case has its poignancy!) It may be that we must acquire the humility of the uncertainty in order to pursue our researches seriously. That is at least a *necessary* criterion, and *may also be* a sufficient one, when one is relatively clear on the question of intellectual and emotional integrity, i.e. when one *has* a wider commitment.

The whole question of integrity, as *my* integrity, must begin with the ego ("I") and extend outward. Its logical extension is an *actual* cosmic unity, in which I can be aware of the Totality in some way. I cannot yet visualize this, nor can I visualize the complexified I-Self which can look both ways through the "window of eternity," seeing some things in detail, but seeing in general as well, and simultaneously knowing the self-consistent nature of the Whole, so that new specifics can be assimilated, and otherness is a joy rather than a shock. But new problems *always* will be posed by this process, and thus new pain. Learning is like birth: the most painful of joys.

Appendix 2

Cosmic Ecology

We will now account for the *spontaneous* generation of an entire, matter-filled, evolving cosmos, and even have some speculations as to a process by which we may have been formed, and may be forming billions of space-time systems like our own. This will also account for the becoming of photons.

As a star evolves, it always becomes more centrally concentrated. Not only does this happen to the star as a whole, but also with respect to the distribution of matter within it: a greater and greater fraction of its mass lies closer to its center in comparison to the entire size of the star. This central concentration intensifies the star's gravitational field in the "core": that part of the star within which nuclear "burning" occurs. The core must become hotter and hotter to keep the pressure up to keep the star from collapsing in response to the increased gravity. The process is largely self-balancing while the "nuclear fuel" lasts, since the squeeze of gravity raises the temperature, which in turn increases the rate of nuclear energy production to supply the needed heat to rebalance the gravity. Thus the star is in a state of continually shifting equilibrium as the process of central concentration proceeds.

An important reason for the continuing central concentration is that the star cannot hold onto its energy. It is leaky. Being hot on its surface, it radiates energy as starshine. This means that the incessant action of gravity has the ultimate upper hand, and the star *must* proceed in its evolution. This is an example of the *fundamental disequilibrium* of the cosmos, which was discussed in Chapter 9. If a balloon didn't leak molecules of air, it would stay at its originally inflated size. When it leaks, however, it gets smaller. In the star, the leaking leads to further concentration of the mass of the star at its center, raising the temperature, etc. We should also note that the energy escaping the star is also lost mass, because of the equivalence of mass and energy. This is quite analogous to the "mass defect" discussed in Chapter 6. This gives gravity a greater and greater "grip" on the material in the core of the star.

In the later stages of stellar evolution, the production of "mass defect" from gravitational centration begins to yield a greater amount of energy than does the process of nuclear fusion. Even when a star explodes, blowing away about half its mass in a "supernova," its nuclear energy production is probably less than the energy released in the production of mass defect.

Eventually, subsequent to the supernova explosion just described, the remaining core, a single, sufficiently massive star, of which there are many billions in our cosmos, will achieve such a terrific central concentration that its gravity will be so strong as to preclude the escape of this energy, i.e. these photons. At this point we say that the star has reached the "black hole" stage.[1] It is a curious fact, as mentioned in Chapter 6, that when the remaining former core, now a "neutron star," reaches the black hole stage, it has created mass defect equal to its entire original mass, so that the neutrons which "depart" from our space-time system have no remaining mass. This is in spite of the fact that the number of neutrons which do so depart is represented by a 1 with fifty-seven or more zeros after it. We also know that there is an infinite discontinuity of space and time from our own space-time system at the boundary of the black hole, which gives added meaning to the term "depart," just used. Since the contracting star *created* that infinite boundary, we are not quite certain that it cannot burst forth again with all of its newly created energy, but we are reasonably confident that, as with human death, departure is a one-way process.

But the matter which once was the core of the star will keep on getting hotter, will keep on producing photons, even though they can no longer escape. There is no reason in principle why the continued collapse of the star, *inside* the black hole, cannot produce an indefinitely large amount of energy (mass) in the form of photons, even enough to multiply the original mass of the star by countless billions. In fact, there is no reason why, inside the black hole, the amount of matter might not reach many times the amount presently in our own cosmos. This was one of the conclusions of Golay's paper quoted in Chapter 6. Let us note that we have not yet reached the point of speculation. At least physicists are firm in their knowledge of the processes so far described.

In Chapter 6, the point was made that under the right conditions matter might come into existence and pay for its new being just by coming into existence. I believe that the "collapse" into the black hole provides the needed temperature and density for precisely this to occur. The cost of all the new "stuff" is virtually nothing. At least it is no more than the single star which underwent the process. This is a speculation, since it occurs inside a black hole which is invisible to us. However, the physical processes which I have invoked are not at all speculative.

Here comes the real speculation, based upon Golay's suggestion.

Since the black hole has become detached from our space-time system, it may be displaced in another dimension, which we may call the fourth spatial dimension, so that if it then expands within that new framework, it need not push out of the boundaries of the black hole as seen in the parent cosmos, just as a two dimensional space which may be represented by a piece of paper does not interfere with another such space when displaced in the third dimension. We may place one piece of paper upon another, and each may be of whatever size with no problem to the other.

Then, since our own cosmos manifests properties which are those of the "hypersphere" mentioned in Chapter 6, it is possible that our own cosmos was once a single star, shrinking and "dying" in some other "parent" cosmos. To repeat, a single star may give birth to a new space-time system, a new whole cosmos which is as large and massive "as it pleases," to use an anthromorphic expression. This would truly be creation from a void, for if our own cosmos is an example, the single star from which it arose was but a trillionth of a trillionth part of that which grew from it.

The trick, again, is that both mass and mass defect (gravitational relationship) come to being simultaneously under the right physical conditions. The mass which was produced was in the form of photons, which completes our search for origins, except for the non-trivial problem of the origin of the first seed of the process. The photons go on, by means of the pair-production process, to produce quark/antiquark pairs and electron/positron pairs, as described in

Chapter 6. This process ends early in the Big Bang, leaving as a remnant the stuff out of which all stars and planets are later made. The pair-production process itself hastens the cooling of the cosmos to the point at which pair-production ceases. At that time, the amount of "matter" in the cosmos is a mere trace compared to the amount in the form of electromagnetic radiation, but since the density of radiation falls off more rapidly than does the density of matter as the cosmos expands, matter eventually dominates the stuff of the cosmos, with radiation being the "trace."

Notes

1. For an excellent discussion of this process, the reader is referred to Hawking's *Brief History of Time*.

Appendix 3

Excerpts from Weisskopf's
Knowledge and Wonder

In our ordinary way of looking at things, the electron must be either a particle or a wave. It cannot be both at the same time. (1963, p. 136)

Quite generally, all measurements which could be used for a decision between the wave and the particle nature of the electron (or any other entity) have the same property. If one performs these measurements, the object changes its state completely in the performance itself, and the result of the measurement applies not to the original state but to the state into which the object was put by the measurement. (p. 136)

The quantum nature, the coarseness of light, makes it impossible to decide between wave and particle. It does not allow us to subdivide the atomic orbit into a succession of partial motions, by particle displacements or wave oscillations. If we force a subdivision of the process and try to look more accurately at the wave in order to find out where the electron "really" is, we will find it there as a real particle, but we will have destroyed the subtle individuality of the quantum state. The wave nature will have disappeared, and with it all the characteristic properties of the atom [in its] quantum state—the simple shape, the regeneration of the original form after perturbation, and all other specific qualities of the atom. (p. 137)

The impossibility of measuring certain quantities' relation to atomic particles is the basis of the famous uncertainty principle of Heisenberg. It states, for example, that one cannot determine with full accuracy both velocity and position of an electron. Clearly if one could, the electron would be recognized as a particle and not as a wave. . . . We know from a great wealth of observations that our objects exhibit both wave and particle properties. Hence the Heisenberg restrictions must have a deeper root: they are a necessary corollary to the dual nature of atomic objects. If they were broken, our interpretation of the wide field of atomic phenomena would be nothing but a web of errors, and its amazing success would be based upon accidental coincidence. (p. 138)

These features, however, do not make electrons less real than anything else we observe in nature. Indeed the quantum states of the electron are the very basis of what we call reality around us. (p. 141)

Appendix 4

The Spiritual Imperative in Physics

The principal guiding fact which underlies this book, and indeed the whole convergence of science and spirituality, is the fact that consciousness has evolved from the primordial hydrogen of the cosmos, that is, out of an *unconscious* condition. The usual statement of this fact is the so-called "Anthropic Principle," which states that since we are here, the nature of the physical stuff which evolved into us must be such that humans are possible. The earliest statement of the Anthropic Principle in this form of which I am aware is that of Pierre Teilhard de Chardin, in *Human Energy,* where he says:

> It is radically impossible to conceive that "interiorized" and spontaneous elements could ever have developed from a universe presumed in its initial state to have consisted entirely of determinisms. Anyone who accepts this starting point blocks all roads that would bring us back to the present state of the universe. On the other hand, from a cosmos initially made up of "elementary freedoms," it is easy to deduce . . . all the appearances of exactitude upon which the mathematical physics of matter is founded. . . . There is neither spirit nor matter [separately] in the world; the stuff of the universe is *spirit-matter.* No other substance than this could produce the human molecule.[1]

Not only is there the recognition that the fundamental entities of the stuff of the universe must be *elementary freedoms,* but also that elementary freedoms can exhibit the "appearances of exactitude" which are so characteristic of physics as a science, and which have led many to the erroneous assumption that science is properly rationalistic.

Formulations of the Anthropic Principle which emphasize the element of time have the advantage that they show forth a process of complexification.

Since evolution is a fact, and since a kind of consciousness exists which cannot be attributed to the primal stuff, our guiding principle is on the most solid of foundations, and must be taken into account. We cannot claim to have understood the physical world until we understand, can explain, the principal guiding fact.

Unification theories in physics presently attack the "other end" of this problem. They attempt to explain how the present elementary particles and fundamental forces arose in the cooling of the Big Bang. They arrive at the primordial hydrogen from time prior to its existence. In accounting for hydrogen, they account for the existence of the proton and the electron, the *constituents* of hydrogen, at a time about one second after the Big Bang. At this time, the quantum-state waveforms[2] upon which the explanation of the guiding fact will be built had not yet come into existence anywhere. Much later, when conditions in the cosmos were sufficiently gentle for the quantum states of the hydrogen (and, by that time, helium) atoms to form, the wave patterns of the electrons began to exert their effects, being then a *new* presence in the cosmos.[3] If spirituality is one late manifestation of the evolutionary process, we must eventually be able to trace the potential for this manifestation to properties of the evolving "stuff," i.e. of the primordial hydrogen. This clearly indicates that we not only need to pursue the ultimate unification theory earlier toward the instant of the Big Bang, but also to pursue some sort of theory forward in time, in the cooling or gentling direction. We need to envision the time in which more and more subtle effects will take place. This, too, will yield a sort of unification theory: showing and explaining the phenomena of the unity which we now must necessarily term "spirit-matter."

One *wrong* path to this understanding is: chemistry is physics "writ large"; biology is chemistry "writ large"; and spirituality is metabiological, i.e. is biology "writ large." While all this may be true enough, the endeavor is presently too complex for us to succeed by discovering a detailed continuity of phenomena along this path.

Fortunately, it turns out that we can investigate spirit-matter with knowledge in hand, or at least *at* hand. We are in a position to document the *principle* by which the complexification of spirit-matter occurs, and by means of which spirituality becomes a natural phenomenon, even when it involves conscious sacrifice of ego-desires. Suggestions for investigations *within physics* abound in this book, beginning with a study of the webbing which occurs in the outer lobes of electron wave overlaps, which are described speculatively in Chapter 1.

First, of course, we must *recognize* that it is indeed spirit-matter with which we are concerned *as physicists* to explain.

This is the first and most concrete form of the spiritual imperative in physics.

The other form of spiritual imperative is to draw implications of the concrete indications which we have, that *something greater* is operating in spirit-matter. I have called this greater something the Patterning, and have drawn some of the implications, in the chapter "Holographic Evolution," in my *Atoms, Snowflakes & God*. It is this side of the imperative that motivates my own efforts as a physicist at present, and which directly informs the structure of Part III of this book.

Notes

1. *Human*, pp. 23–24, 57–58. The writings containing these quotations are dated 1931 and 1936. The "Anthropic Principle," so named by Brandon Carter, has been variously formulated by Carter, Robert Dicke, John A. Wheeler, and others. For a fine discussion, see Edward R. Harrison's wonderful book, *Cosmology*, Cambridge, Cambridge University Press, 1981.
2. See Chapter 1, "What Is Spirituality?"
3. The fact that new phenomena which "could not" (Ernst Mayr, see Chapter 10: "Theonomy") have been predicted from the previous state of the cosmos arise continually also needs explanation. We must be able to account for *this property* of the "stuff" of the cosmos.

Bibliography

Adams, Richard. 1974. *Shardik.* New York: Simon and Schuster.

Auden, W.H. 1969. For the Time Being. *Collected Longer Poems.* New York: Random House.

Bentley, W.A., and Humphreys, W.J. 1962. *Snow Crystals.* New York: Dover.

Blake, William. 1975. *The Marriage of Heaven and Hell.* London: Oxford University Press.

Capra, F. 1975. *The Tao of Physics.* Berkeley: Shambala.

Chayefsky, Paddy. 1962. *Gideon.* New York: Random House.

Clark, R.T. Rundle. 1960. *Myth and Symbol in Ancient Egypt.* New York: Grove Press.

Daniélou, Alain. 1964. *Hindu Polytheism.* New York: Pantheon.

Dyson, Freeman. 1988. *Infinite in All Directions.* New York: Harper & Row, Perennial Library.

Edinger, Edward F. 1985. *Anatomy of the Psyche.* La Salle, IL: Open Court.

Eliade, Mircea. 1961. *The Sacred and the Profane.* New York: Harper and Row, Harper Torchbooks.

Eliot, T.S. 1943. *Four Quartets.* New York: Harcourt Brace and World, Harvest Books.

Ferguson, Marilyn. 1980. *The Aquarian Conspiracy.* Los Angeles: J.P. Tarcher.

Feynman, Richard P. 1965. *Lectures on Physics, Volume III.* Edited by Robert B. Leighton and Matthew Sands. Reading, MA: Addison-Wesley.

Fitzgerald, Edward. 1956. "The Rubaiyyat of Omar Khayyam." *The Pocket Book of Verse.* Edited by M.E. Speare. New York: Pocket Books.

Goethe, Johann Wolfgang von. 1958. "Selige Sehnsucht." *Werke.* Edited by Erich Trunz. Hamburg: Christian Wegner.

————. 1959. *Faust/Part Two*. Translated by Philip Wayne. Baltimore: Penguin.

Golay, Marcel. 1961. Confessions of a Communications Engineer. *Analytical Chemistry*. 33:23A–31A.

Harrison, Edward R. 1981. *Cosmology*. Cambridge: Cambridge University Press.

Hawking, Stephen W. 1988. *A Brief History of Time*. New York: Bantam Books.

Heidegger, Martin. 1961. *An Introduction to Metaphysics*. Translated by Ralph Manheim. Garden City, NY: Doubleday and Company, Anchor Books.

Hitchcock, John L. 1976. *A Comparison of 'Complementarity' in Quantum Physics with Analogous Structures in Kierkegaard's Philosophical Writings, from a Jungian Point of View*. Dissertation 76-9150. Ann Arbor: Xerox University Microfilms.

————. 1986. *Atoms, Snowflakes & God*. Wheaton, IL: Theosophical Publishing House, Quest Books.

Hölderlin, Friedrich. 1980. *Poems & Fragments*. Edited and translated by Michael Hamburger. Cambridge: Cambridge University Press.

Howes, Elizabeth Boyden. 1971. *Intersection and Beyond*. San Francisco, Guild for Psychological Studies Publishing House.

Jaffé, Aniela. 1970. *The Myth of Meaning*. Translated by R.F.C. Hull. London: Hodder and Stoughton.

Jung, C.G. *Collected Works*, Bollingen Series XX. Translated by R.F.C. Hull. Princeton: Princeton University Press.

————. 1955. With Wolfgang Pauli. *The Interpretation of Nature and the Psyche*. New York: Pantheon, Bollingen Series LI.

————. 1956. *Symbols of Transformation. Collected Works* 5.

————. 1959. *Aion. Collected Works* 9_{II}.

————. 1961a. *Freud and Psychoanalysis. Collected Works* 4.

————. 1961b. *Psychological Reflections*. Selections edited by Jolande Jacobi. New York: Harper and Row, Harper Torchbooks.

————. 1963. *Memories, Dreams, Reflections*. Compiled and edited by Aniela Jaffé. New York: Random House.

————. 1964a. *Civilization in Transition. Collected Works* 10.

————. 1964b. With Marie-Louise von Franz, Joseph L. Henderson, Jolande Jacobi, and Aniela Jaffé. *Man and His Symbols*. Edited by C.G. Jung. New York: Doubleday.

————. 1966. *The Practice of Psychotherapy. Collected Works* 16.

————. 1967. *Alchemical Studies. Collected Works* 13.

————. 1968. *Psychology and Alchemy. Collected Works* 12.

————. 1969a. *The Archetypes and the Collective Unconscious. Collected Works* 9₁.

————. 1969b. *Psychology and Religion: West and East. Collected Works* 11.

————. 1969c. *The Structure and Dynamics of the Psyche. Collected Works* 8.

————. 1971. *Psychological Types. Collected Works* 6.

————. 1975. *Letters, 1951–1961.* Edited by Gerhard Adler. Bollingen Series XCV:2. Princeton: Princeton University Press.

Kazantzakis, Nikos. 1960. *The Saviors of God.* Translated by Kimon Friar. New York: Simon and Schuster.

Kierkegaard, Soren. 1941. *Concluding Unscientific Postscript.* Princeton: Princeton University Press.

————. 1954. *The Sickness Unto Death.* Translated by Walter Lowrie. Princeton: Princeton University Press.

Kuhn, Thomas S. 1970. *The Structure of Scientific Revolutions.* Chicago: The University of Chicago Press.

Kunkel, Fritz. 1936. Unpublished Seminar Notes.

Mayr, Ernst. 1982. Biology is not Postage Stamp Collecting. *Science.* 216:119.

Moon, Sheila. 1972. Prolog. *Joseph's Son.* Francestown, NH: Golden Quill Press.

————. 1984. *Changing Woman and Her Sisters.* San Francisco: Guild for Psychological Studies Publishing House.

Morrison, Toni. 1987. *Beloved.* New York: New American Library, Plume Fiction.

Müller, F. Max. 1962. *The Upanishads.* Translated and edited by F. Max Müller. New York: Dover Publications.

Murry, J. Middleton. 1930. *God.* New York: Harper and Brothers.

Neumann, Erich. 1973. *Depth Psychology and a New Ethic.* Translated by Eugene Rolfe. New York: Harper and Row, Harper Torchbooks.

Newbegin, Lesslie. 1986. *Foolishness to the Greeks.* Grand Rapids, MI: Eerdmans.

Patchen, Kenneth. 1969. *Sleepers Awake.* New York: New Directions.

Polanyi, Michael. 1964. *Personal Knowledge*. Chicago: The University of Chicago Press, Harper Torchbooks.

Prigogine, Ilya. 1980. *From Being to Becoming*. New York: W.H. Freeman. Photographs by Fritz Goro.

———. 1984. With Isabelle Stengers. *Order Out of Chaos*. New York: Bantam Books.

Rahula, Walpola. 1959. *What the Buddha Taught*. New York: Grove Press, Evergreen.

Raju, P.T. 1985. *Structural Depths of Indian Thought*. Albany: State University of New York Press.

Renfrew, Colin. 1989. The Origins of Indo-European Languages. *Scientific American*, 261/4:106–114.

Samuels, Andrew. 1985. *Jung and the Post-Jungians*. London: Routledge and Kegan Paul.

Sarton, May. 1974. *Collected Poems, 1930–1973*. New York: W.W. Norton & Company.

Sinnott, Edmund. 1955. *The Biology of the Spirit*. New York: Viking.

Swimme, Brian. 1984. *The Universe Is a Green Dragon*. Santa Fe: Bear & Company.

Taylor, Edwin, and John A. Wheeler. 1966. *Spacetime Physics*. San Francisco: W.H. Freeman.

Teilhard de Chardin, Pierre. 1961. *The Phenomenon of Man*. Translated by Bernard Wade. New York: Harper and Row, Harper Torchbooks.

———. 1969. *Human Energy*. Translated by T.M. Cohen. New York: Harcourt Brace Jovanovich.

———. 1970. *Hymn of the Universe*. Translated by Gerald Vann. New York: Harper and Row, Fontana Religious Books.

Teller, Edward. 1969. Niels Bohr and the Idea of Complementarity. *Great Men of Physics*. Edited by Marvin Chachere. Los Angeles: Tinnon Brown.

Tillich, Paul. 1948. *The Shaking of the Foundations*. New York: Charles Scribner's Sons.

———. 1957. *The Protestant Era*. Chicago: University of Chicago Press.

———. 1973. *Systematic Theology*. Chicago: University of Chicago Press.

van der Leeuw, G. 1963. *Religion in Essence and Manifestation*. New York: Harper & Row, Harper Torchbooks.

von Franz, Marie-Louise. 1970. *Puer Aeternus.* New York: Spring Publications.

Watts, Alan. 1957. *The Way of Zen.* New York: Random House, Vintage Books.

Weber, Renee. 1986. *Dialogues with Sages and Scientists.* London: Routledge and Kegan Paul.

Weinberg, Steven. 1984. *The First Three Minutes.* New York: Bantam Books.

Weisskopf, Victor F. 1963. *Knowledge and Wonder.* Garden City, NY: Doubleday, Anchor Books, Science Study Series.

Werfel, Franz. 1946. *Star of the Unborn.* Translated by Gustave O. Arlt. New York: Viking.

Wheeler, John Archibald. 1989. The Universe Self-Synthesized Quantum-Mechanically. Unpublished Lecture.

———. See also Taylor and Wheeler (1966).

White, Harvey E. 1931. Pictorial Representations of the Electron Cloud for Hydrogen-like Atoms. *Physical Review* 37: 1416–1434.

Whitmont, Edward C. 1978. *The Symbolic Quest.* Princeton: Princeton University Press.

Wittgenstein, Ludwig. 1972. *On Certainty.* Edited by G.E.M. Anscombe and G.H. von Wright. Translated by Denis Paul and G.E.M. Anscombe. New York: Harper and Row, Harper Torchbooks.

Yutang, Lin. 1938. *The Wisdom of Confucius.* New York: Carlton House.

Zimmer, Heinrich. 1951. *Philosophies of India.* Edited by Joseph Campbell. Bollingen Series XXVI. New York: Pantheon.

———. 1962. *Myths and Symbols in Indian Art and Civilization.* Edited by Joseph Campbell. Bollingen Series VI. New York: Harper & Row, Harper Torchbooks.

Zukav, Gary. 1979. *The Dancing Wu-Li Masters.* New York: William Morrow.

Index